# WITH TH
# IN MESOPOTAMIA

BREVET LIEUT.-COL. F. W. LELAND
C.B.E., D.S.O., R.A.S.C.

**The Naval & Military Press Ltd**

Published by

**The Naval & Military Press Ltd**

Unit 10, Ridgewood Industrial Park,

Uckfield, East Sussex,

TN22 5QE England

Tel: +44 (0) 1825 749494

Fax: +44 (0) 1825 765701

**www.naval-military-press.com**

M.T. IN BAGHBAD.

[*Frontispiece.*

DEDICATED

TO

MY SON

"TIMBO"

# INTRODUCTION

I WAS asked a few months before leaving Mesopotamia to put my experiences with the Mechanical Transport in that country into book form. At first I thought it was, more or less, an absurd proposition, but I eventually came to the conclusion that a book on the subject might be interesting to all ranks of the R.A.S.C., M.T., who were in "Mespot."

The book is intended to show the development of Mechanical Transport, and the conditions under which it worked, during the years 1916 to 1918. I do not pretend that it is an exhaustive study by any means, for to make a complete history of the M.T. and recount its doings during the three years in question would require a far abler pen than mine, and the tale would run into several volumes, instead of this modest book for which I am responsible.

It really contains nothing of any great official importance which could not have been obtained in the ordinary course; but in my position as A.D.T. I was able to collect the information rather more quickly than would otherwise have been the case.

I am deeply grateful to several officers for photographs, and to others for short accounts of the doings of their units during some of the operations. The book has been written rather hurriedly, for during the last three months of my sojourn in Mesopotamia I was not at all well, so I trust my readers will pardon my shortcomings. Certain facts, apparently very important, may have been omitted, while others of less importance have found their way into print. Another point which I trust my readers will not forget, is that this book was commenced in September 1918, during my spare time, and was completed in January 1919. Since that time things have happened which could not possibly be included in the following pages.

I wish to thank the Intelligence Branch G.H.Q., M.E.F., for their help in connection with reports on the major operations, and also for the maps they gave me for this book. My thanks are also due to Brigadier-General Ryan, C.M.G., etc. (who relieved Brigadier-General P. C. J. Scott, C.B., as D. of S. and T., M.E.F.) for his kindly assistance and encouragement.

After my return from Mesopotamia the MS. of this book was sent to the War Office for censoring, and went through the hands of the D. of S. and T.'s Directorate as well as the Intelligence Branch. Naturally a certain amount of "cutting" was considered necessary, but I am glad to say that I have received authority to print Chapter XVII as it originally stood.

I cannot close this introduction without mentioning Sergt.-Major J. F. Perkins, R.A.S.C., since it was due to his abilities as a stenographer and typist that I was able to get through this book as quickly as I did.

F. W. Leland,
Lieut.-Colonel, R.A.S.C.

Winchester,
*September* 1919.

# CONTENTS

## CHAPTER I

### LEAVING ENGLAND



## CHAPTER II

### BASE M.T. DEPÔT AND FLOATING WORKSHOP



## CHAPTER III

### COUNTRY AND CLIMATE



## CHAPTER IV

### TYPES OF VEHICLES AND MEN

## CHAPTER V

### EARLY DAYS OF THE M.T.



## CHAPTER VI

### THE ADVANCED M.T. DEPÔT



## CHAPTER VII

### ORGANISATION



## CHAPTER VIII

### OPERATIONS, NOVEMBER 1916 TO MAY 1917



## CHAPTER IX

### OPERATIONS, MAY TO OCTOBER 1917

## CHAPTER X

### OPERATIONS, OCTOBER 1917 TO FEBRUARY 1918



## CHAPTER XI

### OPERATIONS, JANUARY AND FEBRUARY 1918 TO MAY 1918



## CHAPTER XII

### OPERATIONS, MAY TO AUGUST 1918



## CHAPTER XIII

### OPERATIONS, AUGUST TO OCTOBER 1918

# LIST OF ILLUSTRATIONS

# WITH THE M.T. IN MESOPOTAMIA

## CHAPTER I

### LEAVING ENGLAND

Condition of affairs on arrival in Mesopotamia—Short description of the Base, etc.

TOWARDS the end of July 1916, while on one of my numerous visits to the War Office, I was informed that I had just been made an A.D.T. for Mechanical Transport and was under orders to sail for Mesopotamia within a few days. I greeted this news with rather mixed feelings. Pleasure and pain vied with each other as to which should come out on top. It was pleasing to know that I was getting what so many people strive for, i.e. " a job " ; yet the thought of having to go so far away from home to a land I knew nothing about, beyond the fact that there was a place there called "Kut" and that it had fallen, caused me pain. I at once went out and purchased a map to seek the geographical position of Mesopotamia. The small sketches of Kut and Ctesiphon, which had previously been published in the daily papers, gave me little or no information about the place for which I was bound. Having only half-satisfied my curiosity on this point and incidentally learned a little more geography, I handed over the M.T. Depôt then under my command, and obtained a few days' leave of absence in order to make preparations for my departure. My boat, the s.s. *Morea*, sailed from England on August 19, but as it called at

Marseilles, I made arrangements to pick it up at that port. This enabled me to have a week's extra leave.

As this book deals with Mesopotamia, there is no object in my describing the voyage, especially as the majority of my readers have already encountered similar experiences. Several officers, who had already served in Mesopotamia, were on board, and they seemed very much surprised and amused when I informed them that I was being sent out to look after mechanical transport in that country. They asked, "How on earth can mechanical transport run in Mesopotamia? Are you aware that for four or five months in the winter there is nothing but rain; that there are no roads and that the ground is impassable for horses—even human beings get stuck in the mud; while in the spring the country is under water and one is compelled to sit in camps pitched on small hillocks here and there? In addition to this it is impossible to work for three months in the summer, owing to the intense heat." Such remarks were not really conducive to put "good heart" into anyone, and I could only hope that, out of kindness, they were exaggerating possible difficulties with a view to getting me to undertake a less arduous and ludicrous job, than the running of mechanical transport in a country which had such peculiar characteristics.

We spent a few days at Bombay, and, on September 16, 1916, we left for Basrah, the home of the General Headquarters of the Mesopotamian Expeditionary Force, arriving there on the 23rd. Headquarters subsequently moved to a quiet spot on the Tigris called Arab Village, some few miles downstream from the Sanniyat position, which then formed our front line.

The late General Maude had just taken over command, and was busy reorganising the whole force for the winter campaign, which afterwards proved so successful.

Basrah is the usual name for the port in question, yet, strictly speaking, this is not correct. The old city of Basrah or Basora, known by all as the home of Sinbad the Sailor,

THE OTHER SIDE OF THE STORY: VIEW ON ONE OF THE NUMEROUS CREEKS AT BASRAH.

is about two and a half miles inland from the Shatt-al-Arab, and is situated on Ashar Creek, which is a tidal tributary that empties itself into the main river by the small town of Ashar. Picture to yourself a great, full-throated river whose waters, twenty, forty, sixty feet deep, ebb and flow in harmony with the tide which swings up from the Persian Gulf some threescore miles below.

A myriad of artificial creeks, succeeding each other at brief intervals, lead off from the main stream and afford wonderful vistas of tropical vegetation, with abundance of vine and palm-trees; of wild-growing blossoms of passionate hues: such are the "suburbs" of Basrah—a seeming paradise!

A few hundred yards away Ashar bursts upon the view—a port in the making. Twenty or thirty ocean-going steamers and men-of-war strain at their moorings in mid-stream; along the banks, but a few inches above water-level, men of all races paddle in the mud, unloading cargoes. A hundred yards inland you will find, cheek by jowl, the vivid contrast of an Oriental bazaar, where the chief business is the drinking of coffee and the making of never-ending arguments; and of British barracks, where Tommy sits and sweats and dreams of 'Ampstead 'Eath the while he polishes his buttons and curses his luck.

Such was Ashar in the early days of the war.

Basrah was a silhouette cut from the *Arabian Nights*; a city of stifling sand-coloured bricks and of jealously guarded windows; of narrow lanes where Arab and Armenian jostled each other in the comparative coolth of the shaded alleys; of occasional deserted open places from which the scorching heat drove even the pariah dogs away in search of shade. Outside the city walls the howling wilderness defies all attempts at cultivation—or at description!

In Mesopotamia life is restricted to a narrow belt of riparian land within a few hundred yards—or at most a couple of miles—of the mainstream. Beyond these limits there is no water, no vegetation, no life—nothing but hard-baked alluvial sand and the sweltering furnace of a pitiless sun.

Tanooma is the village opposite, on the left bank of the Shatt-al-Arab. Margil, about three miles upstream on the right bank, was chosen for building the various wharves, etc., and the location for various base depôts, such as the Supply Depôt, Ordnance, etc. Between Margil and Ashar the Inland Water Transport docks were in process of being built.

The Tigris and the Euphrates are the two main rivers of Mesopotamia, which, after following their various windings, finally unite at Kurnah, 40 miles above Ashar. From this point to the Persian Gulf the river goes by the name of the Shatt-al-Arab. Palm trees fringe both sides of the river, and also the banks of the numerous creeks. The river is tidal almost up to Kurnah, the reputed site of the Garden of Eden, and the old junction of the Tigris and the Euphrates.

The new junction, and the one on which they were working to get a good passage through the Hammar Lake, was only a couple of miles above Margil. The country just inland from Ashar was merely desert, and was called Makina Plain. Here were situated various depôts and base units for reinforcements. All were in E.P. tents. First impressions of Makina Plain were anything but pleasant. It is wonderful, though, the work which has been put into the Base by all departments, especially that of the Works, to make things as comfortable as possible. But in 1916 they were only starting, and it appeared as if nothing could ever be done in such miserable surroundings. Money had to be spent freely, if any return was to be looked for from the large expedition which was then being organised to beat the Turk in Mesopotamia. I can never forget my feelings when I first experienced the dust and dirt of Makina Plain, and even though this book concerns M.T. alone, I felt that I had to give the reader a little local colour, hence this slight digression.

At this time the following units were in Mesopotamia:

No. 23 Motor Ambulance Convoy (including No. 656 M.T. Company, A.S.C. attached); Base M.T. Depôt; and No. 596 M.T. Company, A.S.C.

No. 23 Motor Ambulance Convoy was composed of Star ambulances. A bad report had been sent home with regard to the defects of these vehicles, pointing out that they were practically useless for Mesopotamia. The report is more than two and a half years old, and yet the whole of the fifty ambulances are still on the road working—so much for that report!

The Base M.T. Depôt arrived in the country about June, and was mobilised as a Depôt and Stores Branch, with the addition of a Workshops Section. In September 1916 this very important unit was situated in a few E.P. tents on the present site, now occupied by the depôt, namely on Makina Plain, about two miles from Basrah. On looking at the photographs the reader will realise the difficulties which had to be contended with in a force unused to handling mechanical transport, and where no buildings suitable to accommodate such a unit were available. Even if there had been any, I am certain that the M.T. came very far down the priority list of allotment.

With regard to No. 596 Company, this unit arrived in January 1916, having come from Egypt. It had a total of 110 vehicles (Peerless), including two workshops and two store lorries, and 400 odd other ranks. The lorries were of the usual 3-ton Peerless type, but owing, presumably, to a shortage of 30-cwt. lorries at the time, they were marked with the words "Load not to exceed 30 cwt.," thus turning them into 30-cwt. lorries. This unit had a detachment of twelve lorries at Bushire, on the Persian Gulf, and ten Napiers at Ahwaz, also nineteen Fiats with 1st and 3rd Corps.

During the year 1916 a few reconnaissances had been carried out with mechanical transport for the purpose of finding roads to various places and also of reporting on the suitability of certain types of vehicles for desert work. Lieutenants (as they then were) Dickinson and Vlasto were chiefly responsible for all the good work done and reports made.

Lieutenant Vlasto, who belongs to a well-known Greek family in Liverpool, had already had much experience of driving lorries and motors in countries where no real roads existed. He had served as a private in the Greek army throughout the Balkan wars of 1912–13, where he also did invaluable work as an M.T. driver, to which Captain A. H. Trapman pays a tribute, and tells an amusing anecdote (*Greeks Triumphant*: Forster Groom & Co., Ltd.).

The Peerless lorry used, though a heavy one, generally managed to get home. With regard to these road reports, the journeys from Basrah to Ahwaz and from Basrah to Nasariyeh stand out prominently as fine examples of what M.T. officers, men, and vehicles can do, even though unused to such conditions as existed in this country.

The Star Ambulance Convoy accomplished a wonderful amount of good work, both at the Base and on the L. of C. right up to Baghdad.

As previously mentioned, the Star ambulances had been badly reported on, owing to the bending of the front axle when tried over various bad desert roads. Without doubt the axles were not intended for such rough usage, yet at the same time one must remember that a defect such as this can often be accentuated by fast driving, over bad and bumpy ground. All bent axles were straightened and strengthened, and new axles were also demanded from England.

I might also mention that the Fiat lorries, of which there were a few in the country, had been doing very useful work in the front line under the command of Lieutenant Vlasto. This vehicle was a special type of Fiat with pneumatic tyres used extensively by the Italian Army in Tripoli, and is one of the most useful vehicles that ever came out to Mesopotamia. It was capable of a useful load of one ton. At this time nine of these vehicles,

LANDING OF THE FIRST PEERLESS LORRY IN MESOPOTAMIA.

THE SAME LORRY A SHORT WHILE AFTERWARDS.

out of a total of nineteen, were off the road for want of spare parts which were unobtainable, and the few lorries that were working had been kept going by robbing the nine derelicts.

Except the mobile workshop equipment of No. 596 M.T. Company and of No. 656 M.T. Company (attached 23rd M.A.C.), there were no workshops available for the repair of M.T. vehicles, since the machinery and plant, etc., belonging to the Base M.T. Depôt could hardly be erected in E.P. tents, and no buildings could be allotted.

Signal units were equipped with motor-cycles, but most of these could be best described as "part worn"; in fact, the more one saw of the desert sandy tracks the less one envied the unfortunate despatch riders who had to ride these machines over such a type of country. Most of these units, too, were considerably under war establishment as regards motor-cycles,and little or nothing could be done in the way of repairing those which were out of action, even as regards merely minor defects.

My readers are now aware of the actual state of the Mechanical Transport of the Mesopotamian Expeditionary Force in September 1916, and can readily understand the necessity that existed for immediate reorganisation as regards: (1) Repair workshops. (2) Establishing the Base Depôt. (3) The supply of reserve vehicles and motor-cycles. (4) The need for reinforcements.

With regard to the last point, 50 per cent. of the vehicles at this time could not be run in Mesopotamia owing to the lack of drivers.

# CHAPTER II

## BASE M.T. DEPÔT AND FLOATING WORKSHOP

Full description of unit's functions—The rise and expansion from date of arrival—Photographs—Splitting up of unit—Short history of the floating workshops.

When Mechanical Transport vehicles have to be used in any great number in a campaign, something more is required than the provision of the vehicles, the drivers, petrol, oil, and grease—" start your engine and off you go " sort of idea. To the ordinary layman, so to speak, this may be the generally accepted idea, but *we* know that with Mechanical Transport vehicles it is the same as with men and animals, reinforcements are required. Spare parts are needed; running accessories, such as tyres and tubes and sparking plugs, are essential; while workshops must be found. A fighting unit cannot be kept up to establishment strength unless properly equipped reinforcements are available, and in this respect Mechanical Transport differs from no other unit: its casualties must be replaced.

When one studies the war establishment of the Army and looks through the pages devoted to various units, such as Supply Columns, Ammunition Parks, Advanced M.T. Depôts, Base M.T. Depôts, etc. etc., and considers the functions of these units, it is at once apparent that some of them are not mobile, and that these require something more substantial than E.P. tents for the proper performance of their duties. It will be seen, therefore, that the M.T. was up against rather a complex problem as regards suit-

THE SECOND FLOATING WORKSHOP.

THE OLD AND THE NEW FLOATING WORKSHOPS.

The up-to-date barge with the old workshop alongside and the two attendant store boats, all dismantled.

able buildings for workshops and stores, in a country where houses are made of little more than sun-dried bricks, and where the walls generally collapse if any great weight is placed on the first floor, i.e. when there *is* a first floor. The few houses that exist are wretched caricatures at the best, while in some cases it is only by courtesy and *faute de mieux* that they bear the title of house at all.

Prior to my arrival, Major Archibald, O.C. Base M.T. Depôt, went down to Base Headquarters and demanded the largest building there was in Basrah for his unit, and he was greatly surprised and perturbed when he was informed that he could not have it—it had already been allotted as a clothing store! At the time this building would have been a very suitable one, but the requirements of mechanical transport were unknown, or unrecognised, with the result that this unit was lodged in E.P. tents on "good old Makina Plain." Once there, steps were taken to get the unit housed as soon as possible, but firstly the machinery had to be erected in a suitable building, and this could not be done until after the building itself was erected. The matter was taken in hand as quickly as possible, but everything was scarce in Basrah (it was a long way from England) at the time, and all building materials, with the exception of the bricks mentioned above and chitai matting and poles (which go by the local name of "bullies"), had to be imported. It therefore took some time to obtain the necessary girders and corrugated iron to make the workshops. With the gradual increase in the mechanical transport, this very important unit had to be increased. Its war establishment was amended on two occasions. The buildings were never completed up to establishment, and even now—September 1918—they are still hard at work making quarters for officers and men; so far as one can see, the work is likely for some time to come to be behind requirements.

The Stores Section was a very difficult section to place

in a suitable locality. Margil, at the time, was undoubtedly the right place for the whole depôt, but all the suitable sites were already occupied; of course, to put up a lot more buildings would have meant a waste of valuable time. A khan (or Eastern caravanserai) on Khandag Creek was finally chosen as being a suitable place for the stores. Those who inspected the khan, when it was occupied by Arab merchants, did not think it possible ever to eradicate the smell. This difficulty, however, was eventually overcome; numerous alterations and large additions were made as the number of vehicles increased, and the space allowed for stores was added to. When the khan gradually filled to overflowing, large corrugated-iron sheds had to be erected, so that at the present day the buildings occupied by the Stores Section form almost a small village by themselves.

One often wonders what would have happened in France had it been a country similar to Mesopotamia, with no suitable buildings and few workmen, and with vehicles pouring into the country at the prodigious rate at which we sent them over during the four years of war.

It would certainly seem a sound policy, and one advocated by Colonel Donohue, Inspector of Mechanical Transport Services, that units, such as M.T. Depôts, should all have so many collapsible buildings as part of their mobilisation equipment, and that, when necessary, these should accompany the unit, thus making it independent of the shortcomings of the country in which mechanical transport might have to work. It would be by far the cheapest plan in the long run, as big rentals have to be paid for suitable buildings in France or, as in the case of Mesopotamia, building material has to be transported enormous distances at great cost of money, labour, and transport, precisely at a moment when these last two are required most for other purposes. It must be remembered that labour at the Front is always scarce, and time is precious, far more precious even than money.

BASE M.T. DEPÔT, END OF 1918.
Covering 42 acres.

Half an acre in extent for stores.

Our tool-room.
BASE M.T. DEPÔT, SEPTEMBER 1916.

As it was, however, this Base Depôt, with the exception of the two khans already mentioned, had to be completely built. It was unfortunate having the Stores Section separated from the rest of the depôt, for this entailed extra housing accommodation being erected close to the stores. The work on all the buildings of the depôt progressed very slowly, though perhaps it was slightly accelerated by the building operations being split up. The workshop buildings were made of corrugated iron, with iron girders let into cement blocks. A large amount of the work was carried out by the Army Service Corps personnel, and, so long as these men were available, it was carried out quickly; but then a halt would come owing to lack of material. Later, large additions had to be made to accommodate all personnel and reinforcements, as these represented various nationalities who could not be mixed together; also extensions and additions became necessary. Sheds to hold the vehicles of the Reserve Vehicle Park had likewise to be erected; shedding had been demanded for these about October 1916. If I remember rightly, 6,000 feet of 18-feet shedding had been demanded from the Works Directorate and was promised by April 1917. When it came, we were unable to get what was estimated for, as other buildings of more importance, so it was said, had to be constructed. You may forecast and foresee, but it is not always possible to obtain, in war time, what you would consider your just rights. About 3,000 feet of this shedding, however, was eventually obtained for the M.T., after much discussion.

Towards the end of 1916 the Workshop Section was fairly well housed, and the tyre press, badly needed, was also in working order. The Stores Section was at work; spare parts were beginning to arrive and everyone felt that things were on the move. Roads were also springing up; the rain had laid the dust, reinforcements once more were available; motor-cars had also arrived and, naturally, the M.T. began to be looked upon as a "moving" force.

The year 1917 was an exceptionally busy one; between January and December the number of vehicles passing through this depôt reached the total of 2,367. Buildings were extended; officers' and men's quarters and messes and recreation-rooms all began to blossom forth, slowly but (more or less) surely.

At the time this unit arrived in Mesopotamia it was never foreseen that mechanical transport would be used to any very great extent, as the War Establishment embraced a Workshop Section and Stores Section. On arrival it consisted of 9 officers and 202 other ranks. At the present date its War Establishment is 26 officers and 510 other ranks. During 1917 it was considered that the Workshop Section of the depôt should be formed into a separate unit, as an L. of C. heavy repair workshop. The War Establishment was got out, and in the month of June the separation occurred, and 962 M.T. Company was formed out of the Base M.T. Depôt. It retained the workshops, etc., which had been erected by its parent unit, and has occupied them until the present date.

In France, vehicles which have been badly damaged and are beyond ordinary company repair find their way to advanced depôts or to the Base. In Mesopotamia very few vehicles indeed were sent for repair to the Base after 1917. No. 962 Company had enough work to do in keeping all the vehicles at the Base and those on the L. of C. in good order, and in addition it had more work thrust upon it owing to the condition in which vehicles were arriving from overseas. All the heavy repairs from the front line were carried out by the Advanced M.T. Depôt, Baghdad, whose work is dealt with in another chapter.

After the capture of Baghdad it was decided that an Advanced Store Section would be necessary and that it should be located in Baghdad, which city, for the time being, was the hub of the Mesopotamian universe. An advanced section, therefore, was sent up during the month of June 1917, under command of Captain Thresh. Two large buildings were taken over. They had no great advantages, and all the disadvantages it was possible to have; all bins for storing parts, etc., had to be made, and tyre racks erected; a few tons of spare parts which were placed on the first floor had the effect of causing most of the walls of the buildings to bulge, and it was at once apparent that these buildings could not be used as M.T. Stores.

A good khan was found, however, on the right bank, which had just been taken over by the O.C. No. 729 M.T. Company, as a camp. This company, of course, had to be turned out, much to their disgust, though Major Snepp recognised that it was entirely in the interests of the service and took it very well indeed. The other half of this walled enclosure, if I may call it so, was occupied by the prisoners of war, and, naturally enough, a jealous eye was cast on this portion, and efforts were constantly made for the whole khan to be allotted to the A.S.C. M.T. After numerous discussions it was finally decided to transfer the prisoners of war elsewhere, and to allot us the whole khan. A large amount of building had to be done inside, though there were approximately twenty to thirty very good rooms, most of which were afterwards used as tyre stores. Even now, in 1918, with the numerous additions which have been made to this khan, there is barely sufficient room for all the spare parts necessary, and two or three extra yards have been taken over for storing timber and material, in the vicinity.

It was considered at the time a better arrangement to send an advanced section from the Base than to have this unit as a section of the Advanced M.T. Depôt, for the reason that one unit only was dealing with stores and that any differences would be settled by that unit alone. (This refers, of course, to shortages in transit between Basrah and Baghdad.) This arrangement has worked in a perfectly satisfactory manner. The losses have been few, and were easily adjusted; under this system it is not a case of one unit trying to make up deficiencies at the expense of another.

The Returns Section, which this unit previously dealt with, was, on or about May 1, 1918, taken over by the Advanced M.T. Depôt, since it was considered to be a more economical arrangement, and, judging by the work of the last six months, this has undoubtedly proved to be of great benefit. It would be as well to mention that the Returns Section deals with the return to store of M.T. articles no longer required by the various units; as a rule the old worn-out article must be handed in before a new one is issued.

During the operations in May 1918 towards Kirkuk, it was found necessary, for the benefit of the companies working on that line, to establish a Field Section of the Advanced M.T. Stores at railhead to enable companies to obtain spare parts, when there were any available, with greater readiness than having to send into Baghdad for them. This Field Section was a very small one, consisting of an officer and a few men. After the Kirkuk operations it was transferred to Ruz, which was the railhead for the Persian L. of C., and later on it was sent from Ruz to Khaniquin, which was considered the farthest point from which this could be economically worked. Now that the railway is under process of construction into Persia, it is considered necessary to establish a large railhead depôt at Pai Tak Pass, and an increased war establishment was submitted to enable the Base M.T. Depôt to expand, in order to meet the augmented needs of the Stores Section at Basrah, the Advanced Stores at Baghdad, and the railhead depôt at Pai Tak. At the time of writing this book there is an armistice, and it is not known whether this will ever eventuate, but my readers will now be aware of the organisation for handling the M.T. Stores which would, under war conditions, be in vogue in Mesopotamia and Persia.

I can fully appreciate the difficulties of the O.C. Base M.T. Depôt during his two and a half years of trial and tribulation at Basrah. He has had to see his Stores Section situated some distance from the depôt lines ; he has seen his beloved Workshop Section, over which he took so much trouble, taken away and formed into another unit ; and he has had various nationalities going through his reinforcement camp, in which matter he has my entire sympathy ! He has also had to split up his Stores Branch to enable an advanced section to be placed at Baghdad. These are a few of the main features which might have, in ordinary circumstances, formed the ground-work for a good "grouse." But, like a good soldier, Lieut.-Colonel Archibald never let them out of his own hearing. Notwithstanding the many trying conditions under which this very important unit laboured, work progressed on all the buildings, and, at the time of writing, about forty-two acres are taken up entirely by this unit.

The following are the various sections, from which my readers may form some idea of this unit's organisation.

| DETAIL. | BRITISH. | | | | | | INDIAN. | | | | | TOTAL. |
|---|---|---|---|---|---|---|---|---|---|---|---|---|
| | Officers. | W. Officers. | Clerks. | S.-Sergts. & Sergts. | Artificers. | Rank & File. | Officers. | N.C.O.s. | Cooks. | Clerks. | Pub. Followers. | |
| Headquarters | 5 | 2 | 4 | 5 | — | 38 | 1 | 3 | — | 1 | 1 | 60 |
| Store Branch | 8 | 1 | 32 | 8 | — | 26 | — | — | — | — | — | 75 |
| Six Store Groups | 6 | — | 54 | 18 | 12 | 108 | — | — | — | — | — | 198 |
| Reserve Vehicle Park | 2 | 1 | 3 | 4 | 16 | 24 | — | — | — | — | — | 50 |
| School of Instruction | 2 | 1 | 1 | 2 | — | 18 | — | 2 | — | — | — | 26 |
| 1st Reinforcement of Personnel | 2 | 1 | 6 | 3 | — | 28 | — | 10 | 8 | — | 16 | 74 |
| Ahwaz Detachment | 1 | — | — | 2 | 6 | 29 | — | — | — | — | 2 | 40 |
| Base Pool | — | — | — | 1 | — | 11 | — | — | — | — | 1 | 13 |
| Total Base M.T. Depôt | 26 | 6 | 100 | 43 | 34 | 282 | 1 | 15 | 8 | 1 | 20 | 536 |

Receiving and issuing spare parts of M.T. vehicles entails a large organisation even to carry on *routine work under peace conditions*. It must not be forgotten that the M.T.

was working in a country where it was unknown; to be efficient it was necessary that fairly accurate forecasts should be made with regard to its requirements. Past experience has shown that the orders which were placed on the Home Depôt, if supplied directly, would have just met the demands of units. Unfortunately something went wrong; little is known here, beyond the fact that spares never seemed to come. When those on order for four companies turned up there were already fourteen companies in the country! (and only spare parts for four!)—a farce which was continually repeated, notwithstanding that orders were placed on the Home Depôt directly we had the information that further units were being ordered out here.

The number of different items which go to make up a mechanical transport vehicle varies from 1,100 to 1,400, according to the type, and when one multiplies the number of types in the country it is at once seen what a large number of entries there must be in ledgers. In addition, there is a card for every single item in every section, so that one realises the enormous difficulties which the Stores Section has to face, especially in a country where 20 to 25 per cent. of the personnel are constantly sick. The number of items at the present moment which the Stores Section have to account for, amount to approximately 25,000. Urgent demands were always put in for by wire; ordinary demands for stock being sent by post.

I have mentioned in this chapter the Persian L. of C., but the operations on this line will be dealt with more fully in other chapters, as well as the reasons why it was necessary to send an expedition so far up this flank.

I consider it very fortunate that we had an officer of Major Owen's experience in charge of the Stores Section at Basrah, from the time of its arrival up to the end of the war. During the whole time I have been out here I do not think I have ever envied him his job. The position of Officer-in-Charge of Stores Section is always a thankless one. The unit under discussion never gave the slightest cause for complaint, neither to this Directorate nor to the Auditors, and officers and all ranks are to be congratulated, especially in view of the extraordinary difficulties under which they were working, quite apart from the abnormal hot weather, of which Basrah is a chronic victim.

I have referred above to the percentage of sick, and I would emphasise the fact that the figures given are correct, for accurate records were kept at the Base in the Stores Section by Major Owen.

It is only fair to say that during the whole time the Mechanical Transport has been used in Mesopotamia, with the exception of a few small items and a certain amount of material, everything required was received from England. Occasionally one or two of the other Fronts sent us certain surplus stores, but this was only late in the campaign, since in the earlier days nothing *could* be spared.

India as a source of supply was of very little use to this force so far as M.T. spares were concerned ; in fact on one or two occasions we have been let down rather badly. They would promise a supply of spare parts, and in these circumstances orders were not placed in England for a period of several months, during which time no spares were received from India, nor was there any information when they would be forthcoming. Ultimately India politely informed us that she was sorry but that she could not supply, and suggested we indent on England. The delay was serious, and in addition it meant that the type of vehicle in question had to be kept on the road in Mesopotamia for twelve months without a single spare part. From India, however, a certain amount of material was obtainable, and a good supply of spring steel was at one time received ; when the springs had been made, however, it was discovered to be nothing more than mild steel. I have since heard an amusing yarn with regard to this same mild steel from Mr. MacPherson, of the Munitions Board in India, who verified the fact that it was mild steel, but that it was dispatched out here as spring steel. There have been numerous cables both sent to and received from Home M.T. Depôt which have their amusing side, but there is only one which I intend to quote.

In April 1918 Troopers (War Office) wired out to know why such enormous demands had been placed for Ford radiators. The reply was to the effect that the life of a Ford radiator in Mesopotamia was from twelve to eighteen months. In September 1918 Ascormetra, otherwise the Home M.T. Depôt, cabled out to say that seventeen radiators were being dispatched forthwith, and that the balance to complete would be sent out at the rate of thirty a month, i.e. a total of 377 for the twelve months. (There were about 3,500 Fords in the country at the time.) Writing now towards the end of 1918, it can be considered fortunate that it is winter out here, which is fairly cold. Most radiators are now just bits of tin patchwork, which have to be mended daily. If the weather was hot, the cars would be unable to carry sufficient water alone to take them over a fifty-mile journey.

Lack of spare parts has been severely felt, the number of vehicles off the road in companies really being no indication that the workshop staff were not doing their duty. Remarks with regard to scarcity of spares will occur throughout this book. I mention it here, as the provision of spares comes under the Base M.T. Depôt. The other sections, i.e. Reserve Vehicle Park, Reinforcements, Stores Branch, School of Instruction, etc., of this unit had all their particular duties, as their names imply. The work of the R.V.P. was naturally of an up-and-down nature, according to the size of the consignments of vehicles arriving, and to their condition on arrival. This section was never idle, but on occasions had more work than it could possibly cope with, and on the whole did very valuable work.

The training-school was really first required for the instruction of 100 Horse Transport men who were transferred to the M.T. owing to the shortage of drivers. Later on it was found that the men coming from England had to be trained on Fords; others had to have refresher courses. With the inauguration of the Asiatic driver this section may be said to have been kept "real busy." The "trained" driver from India had to be retrained. The first batch of 324 who came over comprised numerous castes. The passing out of these gave the following result:

| Total number tested. | Total number of failures. |
| --- | --- |
| 306 | 196 |

Of this number only about 4 passed as first-class drivers, 30 passed as second-class drivers, and the remainder were all third-class.

The driving test was very simple and consisted of starting the engine, driving round a certain laid-out course, and stopping and starting at a given point; reversing on at least two corners and turning round on a 16-feet road; driving over a few dips and bumps; and answering a few elementary questions on the care of the car.

75 marks qualified a man as a first-class driver, 50 to 74 as a second-class driver, and 30 to 49 as a third-class driver.

It was found afterwards that it was practically a waste of time to try to teach the Indian, mechanism. The chief points to which attention was paid were the driving and elementary care of the car, together with a knowledge of taking off and putting on tyres. Even now, at the end of 1918, very few Asiatics have the slightest knowledge of the engine; all they know is that they fill up with petrol and oil, turn the handle, jump inside, and work their gears. If they get a puncture, the majority are able to take off their tyres but are not always able to put a new tube in. This, on convoy work, is generally left to the First Aid Staff, to save time and also to avoid tubes being damaged.

Under these circumstances you can imagine the feelings of everyone on hearing the good news that Indian drivers were being sent, and we thought how pleased the fighting troops would be to have to depend on these men for their daily ration.

Instruction was the keynote ; they were taught to drive in spite of themselves, and to-day, due to the perseverance of all ranks who assisted in this instruction, both in depôts and companies, the Indian is a good driver, and even in cases where he cannot drive, he does his best to keep his vehicle clean.

These men on their return to India, Burma, Mauritius, and possibly Ceylon—Arabs, Jews, and Armenians—should all prove useful members of a civilised society. There are probably a good half-dozen different castes of Indians employed in Mesopotamia, and these, coupled with the other nationalities mentioned (excluding British), give a total of a round dozen of strange tongues spoken in Mechanical Transport units. The land which produced the Tower of Babel also carried on the good work in 1917 and 1918, only we pronounce it " babble " nowadays.

At this time the War Establishment for a Ford Van Company contains 60 per cent. Asiatic drivers to 40 per cent. British, so it speaks well for officers, N.C.O.s, and men that the vehicles manned by such a motley crew are able to move at all. The M.E.F. did their little bit to save white man-power for the exhaustive fighting on the Western Front, but little is known of the difficulties which had to be surmounted in this land which gave us the Garden of Eden.

Before closing my remarks with regard to the Base M.T. Depôt I should like to bring to notice a few points which are considered worthy of interest. During the year 1918, approximately the following arrived and were dispatched up country :

| | Arrivals in the country. | Departures up the country. |
|---|---|---|
| Vehicles . . . . . . . . | 3,300 | 3,100 |
| British personnel . . . . . . | 5,000 | 4,000 |
| Indian ,, . . . . . . . | 3,500 | 3,000 |

The above vehicles exclude motor-cycles.

The total number of Indians tested by this unit was 2,600, whilst 1,200 have had to be completely trained in driving. 1,200 British drivers were tested during the year, and more than 400 trained; while the total number tested and trained for the years 1917 and 1918 were 4,200 and 1,500 respectively. In addition to the above more than 800 artificers were trade-tested.

The above information should give my readers some idea of the many duties which a Base M.T. Depôt has to perform.

During October 1916, orders were received for the move of G.H.Q. from Basrah to Arab Village, and the move was started on October 15, 1916. The D. of S. and T. (Brig.-General P. C. J. Scott) and the Staff of this Directorate left on October 17, 1916. As previously mentioned, there was little or no M.T. up at the front line, and, the reorganising having to start at the Base, I had to remain there for the time being.

Orders for certain vehicles had already been sent home, and information had been received from England that a number were on the way out. There were no mobile workshops in the country available for sending up the line, so some arrangements had to be made whereby the vehicles in the front line and those due to come could be repaired, Arab Village being some 200 odd miles from Basrah. It was decided that a floating workshop should be constructed. For this purpose a *mehayla*, or large native craft, was obtained; the actual tonnage of the boat was about 60 to 80 tons. It is hardly necessary to describe this craft, since a glance at the photograph will show the reader the exact type. The Ark of Biblical times, I should imagine, was similar, but doubtless somewhat larger. Underneath the platform on which the machinery was erected, a good strong floor was made and bins put up for the purpose of carrying a supply of spare parts; this unit acted as a small section of the Base M.T. Depôt, both from the point of view of workshop and Stores Section, up to the capture of Baghdad.

Even in 1916, *mehaylas* were almost worth their weight in gold, and it was only after great difficulty that one of these boats was obtained. The work of fitting it up was undertaken by the O.C. Base M.T. Depôt and the officer in charge.

Another reason why it was necessary to have such a unit was that information had been received from the War office that the two Ford Van Companies on order would not be equipped with mobile workshops, though these were eventually received. It was recognised in any case that mobile workshops would not be available for work with these units for some time to come, and that meanwhile some means must be adopted for repairs. Even the fitting-out of this craft presented numerous difficulties—it was almost impossible to obtain timber, for it was being very jealously guarded at this time at Basrah, owing to the supply being very small. Sufficient, however, was obtained, and the work was put in hand. Captain Wood was instrumental in getting out the design, but when the work was practically complete it was considered by the inspector from the Inland Water Transport to be top heavy, and the whole platform had to be lowered 16 inches. This was completed in twelve hours—a good performance considering that there were thirty-two uprights 6 inches by 4 inches, all of which had to be cut down and fitted. The platform was jacked up while this was being done, and when all was ready, it was lowered into its new position. Captain Sykes, the O.C. of the unit, was responsible for this smart bit of work.

This floating workshop left the Base a few days afterwards, Lieutenant Buckley and about forty artificers of various trades, in addition to the O.C., forming its war establishment. Two smaller *mehaylas* were afterwards obtained—boats capable of carrying about 25 tons—and were fitted out merely for the purpose of carrying spare parts, but this was not done until a month or so after the main floating workshop had left for Arab Village, it then being found that one boat

THE FIRST FLOATING WORKSHOP.

could not accommodate all the stores. This unit did very good work indeed while stationed at Arab Village, and a few days after the main advance on Baghdad began, it was all ready packed up and waiting to be towed up river.

The O.C., by some means, at a time when tug-boats were very scarce, managed to get up river, arriving at Baghdad only a few days after the occupation on March 11, 1917. A suitable building was selected, and this unit was in the position to undertake repairs to M.T. vehicles on March 17.

It would be as well, while on the subject of this floating workshop, to finish off its history up to the present date.

It remained in Baghdad until June 1917, moored close to the building which is now occupied by the Advanced M.T. Depôt. After the arrival of the personnel of that unit, it was found necessary to move the floating workshops down river, as the place was getting rather congested, so it was moored close alongside the bank at Hinaidi (four miles from Baghdad) with its two attendant store boats. It continued to carry on the work of repairs, and also assisted in the general overhaul of the Fords of the two companies which were then out here, namely, 783 and 784 Companies, and also the various vehicles, cars, and ambulances which were attached to it for repairs.

With the increase of the M.T., and the age of the boats in question, it was considered advisable that a *swimender* barge should be applied for. This would enable its machinery and any extra required, as well as the vehicles under repair, to be garaged on board. In addition it would have a double deck, where the personnel could be accommodated upstairs. Sanction was granted for this on October 5, 1917, and the work of fitting out the barge up to a certain point, was given to the D.I.W.T., and a very nice job was made of it. It was put in hand on November 20, 1917, and was completed by January 22, 1918, and arrived from Basrah on February 8, 1918. Numerous additions had to be made to this barge, such as the fitting-up of the officers', N.C.O.s', and men's quarters, the various offices and store-rooms, and also the transfer of the machinery from the old *mehayla*. Captain J. C. Gould, A.S.C., was in charge of this unit at the time, and very rapid progress was made with all the work. It was finally completed about five to six weeks after its arrival at Hinaidi.

About the time the floods were expected, it was found necessary to move this barge three miles farther up the river to a place called Karradah. Owing to the river rising in the early summer, it was found that the channel of the Tigris had shifted once again and that this barge was a danger to shipping using the channel—or, from an M.T. point of view, the shipping was a great danger to the barge—so it was decided to bring it up beyond Baghdad. A suitable mooring was chosen, and this workshop, at the time of writing, is installed about two miles above Baghdad on the left bank.

This unit, in addition to its ordinary functions, acts as parent to two mobile workshops, each consisting of six Packard workshop and store lorries, with the same equipment as for a Ford Van Company, and with the same number of artificers. These are sent out as required to various Corps or areas requiring extra workshop facilities. The whole of the personnel can be housed on board this barge, and the men's quarters are specially fitted up with a double row of bunks on the upper deck. They are airy, cool, and comfortable. A portable fitters' shop for use on shore has also been erected by this unit, for, as a rule, considerably more vehicles are under repair than the space on the barge could possibly accommodate.

On or about June 17, 1918, Captain H. C. Gould, who had business troubles in England, was ordered home, and the unit was taken over by Lieutenant Ainsworth, who is entirely responsible for all the later improvements which have been made with regard to both the barge and the portable buildings on shore. At this time, including the two workshops, the war establishment had been increased to 111, all ranks.

It might be interesting to record here the tools with which the first floating workshop was fitted. They were as follows: 2 small lathes, 1 grinder, 1 electric drill, 1 Austin power plant, 1 treadle drilling machine, and the usual fitters', wheelers', and blacksmiths' tools in addition.

The extra plant fitted on the large barge is as follows: 1 $8\frac{3}{4}$-inch centre gap lathe, 1 power shaping machine, 1 hand shaping machine, 1 Austin power plant, 2 electric drills, 1 sensitive drill, 2 small lathes, 1 grinder.

A photograph of the large and up-to-date barge is reproduced, and a general idea can be formed from this together with the written description.

## CHAPTER III

### COUNTRY AND CLIMATE

Description of country, roads, railways, etc.—Climate and diseases—Short account of a Vauxhall convoy—Some photographs.

In September 1916 we who were just out from home, and had had no experience of the East, found the weather remarkably hot, and, judging by reports from officers with regard to what the months of June and July were like, most of us were very thankful we had not arrived earlier. It was hardly to be wondered at, therefore, that the unfortunate A.S.C. M.T. drivers who had to experience the hardships of the 1916 summer, when ice and fans were unknown, should have gone sick in the numbers they did.

The majority of the M.T. in the country in 1916 were employed at the Base, though No. 596 Company, with over 400 personnel, had small detachments in one or two other places for transport purposes. The heavy lorry up to that time was untried up country.

Provided good houses, fans and ice, and, if possible, good lighting facilities are available in Basrah, the climatic conditions for nine months during the year are very fair indeed, but the months of June, July, and August are, as a rule, anything but nice. There is a very high temperature which sometimes goes up to 122 degrees in the shade, *as it did in* 1917; the heat is, moreover, damp and clammy. The farther up the river you go the drier the climate becomes.

In Baghdad, although the temperature may rise to 124° in the shade, there was no comparing this with 116° in the shade at Basrah. One great advantage of the Mesopotamian climate, as compared with other tropical countries, is its cool nights and a considerable drop in the temperature from the extreme heat of the day. In Baghdad and beyond one could always do with a blanket at night when sleeping.

During the winter months, both at Basrah and up country, the days are usually bright and warm, but once the sun has gone down it gets very cold, and it is easy to realise that during the four seasons of the year in a country such as this the ordinary man who has done little travelling is liable to go sick from various causes due entirely to the climatic conditions. No doubt, in the early days of the Mesopotamian Campaign, numerous reports had gone to various quarters with regard to these conditions. There had already been a Mesopotamian scandal and new arrivals all seemed full of forebodings as to what would probably happen to them during their sojourn in the country, but the end of 1916 and the years 1917 and 1918 were very different from 1915 and the early days of 1916.

Great strides had been made both from a medical point of view and the engineering side, i.e. with regard to buildings, roads, etc.; things were not so black as they were painted. It is rather unfortunate in a way that even now, in 1918, no action appears to have been taken to try to stop the spreading of yarns with regard to the conditions in this country. I always made it a point to ask officers on arrival out here what is still thought of Mesopotamia at home. Practically all the answers have been the same—that their friends never expect to see them back again.

In addition to the heat and cold there are, of course, the rainy and the flood seasons. The former lasts, as a rule, from about November to March, but the rain is very intermittent. Sometimes it rains for a day and then there is a week's fine weather. While the country is wet, travelling is practically impossible for any kind of transport. During the winter 1916–17 there were only about thirteen days on which the Ford vans could not work. On one or two of these days it would have been possible to work, but it was considered a sounder proposition to keep them off the roads and allow them to dry. The soil is extraordinarily sticky —like a mixture of glue and cement—and when wet it is not at all pleasant to attempt walking or driving. The rain also takes a long time to percolate through the soil, and the water lies on the top.

I think some of my readers will remember that section which runs from Kadara up to close on Kizil Robat, which was under water for some days; the water was about 9 inches deep along the track which was utilised by Ford vans, but there happened to be a certain bite in the ground and, notwithstanding the water, convoys were able to proceed.

During the spring of 1918 the rainy season lasted longer than usual and extended into May, and in consequence we had a very cold spring. Like all other countries, the seasons vary to a greater or lesser extent as the case may be. The first floods, as a rule, come down in March, and are caused by the rain-water from the higher levels along the Tigris, which generally have the effect of causing a rise in the river. The second flood in April is due to the snow melting on the mountains, and naturally depends on the amount of snow that has fallen during the winter, which varies in accordance with the severity of that season.

In Biblical times, doubtless, Noah was a weather prophet, having a great number of years' experience, and he foresaw that in a certain year there would be a great flood, and he prepared accordingly. It is quite easy to exaggerate present-day floods over such a level country. A rise of a few extra feet over the ordinary flood-level, and the whole of Mesopotamia practically becomes one vast sea as far as human eye, even aided by binoculars, can reach.

The spring flood of 1918 was a record one, and though

the big bund which is around Baghdad had been built up 2 feet higher than any known flood of recent years, there was only a question of 6 inches more to go before the flood would have been over the top. As a matter of fact this catastrophe would not have actually happened, as the Works Department had made arrangements for cutting the bund some miles above Baghdad, and diverting the flood water by the Baqubah road north of the city.

One of the most trying peculiarities of Mesopotamia, if one might call it so, is the dust. The soil, though apparently hard when dry, very soon cuts up under constant traffic, and a very fine form of dusty sand results. It is very light and is easily blown about; in fact, on a still evening, after a car has passed along a dusty track, it sometimes hangs in the air for an hour at a time. So those who have not done convoy work in Mesopotamia, but who are used to mechanical transport, can well imagine what happens with a long convoy of M.T. vehicles on a dusty track. A side-wind in this country is always considered the convoy's greatest friend.

One can hardly devote a chapter to Country and Climate without writing a few words about diseases. Like all Eastern countries, the towns are naturally dirty, with flies innumerable. These pests, however, seem to make themselves felt mostly in the spring and autumn, the winter being too cold for them, while the summer is too hot. The chief diseases met with out here are smallpox, cholera, enteric, plague, dysentery, malaria, and sandfly fever—diseases from which the M.T. drivers chiefly suffered. While on the subject of diseases it is absurd to think that men should be enlisted or conscripted into an army and be allowed to come out to the East and run the risk of carrying a disease such as smallpox, without being vaccinated. This should have been made compulsory. I hold no brief for vaccination, but where the medical authorities have laid it down that vaccination is essential, it is up to all to see that, for the sake of our comrades, we take all recognised precautions. Notwithstanding the fact that the M.T. driver was almost the first man to spread this disease, there were a great number (at one time 500!) of conscientious objectors. The persuasive powers of the doctors seemed hardly sufficient for the purpose of converting these, and it was left to the R.A.S.C. to do it. I'm glad to say it was done fairly successfully, since, at the time of writing, there are fewer than half a dozen objectors in the country.

While on the subject of country and climate it is rather essential that reference should be made to roads. The roads for the most part are merely composed of the actual soil of the desert, sometimes raised up a foot or two above the ground, but more often than not just a mere track. This soil, if kept watered by artificial means, becomes wonderfully hard and really forms a very good road; but in a country such as this, where water is scarce and roads are necessary, it can readily be seen that road maintenance was one of the most difficult problems which had to be faced.

In the 15th Division, both before and after the capture of Ramadie, great strides were taken to make roads, and the G.O.C., Major-General H. T. Brooking, C.B., prides himself on all the roads in his area, and I must say that they are good. A kind of white, rather sandy sort of stone was obtainable from Ramadie right down to Dhibban on a range of hills, and this was utilised for the building of a road from Dhibban to Felujah. A good road, too, was made from Kadara to Kizil Robat, called the Duwailab road; but for the most part, and looking at it from a mechanical transport point of view, the tracks on which vehicles had to run could honestly not be called roads at all.

During 1917–18 it was brought home to the authorities very forcibly that it was far cheaper to expend time and labour on road maintenance than it was to try to keep pace with the breakages on M.T. vehicles, and this resulted in efforts being made in every area to try to improve road conditions; these efforts were effective. A glance at the map, however, and the measuring of distances over which

VAUXHALL CONVOY AFTER CROSSING SHAFI BRIDGE.
Tigris in the distance.

mechanical transport had to run, will show the reader at once what an extremely difficult problem road maintenance was and always will be. One might almost say that the mechanical transport ran from the Persian Gulf to the Caspian Sea, via Baghdad, a distance of approximately 1,000 miles.

In November, knowing very little about the country, I took the opportunity of taking a convoy of eighteen Vauxhall cars up to G.H.Q., which were then settled at Arab Village. I am putting in a short account of this journey which, though it contains nothing of very great note, will doubtless help to bring home to those of my readers who have never been in the country the road conditions in Mesopotamia. The result of the journey had also the effect of causing still more attention to be paid to road maintenance.

On November 10 the convoy took the road at 11 a.m., two cars being left behind to bring on Colonel Donohue, A.S.C., who was arriving from Bushire in a few days' time. No trouble was experienced until after our arrival at Kurnah, which was reached during the afternoon.

The Vauxhalls' first experience through heavy sand was about seven miles below Sakricha, where there was a stretch of several hundred yards along the railway-line then in course of construction. Although this point was reached about 5 p.m., when it is comparatively cool, all the radiators boiled coming through this very bad stretch; in fact one or two of the vehicles found great difficulty in getting through at all. A halt had to be made for the night (in the open) soon afterwards, for one of the drivers took a wrong turning and went off the track into a ditch. The car, badly damaged, was dug out the following morning. A photograph of the operation is shown opposite page 38.

The "going" was not what one could describe as good, especially the approaches to the bridges, and in my road report I pointed out that it was disgraceful and not fit for any form of mechanical transport.

Next morning, November 11, the damaged car was extricated in a couple of hours. The front axle was badly twisted, but nevertheless the vehicle was able to proceed slowly under its own power, but it was left at Sakricha, for the time being, and eventually brought into the Base M.T. Depôt. The road continued to be bad up to Ezra's Tomb, which was reached during the afternoon. As the convoy crossed the railway-line, one of the cars was damaged owing to the very steep incline, the base chamber of the engine of No. 4 car striking the line. It was brought into the camp at Ezra's Tomb and put on a barge, which fortunately happened to be there, and dispatched to the Base. By this time it was too late to proceed farther that day, so a halt was made for the night.

One has often heard yarns about mosquitoes in various parts of the world from travellers, but I do not think any of those travellers could ever have slept a night at Ezra's Tomb. No man would ever dare tell the truth about Ezra's mosquitoes for fear of being thought an apostle of Ananias. Any of my readers who have slept there will, I am sure, bear me out in this respect. Each one of the party next morning was a "Study in Bites!"

On the morning of the 12th the railway-crossing had to be built up with planks to enable the Vauxhalls to get over without damaging the crank-cases, and the cars were not clear of this crossing until 10 a.m. The going for a few miles from Ezra's Tomb was fair, but when about seven miles out it got very bad and naturally the pace had to slacken. Delay was experienced at Qalat Saleh owing to the bridge not being open for road traffic, and the cars were not clear of this until about 3 o'clock. On looking up the road report of this section I see that it is described as "that part of the country on which the cars ran." One point, about three miles from Abu Sidra, is one of the worst pieces of "road" it has ever been my lot to travel over. The section in question was about half a mile long, and I do not think any of the vehicles went over it at more than

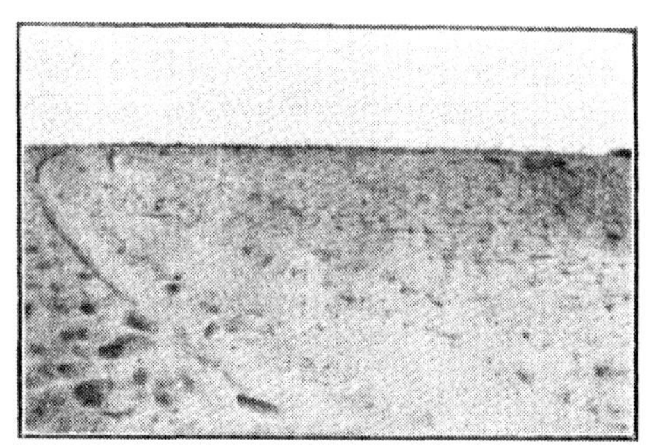

A piece of the road from Basrah to Arab Village, November 1916.

On the road between Ahwaz and Shush, Persia, January 1917.

Road from Hillah to Museib along the Euphrates, during the wet weather.

THREE] EXAMPLES OF "ROADS" IN MESOPOTAMIA AND PERSIA.

about one and a half miles per hour, and yet three buffer springs were broken while it was being traversed. Abu Sidra was reached about 4.30 p.m. The total mileage to date was 99 miles, and the total running hours 12½. *Casualties*, 2 cars *hors de combat*.

On November 13 Amarah was reached about 10.30 a.m. Here one or two cars had to be handed over, and a few men were admitted to hospital, with the result that we could not proceed farther than No. 2 Marching Post that day.

November 14.—The running from No. 2 Marching Post to No. 8 was a distance of about 70 miles. This was the best day's run up to then. It must not be forgotten that nearly all the drivers were inexperienced to Mesopotamian roads and to the various minor mechanical troubles. Incidentally, time was no object and every opportunity for keeping the pace down was taken to avoid breakages. On this day further trouble was experienced with boiling radiators owing to the very heavy sandy stretches and lack of water.

On November 15 we left No. 8 Marching Post at about 9 a.m., and Sheikh Sa'ad was reached at 10 o'clock, where we remained some time owing to the bridge not being open for road traffic. While here I inspected the two Caterpillar Companies which had just arrived. We resumed our journey at 12.30 p.m. for Arab Village. The road, which ran direct to that place, was what one could only describe as a sandy stretch, and the radiators of all the vehicles had to be filled up about eight times in the course of seven miles. Arab Village was reached during the afternoon, and on the two following days the cars were delivered to their various destinations.

The road reports sent in to the D.Q.M.G. and to the Intelligence Branch could not be called reassuring, and it was apparent that strong measures would have to be taken at once to get the roads in proper condition if mechanical transport was to be used to any great extent. It is far cheaper to maintain roads than it is to provide the spare parts, especially when the long distance from the source of supply is taken into consideration.

Writing at this juncture (1918), remarkable strides have certainly been made in the country with regard to road maintenance. Although some of my readers may doubtless smile when I talk of "remarkable strides," recalling to mind the number of vehicles they have had out of action, I shudder to think of what would have happened had less been done to the roads.

All this took time, however, and the companies who came out here in the early days have the satisfaction of knowing that it was their experience which helped to improve road conditions.

Previous to my departure from the Base Major Hodgkinson, Indian Army, attached to the Army Service Corps, Mechanical Transport, in Mesopotamia, had taken up five Ford cars to Arab Village. He gave a very graphic account of his journey and had numerous and interesting photographs of the road from Basrah.

Soon after my report was sent in the work of putting the whole of the road into fairly good order was undertaken, and subsequently convoys had not the same difficulties as experienced by those who left the Base at the end of 1916. Although the road was in a fearful state most of the way up, there was an exception from Amarah to No. 5 Marching Post. Here very good efforts had been made to keep the road in order; in fact, one could say that it was the only place along the whole line fit for mechanical transport.

While at G.H.Q., on this visit, numerous road reports were made by me and sent in to headquarters, and Lieutenant Vlasto was called in to assist, with his detachment of Fiats, in improving the numerous culverts between Twin Canals and Sheikh Sa'ad.

When visiting Arab Village again in March 1917 the improvements in the roads were certainly most marked, and on the majority of them one could travel in comfort at from

JUST BEFORE THE ACCIDENT TO LIEUTENANT LAMPARD, M.C.

A MINUTE AFTER THE ACCIDENT.

twenty to twenty-five miles per hour from Arab Village almost right up to the Hai.

On November 22 a few cars were collected for the return journey, one or two of which had to be delivered on the way down—chiefly Fords.

A start was made at 11 a.m., but there is very little of interest to report with regard to this journey, which, except for numerous delays at bridges, would have been accomplished by the afternoon of the 24th. As a matter of fact Basrah was reached on the morning of the 25th, the actual running time being 18½ hours. There were no involuntary stops on the way back.

The new bridge over the Euphrates at Ghurmat Ali had been completed by this time and made available for road traffic. While on the subject of this bridge it might be of interest to inform my readers that it was the one which was afterwards moved to Baghdad, placed in position, and called South Bridge. It was of a peculiar type, and not suitable for a river of strong currents, so that in the spring of 1918, when the very heavy floods came, it was carried away. I understand that some parts of the bridge even got as far as Amarah. At the time of writing this book the new bridge at Baghdad is almost completed.

The question of roads on the L. of C. was taken up with the Director of Works, the late Brigadier-General Stokes-Roberts, C.B., who was deeply interested in the welfare of mechanical transport, an officer who always did his best to help you out of a difficulty. It was due in a great measure to his work on the L. of C. that roads were made at all passable.

I must now say a word about conditions on the Persian side. In the rainy season there was one great source of trouble on the roads to the units working beyond Kizil Robat up to Pai Tak. There are numerous foothills which, when it rains, collect the water into one central channel, which usually swamps the road in the vicinity. One or two drivers lost their lives in these raging torrents, and Lieutenant

Lampard, M.C., would have been lost but for the presence of mind of an Indian. The latter unwound his turban and threw out one end to Lampard, who managed to catch hold of it and was pulled ashore. These gullies had their amusing side, though not from the workshop officer's point of view. Those where trouble was experienced gradually became known to all drivers, and resulted in their charging downhill, across the small gully with a great bump, and up the other side at a fast speed.

The farther one went into Persia the worse the roads became up as far as Hamadan, but the country seen from the top of Pai Tak Pass in spring and summer is really beautiful, especially to those of us who had spent eighteen months of desert in Mesopotamia. Numerous valleys had to be traversed with varying soils and tracks, and those that were good soon became bad.

Pai Tak Pass itself was no small obstacle to be negotiated. Alexander the Great was supposed to have used this pass, and I was informed that the large archway built half-way down the pass commemorates this passage. The only other pass of note on the road to Hamadan is the Asadabad, rising up to 7,000 feet in seven miles. Captain Aldham was the first Army Service Corps Mechanical Transport officer to experience these joys, he having been selected to proceed with the original "Dunsterforce" in charge of about forty-six Ford vans and six cars. His account of the journey through the snows forms interesting reading, though the details with regard to the numerous dead seen *en route* are rather harrowing. Many seem to have been caught in a blizzard on this pass, and died of exposure. The dead through starvation were also numerous. I witnessed similar scenes even in July 1918.

There are certain good stretches in this long road, but these are all too short. While M.T. vehicles were working this line, as they had to do all the summer of 1918, the wear and tear on tyres was abnormal. Peerless lorry tyres could only go 500–600 miles on back tyres without re-

TYPES OF M.T. DRIVERS IN MESOPOTAMIA.

The key to the group of mixed races is as follows (reading left to right):—*Back row.*—Hindoos.—*Fourth row.*—1, 2, 3, 4, 5, Mussulmans; 6, West African; 7, Italian; 8, Armenian; 9, 10, 11, 12, 13, Indian Christians.—*Third row.*—1, 2, 3, 4, 5, Sikhs; 6, American; 7, 8, Englishmen; 9, Canadian; 10, 11, 12, 13, Pathans.—*Second row, sitting.*—1, Burman; 2, 3, Armenians. 4, 5, Armenian Jews; 6, Manxman; 7, Irishman; 8, 9, Englishmen; 10, Scotchman; 11, Welshman; 12, 13, 14, Mauritians; 15, Pathan.—*First row, sitting.*—1, 2, Burmese; 3, 4, 5, Arabs; 6, 7, 8, 9, Chinese; 10, 11, Mauritians.

tyring and about double that on the front. As the Persian L. of C. was almost in the nature of a surprise and no provision made, all the available tyres were used up in three months, though this represented 100 per cent. for all Peerless in the country, of which there were 285, but only 75 were in use on the Persian L. of C. The consumption of covers and tubes on Packards and Fords was also considerable.

For the benefit of those who have not done mechanical transport work in Mesopotamia or Persia, the following short account of a convoy might not be out of place.

Quite recently an officer was sent out with forty-five ordinary Ford vans, and while returning between Hamadan and Kermanshah, over a distance of forty-two miles, twenty-one front springs and five back axles were broken, in addition to numerous minor troubles. The drivers composing this convoy were approximately half British and half Indian.

This is related merely to emphasise to my readers the difficulty with which M.T. drivers had to contend in this country, and it will assist them when reading the chapters devoted to operations especially, where remarks occur with reference to the hard work done by all Mechanical Transport personnel.

It might be as well to mention in this chapter the question of railways.

At the time of the occupation there was nothing in the shape of a railway between Basrah and Baghdad, and naturally, in view of an advance, the question of railways had to be seriously considered. The first line to be constructed was that between Basrah and Nasiriyeh. This was completed on December 29, 1916, and to assist river traffic it was decided to run the line to Amarah. After the capture of Baghdad the length of the lines of communication was considerably increased from Basrah. The windings of the Tigris from Kut upwards can only be described as extraordinary. In summer, when the river fell, it was at times impossible to navigate, except for very light draught boats. Serious, and possibly disastrous, delays would occur, so it was considered necessary to run a railway-line from Kut to Baghdad. This was completed on July 25, 1917—a remarkably fine performance. I am given to understand that the Turks, when informed of it, could not believe that it was completed in the time.

From an M.T. point of view the railways were a great nuisance. They were generally constructed over the ordinary roads, and while in the course of construction the M.T. had to find a new way to get to their destinations, sometimes using the railway permanent way, and at other times making the best of a bad job. This was, of course, prior to the proper maintenance of roads in the vicinity of railway-lines.

The list I append below shows the dates on which the various lines were constructed :

| | |
|---|---|
| Kut to Baghdad | 25.7.1917 |
| Baghdad to Felujah | 20.12.1917 |
| Baghdad to Dhibban | 18. 2.1918 |
| Hinaidi to Table Mountain | June 1918 |
| Hinaidi to Kizil Robat | December 1918 |
| Baghdad to Tekrit | 17. 8.1918 |
| Baghdad to Baiji | 9.12.1918 |
| Baghdad to Hillah | 30. 5.1918 |
| Basrah to Nasiriyeh | 29.12.1916 |
| Narumah to Amarah | 20.10.1917 |
| Basrah to Amarah | 26.12.1917 |

Before dismissing the question of railways, it should be noted that no remarks have been made with regard to the Decauville light lines. These were used wherever possible and with great success.

The light line will have to be reckoned with in the future, and doubtless the motive power of this will be an internal-combustion engine of some description and not necessarily one that can only run on lines. I believe a certain type of motor lorry with ordinary back wheels, shod with solid rubber tyres and bogey front wheels for running on the line, has been tried with great success in South Africa, when used to take the place of the ordinary steam engine.

NO. 1 WAS TAKEN AT THE TIME THE BRIDGE WAS BEING CARRIED AWAY. THE BREAKAGE CAN BE SEEN ON THE RIGHT.

NO. 2 SHOWS ALL THAT WAS LEFT AN HOUR AFTERWARDS.

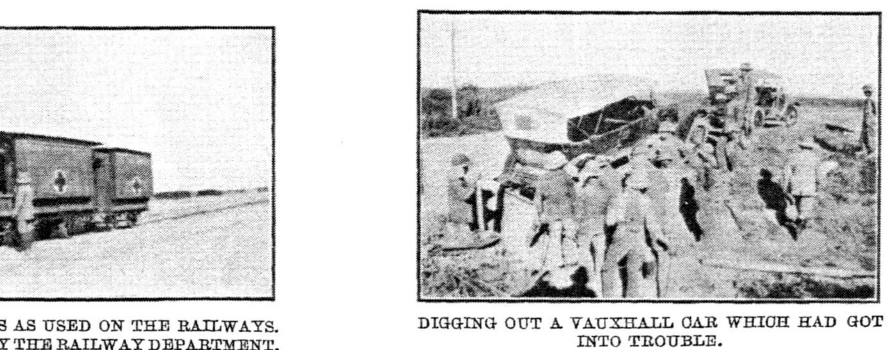

MOTOR AMBULANCES AS USED ON THE RAILWAYS. THESE WERE RUN BY THE RAILWAY DEPARTMENT.

DIGGING OUT A VAUXHALL CAR WHICH HAD GOT INTO TROUBLE.

# CHAPTER IV

## TYPES OF VEHICLES AND MEN

Discussing various types of M.T. vehicles as used during the campaign—The various nationalities who were taught motor driving—Arab skilled labour.

In 1916 there were few types of M.T. vehicles in Mesopotamia, and the country over which an advance might take place was almost unknown. The Peerless lorry was practically used only at the base, though the Fiats were in constant use along the front lines. Their experience tended to prove that the pneumatic-tyred vehicle was essential for desert work.

It is very hard to imagine the condition of the desert when the weather is dry; with troops, guns, and animals constantly passing over the same place day after day, the tracks become like drift sand, and you can dig for a foot or two before getting to a hard under-surface. It will readily be seen, therefore, that solid tyres would be unsuitable and pneumatic-tyred vehicles essential. Twin tyres, too, would be necessary on the back wheels for heavy loads.

This chapter will deal with the types of M.T. vehicles which were sent out to Mesopotamia, and it is not overstating the case to say that, without exception, they all did excellent work.

Since the Fiat lorry had proved itself a good type of

vehicle, the question came up as to whether a similar type could be found among English or American lorries. It was decided that the American Packard would be a suitable vehicle for work in this country. This vehicle was fitted with solid tyres and it was a question of altering the wheels and fitting them with rims to take pneumatic tyres. The War Office wired out to say that this was being carried out, and that two companies, Nos. 729 and 730, were being mobilised for service in Mesopotamia equipped with these light Packard lorries. Later a cable was received stating that owing to the wheels being of assorted sizes trouble was experienced in the conversion, and that these two companies could not be expected to come out equipped with these vehicles. Eventually they came out as Ford van companies.

Notwithstanding this, it may be as well to mention that nearly all the Ford van companies were later equipped with light Packards as workshop and store lorries, all of which had pneumatic tyres. One complete company, i.e. No. 976 M.T. Company, was also mobilised as a Packard company, and has since done very good service in this country. Presumably there was something else besides the size of the wheels which, at the time, prevented these two companies being mobilised as Packard companies. Had they arrived early in 1917 as such, they would have been invaluable in the advance on Baghdad in March.

Mechanical transport was urgently required towards the end of 1916 for the forthcoming winter campaign, and as nothing else could be immediately dispatched from England, it was decided that Ford vans should be used. The chief advantage, of course, with the Ford was that it was light, and this was of considerable importance in the rainy season. These vans could travel for some hours after the rain had begun, when it was practically impossible for a heavier type of vehicle to move, even with non-skid chains.

This vehicle was supposed to carry a useful load of 8 cwt. Actual experience proved that the maximum load was 7 maunds (560 lb.), or when carrying passengers, in lieu of supplies, the total number allowed was three in addition to the driver.

It might be worth mentioning that small cards were printed, and issued to all companies concerned, containing this information, so that all drivers of detached vehicles could be given them. This was deemed necessary in view of the frequent cases which occurred of the overloading of these vehicles. On certain occasions, when the roads were extremely bad, it was not possible to carry 560 lb., and the load had to be reduced to 6 maunds or 480 lbs.

At one time it was thought it would be a useful thing to attach a few Kurds to each Ford van company. The type of Kurd intended was the "carrier." He can generally manage to carry about half a ton on his back, and he walks round the streets shouting "Ba'alak" (meaning "look-out").

These men would have been invaluable at times in carting home a car which had been damaged in an accident or bogged. Once get the vehicle on his back, there would not be the slightest difficulty in his carrying it any distance up to two or three miles. The experiment, however, was never tried, chiefly owing to the large sums of money which these men earn as "carriers" in Baghdad. It would have cost almost as much to have kept one of these Kurds in a Ford van company as it would a 3-ton lorry.

Notwithstanding the numerous breakages and trouble experienced owing to arduous conditions, of which more anon, the Ford has repeatedly proved itself a very suitable vehicle for this country. In addition to carrying supplies, it has been used for the carriage of water, ammunition, troops, Lewis guns and crews, and, on numerous occasions, a Ford has gone right up to the trenches under enemy rifle fire. From a transport point of view, the heavier vehicles, namely, Peerless, Napier, Daimler, etc., have all done very good work in this country, but it is impossible for these heavy lorries to travel unless the tracks are hard.

In addition to the van, the Ford car, as issued to units, etc., gave universal satisfaction. The car used by General

Headquarters, Headquarters of Army Corps and of Divisions was a 25 h.p. Vauxhall. All officers I have met who have used this car speak very highly of it, though a single rear wheel is preferred to the twin. I fancy that this is chiefly due to the fact that, going through heavy sand, the twin wheel brings the dust round with it, and this, entering the back of the car, makes travelling very unpleasant on hot days. Personally I used a Vauxhall for two and a half years during this campaign, and I can say it "never let me down." During this period my car was driven as a rule by Pte. Holmes, and we made the acquaintance of all parts of Mesopotamia and various parts of Persia.

I will return for a moment to the heavier type of vehicle, the Peerless lorry, which has been in use from the Gulf to the Caspian Sea. I have nothing but praise for this vehicle, and also for all ranks of No. 596 M.T. Company, A.S.C., for the arduous work accomplished under very trying conditions during their three years of active service in Mesopotamia.

The types of ambulances in general use were the Ford, Star, and Vulcan. All did remarkable work, but the Ford, owing chiefly to its lightness, was considered the most suitable. One disadvantage of this vehicle is its small carrying-capacity for patients as compared with the two heavier types just mentioned. The great overhang, too, is a drawback which might be remedied. It has been considered that it would be a great advantage to have the two lying-down cases on the same side, one above the other; shorten the body and bring the ends of the stretchers and the body on the near side immediately over the dash. This would have the effect of distributing the load to a greater extent. It was suggested in 1917, but owing to the great amount of work already in hand, it was not considered advisable to attempt to make any alterations. During 1918, however, the 3rd Corps undertook to alter one of these ambulances and give it a good trial. Up to the time of writing no reports have been received with regard to this.

OFF-LOADING CATERPILLARS ON TO A BARGE, BASRAH 1916.

These were the first of their kind seen in the country.

A NEW USE FOR THE FORD.

Towing some trucks along the Decauville Railway between Baghdad and the Euphrates.

Two other types of vans were employed with M.T. units—namely, the Talbot, 1-ton useful load, and the Napier, of similar capacity. The Talbots were issued to Ford van companies as first-aid vans, and did very good work, the body being just capable of carrying a broken-down Ford. The Napier was used by an armoured-car battery, and I understand that it gave satisfaction. The supply from home was limited, and at the end of 1918 the Crossley van, well known as the R.A.F. tender, was also taken up by the R.A.S.C. and acted with its usual good behaviour.

Although this book deals with the M.T. as a whole in Mesopotamia, the events contained therein deal more particularly with those vehicles used for transport purposes. A few remarks regarding other lorries and vans which were used might be interesting.

The "caterpillar" tractor, for example, used for the carriage of guns, on occasions did very good work carrying ammunition and sometimes supplies. Each "caterpillar" company was equipped with a few 5-ton Fowler trucks. The "caterpillars" were also used for agricultural purposes during the lull in the fighting, and several of them were responsible for the ploughing up of considerable acreage in the neighbourhood of Baghdad. They were also used to drag a heavy road plough, when the condition of the tracks rendered it necessary to level them.

The anti-aircraft gun-lorries were all Thornycrofts, and it was really marvellous the way in which these vehicles got through in the advance on Baghdad, the last few miles from Ctesiphon onwards being one vast sand-drift. The Leyland lorry was used by the R.A.F. chiefly at Basrah and Baghdad, and it gave universal satisfaction. This force depended on the Crossley tender for work across the desert, and into Persia during all seasons of the year.

The Signal units were equipped with Star vans, and these vehicles also did good work, though at times they were overloaded. This was owing, no doubt, to the large covered-in body, which to the ordinary M.T. driver looked capable of taking a load of 2 tons instead of 15 cwt., its authorised load in Mesopotamia.

There were numerous batteries of light armoured cars, for the most part Rolls-Royce, though the Locker-Lampson Armoured Car Brigade had come out equipped with Austins. These were afterwards dispatched to Persia. The O.C.s and workshop officers of units equipped with Rolls-Royce armoured cars can be congratulated on the creditable work they did, notwithstanding the fact that on numerous occasions there was a shortage of spare parts.

With regard to motor cycles, there were thirteen different types in the country, out of ninety machines. The number of tyres had to be reduced, and India was requested not to allow units and departments to bring over to Mesopotamia motor cycles of other makes than Douglas or Triumph, owing to the difficulty of spare parts. It was not foreseen in 1917 that there would be many more than about 250 motor cycles required for this Front, nor that with the advance on Baghdad everything would increase and expand at once; at the time of writing there are approximately 1,100 motor cycles in the country, of which about 850 are in daily use. It is all very well in a campaign which is prepared for beforehand to say such and such a type of vehicle will be used, but in Mesopotamia one had to take advantage of whatever type was available.

The Napier about the middle of 1916 had been condemned as unfit for service in Mesopotamia, but at the present moment there are eighty-six Napiers here which have done splendid service, especially up on the Persian L. of C. The Daimler was never considered suitable for desert work, yet it has proved its worth over and over again, and in conjunction with the Napiers has done very fine work on the Persian L. of C.

Once a certain type of vehicle has been received, there is the difficulty of keeping up reinforcements of the same type. The light Packard lorries, Daimlers, Napiers, Star vans, are all in constant use out here, yet no reinforcement vehicles of these types have been available during 1918. It then became a question of demanding on England one Peerless lorry for every 30-cwt. vehicle required.

In a country such as Mesopotamia it is rather a difficult matter to legislate as to what type of vehicle is most suitable. Where cantonments exist, or towns in which troops may be quartered, good roads would very soon spring up, and, when labour is available, these could easily be maintained; thus the heavy type of lorry would become an economical proposition and much more suitable than light vans originally brought out for work over the desert.

This was proved on leaving the plains of Mesopotamia and going into Persia, for beyond Hamadan, directly the macadamised roads were struck, the Ford proved itself a most uneconomical proposition compared with the Peerless, and only the exigencies of the service rendered their employment necessary. One might, however, take it as a general rule that for a country such as this a lorry of the Fiat type with twin rear pneumatic wheels, weighing about two tons empty, together with light vans of the Ford type, are the most suitable vehicles, from a Mechanical Transport point of view, for the carriage of assorted supplies and material, or even troops. Had numbers of the Fiat been available, they would have been a more economical proposition in Persia, considerably more economical than the Peerless, the replacing of tyres on which is a most expensive item.

While on the question of tyres, it might be as well to say a few words on the subject of rubber. In this country the Fiat and Packard would generally average 1,000 to 1,500 miles on the outer covers. This does not apply to Persian roads. The Ford vans on occasions have reached 3,000 miles during the winter months. During the summer the mileage per cover is considerably reduced, due to a certain extent to the excessive heat experienced, and the very fine dust which gets in under the covers and chafes both tube and cover. This is also in great measure due to the fact that drivers do not pump up their tyres to a sufficiently high pressure. In a way one can hardly blame the driver. All pumps do not have pressure gauges, and if they do they very soon go out of action.

I know that I shall never succeed in impressing the English reader with the very vaguest idea of what it feels like to pump up a tyre to full pressure under the scorching sun of Mesopotamia. Here, if you could find any shade (which is impossible) and a thermometer that would stand the strain (which is absurd), you would find that it registered anything between 120° and 140°. At this temperature the sweat streams off you whilst sitting passively in a draught (if you can find one). The exertion of fitting a tyre increases the stream of sweat to a torrent. The acute exertion of pumping it hard produces a full-bodied river of dust-laden perspiration. Every time the back is bent on the down stroke the sun strikes like a hot iron upon the spine, and the myriad flies that rest on the man's clothing, quenching their thirst upon his perspiration, rise at each movement and buzz about his face.

This was possibly the chief reason why drivers did not pump up their tyres sufficiently. Then again 1918 marked the inclusion of Indian drivers and other nationalities in the War Establishments of Ford van companies, which naturally led to further tyre trouble, and a corresponding reduction in the mileage per cover. One realises the difficulties, therefore, in ordering spare parts, including covers and tubes, and the O.C. Base M.T. Depôt can pat himself on the back and say, "Well, it was no fault of mine that the spares were not available; the want was all foreseen, and the necessary orders placed."

From 1916 to the end of the war we were never short of Ford tyres and tubes, except, possibly, for a day or two occasionally. Then the shortage was due to barges running aground between Basrah and Baghdad.

Notwithstanding the fact, therefore, that there would be a considerable waste in personnel proportionate to the weight carried per vehicle, it was decided by General Maude, late in 1916, to ask for ten Ford van companies for work in

Mesopotamia; this subsequently proved to be a very wise decision. No difficulty was anticipated at home in the supply of the personnel or vehicles, and arrangements were made to dispatch them to Mesopotamia as quickly as possible. I say that there was no difficulty with regard to the supply of personnel, but, doubtless, it was always a difficult problem for the home authorities.

At the same time it must be remembered that the years 1915 and 1916, as regards the Western Front, were not remarkable for any great advances of the Allied Armies, so that the wastage of Mechanical Transport companies on that Front was not considerable.

The type of man employed as a Mechanical Transport driver up to 1916 was both physically and mechanically superior to the type which was raised in after-years. I trust my readers will pardon such a remark, but numbers of A.S.C. M.T. came out to Mesopotamia who were physically unfitted for hard work in the East, and one can only admire the way in which these men tackled the very arduous jobs set them. A number went sick at Basrah almost the day they arrived, and on several occasions medical officers have reported that these men should never have been sent out. I am bringing in this question of physical fitness of M.T. drivers at this point so that my readers can grasp later on in the book the fact that in the numerous operations which took place in Mesopotamia, both before and after the fall of Baghdad, the Mechanical Transport did their share of work with a large proportion of men who were physically unfitted for the hard work which they had to perform; this is all the more surprising when one thinks of the good work done. Once the M.T. companies began to settle down in the winter 1916–17, most of them were informed that the only things they had to worry much about in Mesopotamia were the heat in the summer months and the flies in the spring and autumn.

It was generally acknowledged that during the hot months of the summer no work could be done. Everybody had to be in his house or tent at about ten o'clock, and it was dangerous to go out from that hour until about four in the afternoon. The heat is great, as everyone who has spent a year or two in Mesopotamia will admit, yet the hours worked by the Mechanical Transport during this campaign were far longer in the summer than they were during the winter—the chief reason being that there was more daylight!

Brooding over the stories they had heard in England before their departure, a number of men went sick immediately they arrived.

The M.T. driver, notwithstanding his hard lot, was always cheerful. To the ordinary layman it would appear easy work, sitting on a nice comfortable seat holding the steering wheel of a motor van or car and going over the desert at between twenty and thirty miles an hour. It is, however, an education in itself for anyone to "tail" a convoy of Fords over a fifty-mile run along Mesopotamian roads. It would be a good thing if Generals and staff officers could be induced to accompany the last car on any of these convoys just for an hour or so, say, in the middle of July. After such an experience, doubtless, more thought would be given, and a little more sympathy extended, to the poor old M.T. driver in the hot days of summer. It is not my intention to try to make out that the M.T. driver has not had his measure of praise from Generals and other officers under whom he has served; but one often heard remarks to the effect that the M.T. driver on the whole had an easy time, or to use the common expression, had a "cushy job."

Numerous extracts will be quoted later showing that the services of the M.T. personnel were very much appreciated, but at the same time it must not be forgotten that on the whole, during these three years, the Mechanical Transport was, for the most part, undoubtedly overworked. This fact was brought to notice on numerous occasions and recognised, but owing to the chronic shortage of transport, the exigencies of the service were such that it could not be avoided. As more transport arrived in the country so further operations were contemplated, and it is safe to say that we seldom, if ever, " had anything up our sleeves " to attempt to give a well-earned rest to any unit, the only exceptions being during severe rain.

The discomfort of camp life during this period, and the bringing-in of derelict vehicles which had to be abandoned every two or three days, can hardly be called a rest. It was on these occasions, however, that the Mechanical Transport driver was as cheerful as at any other time of the year. All M.T. companies had the happy knack of making themselves at home, and their camps were, as a rule, models of comfort and cleanliness. These men always had what might be described as a fairly comfortable home to go to, even though they had often to wade through mud a foot deep to get there.

Towards the end of 1917 letters constantly were received from the War Office explaining the difficulty incurred in obtaining the necessary number of reinforcements, in view of the large call made by the Western Front, not only to replace wastage, but also to form new units. Mesopotamia is a long way from England. It is not so far from India. Coloured taxi-drivers were already in use in Bombay and other large towns, and it was thought possible that India could be called upon to materially assist with the extra personnel required.

It was therefore definitely settled during September 1917 that Indians should be trained as Ford drivers, but the first batch did not reach this country until January 1918, and, as mentioned in Chapter II, the results on their being tested by the Base M.T. Depôt were anything but reassuring. However, the Mechanical Transport are nothing if not optimistic, and all ranks persevered.

When these mixed companies were formed, 40 per cent. of the total number of drivers were Indians, and the remainder British. At the time of writing the war establishment of these units contains 60 per cent. Indians and 40 per cent. British, and it is intended to reduce the latter to 20 per cent. and increase the Indians to 80 per cent. This would still give each company a fairly strong and most necessary supervising British staff. In addition to these mixed units, Burmese companies also came out. At the present moment there are two of these companies at work in the country, and three more are expected shortly. There is also a Ford van company for Arabs, Armenians, etc., but this unit was only employed as a rule in and around Baghdad. There were also prospects of raising a good company in Ceylon, and application was made for sanction to form one, but nothing transpired.

Notwithstanding the tremendous amount of raw material which India could be called upon to train as Ford van drivers, they cabled at the end of 1917 to the effect that there were good prospects of raising an M.T. company in Singapore. This would be composed of Malays and Chinese with Eurasian artificers and N.C.O.s ; 10 per cent. of the Chinese and Malays would be English-speaking, but the latter not of very high standard. It was decided by the Director of Supplies and Transport that there were already sufficient nationalities at work.

The language question was, of course, a difficult one, but with regard to Indian companies, this was overcome to a certain extent by asking India to supply havildar-majors (sergeant-majors) who could talk English. However, very few of these were forthcoming. Officers, N.C.O.s, and men have all tried to pick up a little Hindustani, and a number of the drivers have picked up a little English. In this way the companies have managed to carry on.

A number of Indian Army officers were originally asked for to instruct officers commanding companies in the customs of the natives and also in the various castes, as a precaution against trouble that might ensue through ignorance of the different religions. These officers proved extremely useful, but were only attached for very short periods. I saw a Hindu in France objecting most strongly to having to take over a carcass of a dead goat on which a fly had settled which in its peregrinations had been seen on the goat issued to a Mohammedan. A number of R.A.S.C. officers were attached to Indian regiments for two months for the purpose of taking up Hindustani, and also of learning the customs of the natives, which was a good experiment. On the whole, however, the language question has not been a serious one, since on convoy work, with the Indian, it is a case of following the crowd until his vehicle breaks down.

In the first batch of Indians to arrive in this country were included the following: Christians, Parsees, Bengalis, Brahmins, Hindus, Sikhs, and Mussulmans. Anyone with a knowledge of the East will readily understand the difficulty in trying to complete units with the same type of driver, and also to keep all the religions and castes separate, as far as possible. The Sikhs and the Hindus have turned out to be the best drivers among the Indians.

When the Indians first came out to Mesopotamia they used to get very tired. They would muffle up their faces in their turbans when on convoy work and go to sleep. The van driven by the Indian could often be seen suddenly swerving off the road for no apparent reason, and then turning on its side. The only reason for this accident was that the driver was asleep. Directly the van turned over, the Indian, who never seemed to be hurt, would at once jump out, produce an oily rag from somewhere, and start cleaning his car, after which he would sit and wait until the first-aid party came along to help him to put the car on its "legs" again. Usually very little damage resulted from these accidents in the desert.

During 1918 the Ford van considerably increased the radius of action of the force on the various operations, while it must not be forgotten that very nearly 50 per cent. of the drivers were Indians. On the whole, they can be looked upon as an agreeable surprise. The doggedness and perseverance of the instructors, combined with the simplicity of the Ford, was one reason which made the Indian driver a possible proposition in the time. There was a good school of instruction at Rawal Pindi which assisted, in a great measure, to train the Indians who were afterwards sent to Mesopotamia. At the same time I must add that we considered that these men were only partially trained on arrival. They were tested, and as a rule re-trained again at the Base before dispatch up country.

An Indian, if trained on a Ford car and proved to be a good driver, would, if put on a Ford van (which is the same vehicle with a slightly different body), be all at sea, and would declare that he had never been instructed to drive that type of vehicle. Even of the men who had qualified in India, nine out of ten totally failed to pass out as second- or even third-class drivers at the Base M.T. Depôt. The same remarks apply again on their arrival in Baghdad, only to a somewhat lesser degree. Then again, when posted to companies, there were more strange surroundings and rather difficult work (including convoy work over all classes of roads and country), so that it took some time before these men could be considered efficient drivers.

Lieutenant-Colonel Dickinson, A.S.C., was sent over from this force with a view to helping the people in India with regard to the training of the Indian driver. He brought out all the weak points and made his report on arriving back. From a practical point of view I do not know that his visit improved the Indian drivers. They still seem to arrive in much the same state as they did before his mission. However, the Indian authorities were by this visit made aware of the fact that we were not quite satisfied with regard to the driving capabilities of their recruits.

It is very hard on Mechanical Transport units, especially in a campaign where days of rest are unknown, getting a class of driver to whom most of the officers could not talk in their own language and whose driving capabilities were doubtful. I do not think the home authorities realised what a difficult matter it was, and it is only those who have experienced it, and seen the results of the training given, who realise what a hard job the Mechanical Transport officer had in this campaign.

The Burmese driver was far quicker in picking up the driving and the care of the car than any of the Indians, and for some time after their arrival in the country all these men showed remarkable keenness. This was all the more surprising in view of the fact that the Burman when at home is particularly lazy.

The Burman, as a man, is a jolly little beggar, and he seemed to be contented with his lot, however hard it might be. Their one great wish was to get under fire, and if possible have a smack at the Turk. On several occasions they did get there and seemed to like it. A number of Indians, too, came under fire and behaved splendidly.

One officer commanding a unit told me that a Ford had seven bullets through it in an afternoon at various places, four or five of these passing the canopy just above the driver's head, whilst he was lying asleep on the front seat. The driver, who was an Indian Christian, put his escape down to the fact that he had made a pillow of a Bible, and was thus saved from an untimely end.

The Arab, Armenian, Jew, and Chaldean have all been tried here in Baghdad, and they have also been employed in the neighbourhood. The Arab, on the whole, is the better man, but the class from which the drivers were taken was not a good one. Presumably, the better-class Arab did not come forward in any numbers to be trained in motor driving. Possibly the pay was not a very great attraction in 1918, when it cost the ordinary native about Rs.2 per diem to live. The Armenian is lazy and very cute; during his training period he was almost too cute. He found it an easy matter to absent himself when he thought it was not his turn to be taken out on instruction.

Some of these Armenian drivers were, at one time, sent up country on some minor operations owing to shortage of transport on that particular part of the line; on going through a certain village they had the misfortune to run down two or three Arab women and kill them. The Arabs thought this act was intentional, and that night took the opportunity of setting fire to a large stack of Government hay by way of revenge. The feud between the Arab and the Armenian is almost as great as that between the Turk and the Armenian.

Each Mechanical Transport company which had a mobile workshop was allowed the following establishment of native artificers: 4 fitters, 2 blacksmiths, 2 carpenters, 2 strikers, 1 tinsmith, 1 trimmer, and 4 cleaners.

This additional establishment was necessary because the twelve artificers with the ordinary mobile workshop (and four extra vulcanisers in a Ford van company) were totally inadequate to cope with the repairs to 130 Ford vans, to say nothing of the requirements of the other extra vehicles in each company. The Advanced M.T. Depôt also had a considerable number of native tradesmen, consisting of Arabs, Jews, Armenians, and Chaldeans of all classes and trades. The total number of native artificers employed with the M.T. at the time of writing this book is about 750.

One is being constantly asked by G.H.Q. how many British ranks have been saved by the employment of native artificers. This is a very difficult question to answer, as the companies were not sufficiently equipped with workshop personnel, and it is difficult to compare the two types. A number of these fitters and turners were quite equal to British personnel, yet, at the same time, one could hardly say that British personnel was being *saved*, because the more work there was to be done, the more artificers were required. There was never actually a saving on a war establishment, as each unit had to take on more labour to cope with the extra work entailed by the severe road conditions, to say nothing of the climate and the resulting wastage in personnel.

There was also the question of supervision. At one time, wherever a native was employed, it was always necessary to have a white supervisor, as he could not be left alone to undertake a job which was a little difficult.

Among the tradesmen found in Baghdad, the following were, with little training, turned into skilled artificers: tinsmiths, carpenters, blacksmiths, wheelers, coppersmiths.

It took a considerable time to instil even a rudimentary knowledge of the other trades, though there were naturally a few exceptions in every case. Chinese carpenters and masons were also employed constantly by the Base M.T. Depôt, and did very useful work.

The Mauritian is another type of man who has proved a successful motor driver. These men originally came over to Mesopotamia with a Labour Corps. A few were found who could drive, and authority was granted for a company to be formed out of this Labour Corps, reinforcements for which would be made up in due course from Mauritius. At the time of writing a sufficient number have not been trained, but forty or fifty of them have been driving vehicles at the Base to the entire satisfaction of the authorities. The language difficulty is not very great, as the majority speak French, and most of our Mechanical Transport officers have got a smattering of this after a year or two in France.

At one time in the Advanced M.T. Depôt a few good fitters were found, but after a month or two's instruction in I.C. engine work, by which time they could practically undertake an overhaul, some of them disappeared—presumably to take their wares to a better market. The matter was reported, and owing to the very stringent measures now in force with regard to native labour, missing men would at once be traced. It had the effect, however, of starting a system whereby these native fitters were only employed on one job in connection with the overhaul of any vehicle, so that even after six months' instruction these men would only be highly skilled on that particular job on which they had been employed, but they were of little use as all-round mechanics to anybody requiring an artificer.

When you are dealing with a vehicle like the Ford, it

is most essential to get a large return for your money. It is also necessary to keep your men employed on the "one man one job" principle.

I have now gone through the various types of men employed, including the British, and it is at once apparent that the M.T. in Mesopotamia was of a cosmopolitan nature. Under the circumstances it is wonderful that they did such fine work. I have met the British driver in many parts of the world, "carrying on," but I think the way they "stuck it" in Mesopotamia, and all through Persia, right up to the Caspian Sea and into Baku, is nothing short of marvellous. I do not think this will be denied when the long hours, long journeys, heat, dust, dirt, flies, disease, and innumerable mechanical troubles they had to contend with are taken into consideration. Well, just doff your hats when you meet them!

Of all the various types of men employed with the M.T., I might have mentioned the Eurasian, but he has not been used out here to a great extent. In the few isolated cases in which he has been utilised, he seems to have crept in disguised as an Englishman!

# CHAPTER V

## EARLY DAYS OF THE M.T.

Arrival of new units at the Base—Formation of a "Pool" for cars—Remarks on shipping—Reinforcements—Inspection at Ahwaz and Nasiriyeh—"Wangles" and exchanges.

About the end of September 1916 the following units were under orders to proceed to Mesopotamia:

| | |
|---|---|
| Nos. 783 & 784 . . . | Ford Van Supply Columns |
| ,, 788 & 789 . . . | Caterpillar Companies |
| ,, 729 & 730 . . . | Light Packard Companies |
| ,, 773 M.T. Company . | Attached No. 33 M.A.C. |

One or two Anti-Aircraft Sections were also included.

It will at once be seen that efforts had to be made by the O.C. Base M.T. Depôt to get ready for the reception of these units, as doubtless they would shortly be followed by others as soon as the necessity for mechanical transport was fully realised. In view of the near approach of wet weather, steps had also to be taken by No. 596 Company to improve their shops and stores and the parking-grounds for vehicles, together with the roadways leading to them. So far as the Base was concerned, too, it was decided that a Pool of cars was essential. A camp at Makina and Margil had been started and there was no rapid means for officers to get about, and as soon as cars became available a certain number were allotted as the Base Pool. A suitable building had to be constructed, and this small unit was run as a section of the Base M.T. Depôt. At the beginning it consisted of one or two rather old-fashioned cars which had been received from headquarters in exchange for new ones, but, notwithstanding, these cars did very good work in spite of considerable difficulty in keeping them on the road.

I should like to mention one or two points with regard to the stores. All the petrol and oil which was sent up country for the use of Mechanical Transport vehicles had been issued to No. 596 Company, owing to this unit having a detachment of Fiats in the forward area, and this company was responsible for its distribution. This method was soon cancelled, and the ordinary procedure for issuing these commodities brought into use. A lot of trouble had also been caused through loss of stores owing to the method of loading and tallying—any cases which were marked "machinery" seemed to find their way into the E. and M. Section of the Works Department at Basrah, while spare parts got transported up and down the line wherever the people in charge of the *Mehaylas* or barges thought they would like to go. It was very difficult to trace consignments. This difficulty, however, was soon overcome by placing proper tally clerks on board the boats, together with representatives from units, but this, at one time, was a very serious proposition owing to the shortage of personnel.

During 1918 the shipping at Basrah was working like a large port at home, and, beyond damage to vehicles on the way out, I have nothing but praise for the way in which all vehicles and spare parts were handled. At the time of my arrival, even Peerless lorries had to be off-loaded from the steamer to a barge and from the barge on to a pier built of sandbags and a few iron rails. The pier was very unstable, and the task of off-loading all vehicles was entrusted to No. 596 M.T. Company, because they were experts in handling heavy vehicles. I think, out of two or three hundred vehicles which were landed, there was but one accident.

A large wharf was in process of construction during September at Margil, and when this became available no difficulty whatsoever was experienced in bringing big ships alongside and off-loading all classes of M.T. vehicles. Whenever possible vehicles such as "caterpillars" were off-loaded direct on to barges and sent up country. This was done in the case of No. 788 and 789 Companies. One source of trouble, however, with regard to the off-loading of Mechanical Transport vehicles was the unsatisfactory way in which the cargo of ships had been loaded in England. This would very often result in a few M.T. vehicles being off-loaded ; then a halt of some days would intervene, while other cargo had to be got out, before the remainder of the M.T. vehicles could be tackled. Occasionally it happened that twenty or thirty vehicles had to be off-loaded ; then there would be a more urgent call for the wharf and the ship would go out into mid-stream again, to remain perhaps a week before it could be brought alongside.

I have been given to understand that up to the middle of 1916 ships were lying in the stream with stores and could not be off-loaded for two or three months, and I believe there were even longer delays. No. 695 Company, Base M.T. Depôt, was the victim of one of these long delays, both as regards its vehicles and stores. The former, which came out as deck cargo, suffered considerably from weather. The loading of a number of these boats from home was a constant source of trouble. Vehicles seem to have been dumped down in the hold, and to prevent them rolling in the ship, cases of ammunition and iron pipes were utilised to wedge them tightly. The damage resulting from such a method can well be imagined. There are one or two cases of vehicles having been so badly loaded in England that even the captain protested!

It is hardly fair perhaps to criticise in this manner, as undoubtedly the submarine peril necessitated the rapid loading of ships in order that advantage could be taken of certain orders given for their sailings on specific dates and times. But so far as this country was concerned, the matter was a serious one, for it was of little use sending M.T. vehicles out to Mesopotamia which required rebuilding on arrival.

It had been reported to G.H.Q. that there were a very wonderful tractor and some ditchers with the Anglo-Persian Oil Company. All these vehicles had been employed in laying the pipes in the oil-fields to Abadan. The tractor had a big, powerful engine and broad wheels of the traction type, and during the laying of the oil-pipes by the Anglo-Persian Oil Company it was capable of towing a load of 40 tons. This tractor and two ditchers, after numerous delays, were placed on a barge and brought down from Ahwaz to Basrah.

There was a delay during the journey, as the barge ran aground, and the A.S.C. officer and his staff were left high and dry for two or three days without any rations. The tractor and ditchers were eventually landed at Basrah and given a trial. The ditchers made a small bund for the Inland Water Transport, and it was at once seen that they would be of very little use to the force. The tractor was given two or three days' trial on the road between Basrah and Shaiba, but it did not prove successful. Both the engine and the trucks got badly bogged, although taking a very light load. They were sent back a short time afterwards.

During the month of November the personnel of Nos. 783 and 784 Companies and the headquarters of Nos. 788 and 789 Caterpillar Companies arrived.

A consignment of Vauxhall cars was also landed. Most of them were needed up country, so I decided to take them up myself. Colonel Donohue should have accompanied me, but it was easier for him to get to Bushire than it was for him to get away.

THE TRACTOR FROM THE ANGLO-PERSIAN OIL COMPANY.

This chapter regarding the early days of mechanical transport would appear to be somewhat disconnected, but that is, in a way, unavoidable when the narration of a number of different events is crowded into a few pages. Also I have endeavoured to take the events in the actual order in which they occurred; this has had the effect of making the chapter appear slightly disjointed.

The situation of affairs from a mechanical transport point of view had been reported to the War Office in two long letters during the month of September 1916, so that at the end of October they were fully conversant with the whole situation. Reinforcements began to arrive in October, and No. 596 M.T. Company was able to put a number of extra vehicles on the road. The same may be said of No. 656 Company, attached to No. 23 Motor Ambulançe Company. In addition the Base M.T. Depôt began to get a " move on " with the various buildings.

The s.s. *Demosthenes,* one of the few ships mentioned in this book, brought out the following R.A.S.C. M.T. personnel to this country:

| | |
|---|---|
| Officers | 11 |
| B.O.R. | 405 |
| Blacksmiths | 14 |
| Fitters and turners | 44 |
| Electricians | 9 |
| Vulcanisers | 4 |
| Wheelers | 12 |
| Tyre press details, etc. | 82 |
| Total | 581 |

These men were passed through the Base M.T. Depôt, and the companies were once more brought up to war establishment. It would indeed have been very satisfactory if a ship had arrived in 1918 bringing a similar number and similar type of men as reinforcements. With the introduction of Indian drivers, the drafts from England gradually decreased, and the recruit driver or mechanic received during 1918 was of a different class from those of 1916.

During October the derelict "Fiat" lorries had been sent down river, and the Base M.T. Depôt was making efforts to get these vehicles once more fit for the road. In the early stages of overhauling the work was somewhat crippled for lack of the necessary "spares," but these arrived towards the end of the year. Not long after, all these useful vehicles were sent up the line, and were hard at work from early in 1917 up to the time of my departure from the country.

Colonel Donohue, Inspector of Motor Transport Services, arrived towards the end of October, and, beginning with Bushire, made numerous inspections throughout the country.

From the foregoing it is seen that things were "brewing up" from a mechanical transport point of view. There was already practically every type of unit in the country, i.e. Heavy Supply Column (Peerless), Light Supply Columns (Ford vans), Ford Ambulance Convoy, "Caterpillar" Companies, Light Armoured Motor Batteries, and Anti-Aircraft Sections. It was conceivable that all these units would be considerably augmented in accordance with the operations which were contemplated, and, naturally, provision had to be made for supply and repair.

As previously stated, it was known in November that ten Ford van companies were ordered, though in view of the fact that our forces were settled down in front of the Sanniyat position, it seemed questionable if these would ever be required. General Maude, however, was aware of what he wanted, and he was determined to get it. Had all the other motor companies ordered been in Mesopotamia at the time of the advance on Baghdad, they would have been of incalculable value.

November, on the whole, was a very busy month. A fair number of Mechanical Transport personnel and vehicles had arrived, and were got ready for dispatch up the line. No. 33 Motor Ambulance Convoy was ready, and on November 7 it left Basrah, with Captain Houston, R.A.M.C., as O.C.

The officer commanding the Army Service Corps Company, No. 773, was then Captain Vallat. This unit on the whole travelled very well indeed, and was the first complete M.T. unit of any size to undertake the journey by road to Sheikh Sa'ad. All the ambulances were fitted with shock absorbers, which, together with the step at the back, were chiefly instrumental in saving back axles. These steps afterwards proved a source of trouble and annoyance, and those which were not broken by continually striking the ground had to be removed.

On November 30, No. 783 M.T. Company A.S.C. was dispatched from Basrah under the command of Captain Gibbons, but consisted only of 100 vans, 5 officers, and 150 other ranks. The remaining vans to complete its war establishment of 130 had not arrived, neither had their workshops or store lorries. This question was under discussion with the War Office. They said no workshops would be sent with a Ford van company, but, on urgent representation being made, it was decided to send them, and a request was made that they should be of the light Packard type with pneumatic tyres, if possible. The majority of Ford van companies were afterwards equipped in this manner.

Ford ambulances were also dispatched to the front line during this month to complete field ambulances of divisions. No. 783 M.T. Company had numerous troubles on the way up, but although these were a source of annoyance at the time, the reports sent in by the officer commanding were of great advantage to companies who later went up the line, and prevented them from suffering in a similar manner. In December the remaining Ford vans and store lorries of No. 783 Company, and those of No. 784 Company arrived. The latter company got ready at once for Sheikh Sa'ad. It left the Base on December 19, 1916, and reached its destination on Christmas Day. The company was at that time under the command of Captain Pelly, A.S.C.

During this month some of the details of No. 729 Company A.S.C. arrived. After September 1916 various consignments of vehicles began to reach the Base, and by the end of the year there was a considerable number in the country. The table below shows the exact figures on December 1, 1916 and on December 31, 1916:

| | December 1, 1916. | December 31, 1916. |
|---|---|---|
| Lorries and vans | 330 | 472 |
| Motor cars | 101 | 126 |
| Motor cycles | 264 | 310 |
| Ambulances | 144 | 147 |
| Caterpillars | 8 | 8 |
| Fire engines | 3 | 3 |
| | 850 | 1066 |

With regard to this table it may be interesting to record here the figure of merit showing the numbers under repair. At this time naturally no great amount of hard work had been done by the rolling stock, so the actual percentage of vehicles and motor cycles under repair was comparatively small. The following short table gives the approximate state at the end of 1916:

| | |
|---|---|
| Motor lorries | 7 per cent under repair |
| Motor cars | 4 ,, ,, ,, |
| Motor ambulances | 2¾ ,, ,, ,, |
| Motor cycles | 4 ,, ,, ,, |
| Average, say | 4½ ,, ,, ,, |

At this time a number of the old motor cycles with Signal units had been withdrawn and condemned. New machines had been issued, leaving the actual percentage of working motor cycles rather higher than was expected. Signal units always did remarkably well, as will be seen later in another chapter.

It may be observed that no figure of merit is shown in this book regarding vehicles under repair in 1918, this being due to the fact that the bulk of vehicles out of action were for merely minor repairs, and on operations even minor repairs were sometimes impossible. The number of Fords out of action on occasions reached the total of about 800, but two or three days were sufficient to put 350 of these on the road again. It would therefore be unfair to give such a figure as an average. These remarks are somewhat premature, but are included in this chapter in view of the foregoing figure of merit for 1916.

I took a trip on January 20, 1917, to Ahwaz to inspect the mechanical transport there, and also with a view to making a report upon the roads. The vehicles employed in that locality were the 30-cwt. Napier lorries, carrying supplies from Ahwaz to Shush, a distance of almost eighty miles over ordinary desert road. The soil was similar to that of Mesopotamia, and, after wet weather, certain parts of the road were practically impassable. There were no speedometers on any of the cars at Ahwaz, and the distance in a way had to be guessed. I believe there was a very ancient book in the library at Ahwaz which gave the distance as so many "parasangs," or such measurements as were in vogue at the time of Alexander the Great. When worked into ordinary English mileage, the distance from Shush to Ahwaz figures at sixty odd miles. I understand this was the official distance, and the A.S.C. officer commanding this detachment often received complaints as to why his lorries took such a long time to cover the distance. When measured later by speedometers, the old and officially adopted measurements were found to be inaccurate!

The facilities at this time for repair to W.D. vehicles in this district were practically nil. A mobile workshop was afterwards ordered from England, and, later, the machinery of this was dispatched to Ahwaz for the purpose of carrying out repairs. This detachment has given the greatest satisfaction, the number of vehicles on the road always being about 80 to 85 per cent. of the total number available. With regard to the work I would like to mention that on several occasions the detachment of Napier lorries did over 1,000 miles in a fortnight, and this during the winter! In a country like Mesopotamia, machinery is scarce, and in the early days at Ahwaz, prior to the ordering of the mobile workshop and pending its arrival, efforts were made to obtain some suitable machinery off the s.s. *Persepolis*, a Persian boat. The acting Civil Commissioner was approached with a view to getting this ship to Basrah. The boat was ordered up, but unfortunately only arrived about the same time as the machinery from England.

Notwithstanding the fact that the A.S.C. was instrumental in getting the boat to Basrah, I understand that on the day it arrived there was a great rush of all departments dealing with machinery to get hold of the lathes and drilling machines on board. I was not able to join in this rush, being at G.H.Q., but a wire from the Base informed me that all the machinery had been stripped down, and that there was nothing left for the unfortunate A.S.C. M.T. On the matter being represented to D.Q.M.G., however, a wire was sent to the Base, and we were able to obtain some of our just rights, though the machinery, for the most part, was unsuitable. Still, a very good lathe and drilling machine were forthcoming, which have since been in constant use.

The next large batch of Mechanical Transport which arrived between the latter end of 1916 and the beginning of 1917 was as follows: No. 729 M.T. Company, No. 730 M.T. Company, 13th and 14th Light Armoured Motor Batteries and Workshops, 92nd and 93rd Anti-Aircraft Sections, 49th and 50th A.O.D. Travelling Mobile Workshops.

With regard to the first two companies, the officers and personnel had all arrived, but no notification had yet been received from the War Office with regard to the vehicles. Notwithstanding the fact that both these units were sent out at a moment's notice (and indeed one or two officers were unable to see their families before departure), the vehicles of No. 729 M.T. Company did not arrive in Mesopotamia until the end of May 1917, and those of No. 730 Company until the beginning of August.

This resulted in the officers, N.C.O.s, and men all eating

their hearts out with impatience during the advance on Baghdad and the subsequent fighting, to say nothing of the numbers that went sick and were being evacuated to India. Had the vehicles of these two companies also been available, it would have made a tremendous difference to the troops on the march up.

These two units, therefore, had to remain all this time in the vicinity of Basrah and were camped on Makina Plain. They spent most of their time in beautifying their camps and making numerous improvements and additions to camp life in Mesopotamia ; in fact, the lines of No. 730 M.T. Company were a model of what a camp should be. These two companies originally mobilised in England with the light Packard lorry fitted with solid tyres, which were taken away from them prior to their departure from England. In Mesopotamia they had to be mobilised as Ford van companies, so that the personnel had to be trained at Makina on Fords. This work was unfortunately a bit slow, as there were very few spare Fords in the country. By the time these two companies were ready to move up country, each of them had lost about 40 per cent. of the original personnel from England—a fact particularly to be deprecated since they had a good type of driver with them.

Shortly after my trip to Ahwaz I went up to Nasiriyeh by train on inspection duty. The 14th L.A.M. Battery was stationed here, and a few ambulances. The O.C. of the former unit, Captain Somerset, M.C., was a regular "fire-eater," and complained that up to the present he had not had his armoured cars in action. All he had done was to escort "tourists" out to Ur of the Chaldees, the birthplace of Abraham.

Later on, however, this officer had no need to complain when the 15th Division moved up from Nasiriyeh. I think this unit has seen as much of the fighting as most units in the country. Nasiriyeh was the place where I had my first experience of Mesopotamian rain ; this started about half an hour before the train was due to go out. Although the ground is very flat between the Supply Depôt and the railway-siding from which the train left, a matter of 100 yards, it had been converted into a pond about 6 inches deep during that short space of time. I have only once since seen rain in Mesopotamia as heavy, and that was practically the first rain which took place in November 1918.

I have now detailed the Mechanical Transport in the country at the end of 1916 and the beginning of 1917.

It is not my intention to specially mention the arrival of the numerous other Mechanical Transport units which came to Mesopotamia, or describe any of their journeys up river. Sometimes these were accomplished by road, and sometimes by river ; in the latter case only when sufficient tonnage was available or the roads impassable.

The experiences of the first two companies going up made it clear that the reinforcing of the back and front springs of the Ford would be absolutely necessary; so, as each company of Ford vans arrived at Basrah, this work had to be taken in hand. The home authorities were asked to make the alteration for all companies leaving England, but it was not until 1918 that this was done. Other remarks with regard to the reinforcing of front springs, however, will be dealt with in a later chapter on improvements to the Ford which were found necessary in this country.

As this chapter is headed "Early Days," it was necessary to enumerate in detail the actual companies which were out here during the latter part of 1916 and the beginning of 1917. All M.T. units, however, which came out to Mesopotamia are shown in the chapter devoted to that subject.

Looking back on these early days, one laughs heartily over the numerous dodges and "wangles" which went on between various departments in order that one department might get hold of something which another had, but did not wish to part with, occasioned by short supply.

It was one constant beg, borrow, or steal, and many indeed are the amusing incidents which were brought to my notice. Swoppings, too, such as that of a 10-inch lathe for a small stationary engine, a milling machine for a lathe, etc., and even loans to one department of machines for a matter of two or three weeks, pending the arrival of their own, were of common occurrence. All departments pulled together for the common good. [*And the devil take the hindmost.*—Ed.]

The last few months of 1916 cemented a firm friendship between various corps and departments, especially those dealing with machinery, such as Works, Ordnance, and I.W.T., not forgetting the A.S.C.

Here is an example of what might be described as a real exchange: The I.W.T. were very anxious to try a Ford engine in a *bellum* (native craft). It was expected that the Ford engine would be able to propel a 10-ton *bellum* at a speed of 8 to 10 knots, in which case they would have been extremely useful, as fast-moving river transport.

General Gray, D.I.W.T., had ordered out a certain number of motor cycles from England for the use of their department. These had just arrived, and I was doing my best to get hold of a number of them owing to the shortage that existed at that time with the A.S.C. M.T. An exchange was eventually effected, and the I.W.T. became richer by one Ford engine, while the Mechanical Transport benefited to the extent of twenty Triumph motor cycles!

# CHAPTER VI

## THE ADVANCED M.T. DEPÔT

The beginning of this unit at Amarah—The move to Baghdad—Short account of its work—Statistics.

IN 1916 it appeared as if a " stalemate " had set in with regard to operations in Mesopotamia, and that much the same sort of trench warfare would be carried out as was then in vogue in France. This being the case, it was decided that there should be a Mechanical Transport heavy repair unit nearer the front line than Basrah. Amarah was fixed on as the place for this workshop. It was a healthy place, and only a matter of 100 miles by road from Arab Village. Derelict vehicles could be sent down by river, as at the end of 1916 there was sufficient river tonnage available for this purpose.

It had been reported that materials for the building of these shops, with the exception of the roof, were already there. Owing to the scarcity of building material farther up the line, it was not possible to erect these shops elsewhere. Sheikh Sa'ad would at the time have been a suitable place, but since it was entirely a question of tonnage, it would have been impossible to get sufficient building material up so far without interfering with more important supplies.

PERSONNEL OF THE ADVANCED M.T. DEPÔT, BAGHDAD, CHRISTMAS 1918.

Plans were prepared for these shops and submitted to the Inspector-General of Communications for approval. After a matter of some two or three weeks this was given. Major Hodgkinson, Indian Army, who was attached to the Mechanical Transport, Mesopotamia, was sent up in conjunction with the Assistant Director of Works to discuss the plans, the site having already been selected by Major Owen, D.S.O., Chief Inspector Mechanical Transport. Suitable materials and those obtainable on the spot were selected, and the work was to have been commenced as soon as possible. This did not actually begin for some weeks.

At length a start was made, and Major Hodgkinson was dispatched with a party of A.S.C. personnel from the Base M.T. Depôt to assist in the building generally, and to clear the site. This personnel also formed the advance party of what was eventually to become the Advanced M.T. Depôt, and the erection of the machinery, etc., was to be left in their hands. Bricks and all building materials at this time were scarce, and very slow progress was made. Lieutenant Stonewall-Jackson, A.S.C., assisted Major Hodgkinson.

Just as things began to get going nicely a wire was received ordering Major Hodgkinson back to India, apparently to start a training school for the training of native drivers. His place was taken by Captain Sutcliffe, A.S.C., who afterwards commanded this unit. With regard to the training school, Major Hodgkinson wrote me two months after his arrival in India that he had been doing nothing up to date beyond sending in one report. I think they might have left him out in Mesopotamia.

The machinery was loaded and sent up river at the end of January, but it was not until the beginning of March that the power engine was placed in position. By this time, however, the Turks were in full retreat, and on or about March 17, after our entry into Baghdad on the 11th, a wire was sent ordering all work to cease in this unit, which was to proceed to Baghdad. It was fortunate in a way the buildings took so long to get started, as practically nothing had to be dismantled. The actual building itself came in very useful afterwards as a petrol store for the Supply Depôt. The machinery and material were loaded on barges and dispatched up country. Barges were scarce at this time, owing to our great advance.

The tonnage allotments for the various departments was jealously watched by G.H.Q. Captain Sutcliffe, however, succeeded in convincing someone that there were roughly 80 tons of machinery, etc., to load, instead of the 200 tons which were actually there; he got everything up to Baghdad on or about April 8, 1918. This was all off-loaded and placed in the building which is now used by the Advanced M.T. Depôt. A photo is given showing the difficulty of landing a heavy article, such as a fly-wheel, in Baghdad at this time. Such was the beginning of this large and very important unit.

As mentioned in a previous chapter, the floating workshops were anchored off this building at the time, and it was due to Major Sykes' pre-war knowledge of Baghdad that this serviceable building was obtained. I inspected it on March 17, 1917, and after having a good look at numerous other buildings was convinced that it was the most suitable. There were also possibilities for expansion in the immediate neighbourhood.

It would be as well to mention that the building which was taken over in Baghdad was the old German Technical School. It had apparently been used as a munition factory by the Turks, judging from the material left behind, which included bronze, lead, and shell cases. The Turks prior to the evacuation of Baghdad, had attempted to blow up this building. They succeeded in the case of the machine shop. Part of the walls and the whole of the roof had been blown up, and the machines were buried beneath the débris. The power unit had also been destroyed by dynamite. Twenty-five sticks of dynamite were taken out of various holes in the walls; apparently the person or persons responsible for placing the destructive charges had been in a hurry. The work of clearing the machine shop was begun at once, and the various lathes, etc., on being unearthed were found to have suffered very little damage, and all these machines have been in constant use since April 1917.

The large building on the opposite side of the road, formerly used by the Turks as a training school, had also been blown up. This was taken over, and this unit has gone on expanding ever since March 17, 1917. Even at the present time, with one or two buildings not quite completed, it might almost be considered one of the best Mechanical Transport workshops it is possible for an Expeditionary Force to possess. If you asked either the officer commanding, Lieutenant-Colonel Carty, M.C., or any officers who have been employed there, they would tell you " It is the finest unit in the British Army ! " Practically all the officers who have been through this depôt have served on two or three other fronts.

The first O.C. of the depôt was Captain Sutcliffe, but, unfortunately, this officer, when things began to get lively, was invalided out of the country, Captain Porrit acting as temporary O.C. The unit was afterwards taken over by Major Sykes, and later, in March 1918, by Major (now Acting Lieutenant-Colonel) S. W. Carty, M.C.

Extra machinery has been added, brought down even from Persia and collected wherever possible. The war establishment has also been considerably augmented, and in August 1918 it reached the following figures: 21 Officers, 467 B.O.R.s, and 52 I.O.R.s.

In addition to workshops, this unit comprised a return section, reinforcements, reserve vehicle park, and a training school. There were approximately 350 native artificers employed, and these men took some time to train before they were of use.

When dealing with vehicles of the Ford type it is necessary to follow the principle of " one man, one job "—a principle which has resulted in a constant output of thirty overhauls per week. (The term overhauls includes the complete rebuilding of all wheels, reinforcing of bodies, the complete stripping down off the vehicle of every bolt and nut, and the reinforcing of each side member with a plate. It also means the making of new front and rear cross members.) When the work entailed is thoroughly realised, it will be seen how difficult it was to maintain the Ford in Mesopotamia. The workshops were practically split up into two sections, i.e. Ford Section and Miscellaneous Section, the former dealing with Fords and the latter with all types of vehicles, including caterpillars, lorries, cars, and ambulances of all kinds.

The shops, of course, work for the workshops as a whole, there being no special foundry or forge allotted to either section. In addition to the complete overhauls in the Ford section, approximately forty to fifty minor and heavy repairs were also carried out. The average number of overhauls in the miscellaneous shops was two to four a week, and about twenty minor and heavy repairs.

It was recognised in March 1917 that if mechanical transport was to be increased, naturally the Advanced M.T. Workshops—as they were then known—would also have to be increased. Though not exactly the place one would choose for such an important unit, it must be remembered that good and suitable buildings were scarce; it was impossible to get new ones, and work was pouring in which had to be tackled immediately. There is no need to go into questions with regard to the numerous additions, the only trouble experienced being in obtaining authority to pull down the various Arab houses or hovels in the vicinity to allow for expansion.

The position of this depôt has been often criticised.

To carry out its functions it should be: (1) near a railway-siding or terminus; (2) close to a river; (3) large space available in vicinity for expansion; (4) large parking ground; (5) large buildings suitable for all kinds of shops and stores.

ADVANCED M.T. DEPÔT, FORD SECTION.

A BAY IN THE MAIN ERECTING SHOP, ADVANCED M.T. DEPÔT, BAGHDAD.

74|

I often wonder what would have happened had a site with these facilities been chosen, for a site it would only have been. I am sure no work could have been carried out for months, or even years. The only railway at the time was on the right bank, and there were no buildings available. The actual position was on the river, our only means of communication with the Base. The buildings, too, were the best in Baghdad for the purpose ; expansion merely meant the pulling-down of hovels, and the extension of the Kut-Baghdad line ran within 300 yards of the depôt, which included a siding, though the latter did not exist when the unit was formed.

There are one or two photographs of the depôt which will give some idea to my readers who have not seen it. It is a pity that a whole series cannot be shown. As I have said, there are two main sections, i.e. Miscellaneous Section and the Ford Section. Practically all the buildings which were available and have since been built are required to maintain these two sections. The reserve vehicle park and the body-building shop had, unfortunately, to be removed about a mile away from the main building. This was rendered necessary owing to the rapid expansion of Mechanical Transport in Mesopotamia.

However, there is little or no disadvantage in having the body-building shop, or even the reserve vehicle park, situated some distance away ; this is a frequent occurrence in large motor works in England and other parts of the world. The total space occupied by the unit is naturally large, and there was no place in the city capable of accommodating the whole of it without large demolitions. Advantage was taken of every square inch of ground available, even up to, and including, a street which formerly ran through the middle of the depôt. At that time there were private dwellings down one side.

When watching building operations it is readily understood why the donkey is so popular in the East. The Arab does not over-exert himself when working, and it requires very little effort on his part to make up a load for a donkey. When working for the War Department, each donkey carries between 20 and 30 lb., yet when carrying the Arab's goods and chattels the weight is usually about 150 lb. Much time is therefore taken in running up a building in this part of the world; the Mechanical Transport had often to turn out vehicles to draw bricks in order to get a "move on" with various M.T. buildings in course of construction. If this had not been done it is difficult to say how long the buildings would have taken to complete. There were practically no civilian transport vehicles available in Baghdad at the time.

Transport and labour have always been a constant source of trouble in this country; it is fortunate that there are so many boys available for work. They seem to start work at the age of seven or eight years, and from that time until they are fifteen they are jolly little beggars and work hard. They are like the ordinary British urchin: they have a keen sense of humour, and are always up to mischief. At the age of fifteen they begin to feel their manhood, and most of them degenerate. It is hoped the new régime, under which they have been working, and will doubtless work in the future, will considerably improve the rising generation. When one sees the numerous gangs of these youngsters working, and realises all the improvements put into this country since the British occupation with regard to roads, buildings, etc., it is astonishing to think that most of it has been carried out with boy and woman labour.

I have introduced these remarks regarding boy labour into this chapter as Colonel Carty and myself had many a good laugh watching the rate at which the labour employed on the buildings worked, even though we knew that we were dependent upon this type for rapid completion. It was typically Eastern, and though amusing it was at times very exasperating. One knows that the tremendous number of women and boys employed must have cost a large sum of money, yet at the same time conditions out here were such

THE FORD VAN AS IT USUALLY ARRIVED IN BAGHDAD FOR OVERHAUL IN 1918, AFTER BEING "DAMAGED."

READY FOR ROAD TEST AFTER OVERHAUL, ADVANCED M.T. DEPÔT, BAGHDAD.

DIFFICULTIES IN LANDING A TWO-AND-A-HALF-TON FLY-WHEEL AT BAGHDAD, 1917.

that this could not be avoided. The work had to be carried out.

So far as one can foresee, Mesopotamia is going to be a thriving country in the future, but I think the labour question here will always be a serious proposition, especially if the education of the natives makes an advancement.

In the early days in Baghdad this unit was repeatedly called on to do various kinds of work because it had an oxy-acetylene welding plant which enabled the Railway Department to place several engines in commission shortly after the capture of Samarah. These engines had been damaged by the Turks prior to the evacuation of that town. The unit was also responsible for the conversion of two Leyland armoured cars into anti-aircraft lorries.

These two armoured cars originally came out to this country with No. 6 Light Armoured Motor Battery. They were about 40 h.p. Leyland lorries and of a bastard type, for which spare parts were practically unobtainable. They were fitted with solid tyres, and with the armoured plating on them must have weighed somewhere in the region of seven tons when fully loaded. As armoured cars they were of no use in this country, and it was decided to convert them into anti-aircraft gun lorries. The design was partially got out by Captain Wood, who at that time was attached to the Directorate of Supplies and Transport. They had the ordinary drop sides, and the design of the screw jack was considered sound, there being a ball joint at the bottom which admitted of the feet (on which the screw jack rested) being placed on a slightly uneven surface. I have never heard of any complaints being received from the officer commanding the Pom-pom Section to which these lorries were allotted.

At the time of Colonel Donohue's visit to Baghdad he had already suggested the conversion of four Peerless lorries for use on the railway. The brains of several officers were concerned in the construction, but Major Vallat was responsible for the main features of the design. Material at the time was almost impossible to obtain. The wheels of the trucks on the railway were useless, being too large, and finally a number of old tram wheels off the Kadhimain tramway were made to suit the purpose. The illustrations will show what this vehicle looked like on the line. During the past eighteen months they have done invaluable and economical work for the railways.

One of the chief troubles with buildings out here is the foundations. They are more or less built on mud, and when close to the river there is always a tendency for these to subside. This has been proved on two or three occasions. Extra weight placed on the top floor causes buildings to collapse, or the placing of, say, a 30-h.p. gas engine in a room causes vibration, and sometimes with very disastrous results. The power unit of the Advanced M.T. Depôt at the present moment is occupying its third home in the building. These buildings at first sight seemed to have been strong enough, the walls being about 3 feet thick, and with a very good arched roof under the first floor. No doubt a certain subsidence was caused owing to the buildings being situated near the river-front, and the scouring action of the river when in flood doubtless undermined that portion which eventually collapsed.

Not only did the buildings collapse, but a considerable portion of the front wall bordering the river was also carried away. The Royal Engineers got to work on it, and in a short time made a good job of the river-wall. It has now a lasting appearance.

As a unit, the Advanced M.T. Depôt was in the limelight, so to speak, being situated in Baghdad. By limelight I mean that it had to take a place in the forefront of Mechanical Transport units, as so much depended upon its output. Not only was the output of thirty overhauls per week consistent, but all new reinforcement vehicles arriving from overseas had to be seen to.

In view of the sad shortage of spare parts, a disease from which this force suffered throughout 1917–18, the

IN THE MARKET-PLACE

advanced depôt was called on to manufacture numerous articles.

It must not be forgotten, when dealing with anything in the nature of spare parts in Mesopotamia, or even with the obtaining of material, that every known remedy had to be tried in order to get various kinds of materials. No M.T. officer is worthy his salt if there is any material in the neighbourhood and he is unable to get it!

Numerous inspectors have been round the workshops of this depôt, and all have come to the opinion, both as regards the patchwork as applied to the Ford car and the labour-saving dodges in vogue, that these were reduced to a fine art.

The late Commander-in-Chief, Lieutenant-General Sir Stanley Maude, took an exceptionally keen interest in this unit, and visited it on two or three occasions. The present Commander-in-Chief, Lieutenant-General Sir William Marshall, was also interested, and paid it several visits.

The Returns Section was originally part of the Advanced M.T. Stores, but it was considered essential to transfer it to the care of the Advanced M.T. Depôt. All unserviceable parts of M.T. vehicles are handed in to this section, as it is well known that no new parts can be issued to units unless the old parts are returned. All these apparently useless parts are sorted, irreparable parts are put on one side, and if not required for other purposes are sorted into various scrap-heaps.

Articles of use are all carefully checked, put on one side, and brought into stock. Those which are suitable are issued to the Stores Section of the Advanced M.T. Depôt for the overhaul and repair of vehicles, and any parts which are not required are handed over to the stores, where they are taken on charge and issued to units as new parts.

To give my readers some idea of the salving of M.T. spare parts in a force as small as this, the following are a few of the items which have been collected, repaired, and made serviceable during the past six months: outer covers, 500; inner tubes, 5,000; sparking plugs, 4,000.

As far as possible, nothing is wasted. All scrap rubber is dispatched to Kirkee Arsenal, India, and the unserviceable solid tyres with their steel rims are sent to England.

While dealing with the subject of rubber tyres, I should like to mention before closing the chapter that the tyre presses both at the Base and the Advanced M.T. Depôt have done an enormous amount of work in this country. Thousands of tyres have been pressed on, and the records to date show there have not been more than half a dozen burst bands. It is needless to specify the makes ; all the makers are to be congratulated.

Since writing this chapter the year 1918 has come and gone, and on looking back at the work of the unit for the past year, I think it would be interesting to publish a few facts with regard to the work carried out.

The period I take is from March to December—ten months.

The following was carried out in the Miscellaneous Shops: 81 overhauls, and 637 minor repairs.

Among the complete overhauls are included two "caterpillars" and six Horch lorries, the latter being some of the vehicles captured from the Turks at Kirkuk.

Spare parts were unobtainable and a large amount of manufacturing work had to be performed.

In the Ford shops, the following is the record: 1,000 Fords rebuilt and overhauled in ten months ; 793 Fords repaired.

Thus in ten months 1793 Fords were passed through these workshops—a remarkably fine performance, all things considered.

A résumé of the work and the weekly report from the O.C. unit was sent in to G.H.Q., and has received high appreciation from the General Officer Commanding-in-Chief.

This is given in the chapter devoted to that purpose.

A CORNER OF A COPPER MARKET: NOTE THE STRONG LIGHT-AND-SHADE EFFECTS

## CHAPTER VII

### ORGANISATION

Number of M.T. companies in the forward area—Formation of columns—Functions of the D. of S. and T.'s Directorate—Circulars—Dispatch of stores—List of spare parts for units—Statistics.

IN view of the fact that conditions in Mesopotamia from a mechanical transport point of view were rather different from those in France, it would be as well if a short chapter were devoted to the organisation which was in force during 1917 and 1918.

The number of companies to be handled were made up as follows:

| | |
|---|---|
| Ford Van Companies | 22 |
| Peerless Company | 1 |
| Packard Company | 1 |
| M.A.C.s | 5 |
| Caterpillar Companies | 8 |
| Workshop Repair Unit with L.A.M. Battery | 1 |
| Base M.T. Depôt | 1 |
| L. of C. Repair Unit Base | 1 |
| Advanced M.T. Depôt | 1 |
| Floating Workshops | 1 |

From the time that the late General Maude took command out here, the force can only be considered as a very highly centralised one. Thus the mechanical transport was also centralised, and the detailing of the bulk of it was done from the office of the D. of S. and T. With regard to the Ford van companies, it was not considered an economical proposition to allot, say, four to each division, because there was a considerable amount of time during the year in which they might be lying idle. They were, therefore, all administered as Army Troops, and were directly under the orders of G.H.Q.

It was decided towards the end of 1917, owing to the number of companies which had to be handled, that it would be necessary to form three companies into one column under the command of a lieutenant-colonel. This was done, and four columns were made as follows :

No. 1 M.T. Column, commanded by Lieut.-Col. Snepp, D.S.O.
,, 2 ,, ,, Lieut.-Col. Pelly, D.S.O., M.C.
,, 3 ,, ,, Lieut.-Col. Gibbons, M.C.
,, 4 ,, ,, Lieut.-Col. Dickinson.

Operations which took place after the fall of Baghdad were, as a rule, either on the right or left flank or up the centre, and concentrations of mechanical transport took place accordingly. It became apparent at once that it would be impossible to keep columns intact, so column commanders in reality became group or area commanders. In other words, they were allotted to companies which happened to be working for the time being in their area. These companies were constantly changing their columns, and, in addition, the strength of the columns varied considerably. At one time No. 3 Column had as many as twelve companies under its control.

Originally small concentrations took place for minor operations, where it was essential that a Mechanical Transport officer should be placed in charge, because the Staff of Divisions, etc., were unused to handling mechanical transport and were unable to work it economically. As more companies became available, so the radius of action of the force increased, and concentrations of mechanical transport augmented considerably, reaching as high as 1,200 vans for one specific operation. One L. of C. M.T. unit, Headquarters, Basrah, was responsible for the repair, maintenance, and supervision of all mechanical transport on the lines of communication. It had a War Establishment of the ordinary Ford van company, with additional sections added as required, the sections giving supervising staff and extra repair facilities to cope with the increased number of vehicles. This unit, No. 1056 Company, was also instrumental in bringing the Mauritian motor driver into the limelight, and did very good work. There was another company also stationed in Baghdad which was an L. of C. unit. It had a slightly different War Establishment, owing to the fact that it employed Arab and Armenian drivers instead of British and Indian.

The Peerless company was originally stationed at the Base, but on the fall of Baghdad it was found possible to work these vehicles over the desert, and the whole of the company (with the exception of twenty-five vehicles, which remained for Base work) were brought up to the forward area. No. 976 (the Light Packard company) had, in addition to their forty-eight lorries with pneumatic tyres, a further section consisting of our old friends the Fiats added to it. This was for the purpose of grouping these vehicles into a company which was properly supervised, as previously repairs had to be carried out by the nearest workshops. These companies were also grouped in under the command of one of the columns.

The motor ambulance convoys are, of course, medical units, though shown as Army Troops. During operations they were attached to Corps and Divisions and administered through the D.M.S. The "caterpillar" companies were also designated as Army Troops, and were administered through the B.G.R.A. of the Corps. There is no need to describe the functions of the workshop units, as my readers are already aware of these in previous chapters devoted to them.

Each Division had a certain number of mechanical transport vehicles, such as motor ambulances, allotted to their field ambulances, while motor cycles were found for the divisional Signal companies. There were also headquarter cars of the Corps, Divisions, etc. It was found necessary for all these vehicles to be supervised, and for this purpose a Mechanical Transport inspecting officer was attached to each Division. He was responsible for the inspection, minor repairs, etc., of all the mechanical transport attached to the Division. This officer had a small first aid staff, consisting of a sergeant-fitter, two drivers (handy men), one Talbot first-aid van, and one motor car. They formed a very good connecting link between the Division and G.H.Q. Though none were attached to either the 1st or 3rd Corps, the Mechanical Transport inspecting officer situated nearest the headquarters of the Corps was responsible in the same way for the vehicles of that Corps.

After the occupation of Baghdad, the demand for motor cars increased considerably: the country had to be exploited; the Political Department required representatives in various outlying districts; the Department of Local Resources sprang into being on a large scale; Irrigation, Agriculture, the Works Department increased, and roads had to be made. As no motor cars were available, Ford vans had to be allotted. There was consequently a large number of vans on detached duties from the various companies; one time the figure reached 220. They were always a source of trouble and annoyance to both this Directorate and the officers commanding the units from which the vehicles were detached.

It is also bad for drivers to be constantly away from their headquarters, and attached to other departments who know little or nothing with regard to the upkeep of this class of vehicle. Drivers get careless; supervision is sometimes impossible owing to the distances at which vehicles go from their headquarters; losses of equipment are numerous; and when the driver goes sick there is great difficulty in replacing him. As far as possible the vehicles were always detached from the company nearest to the locality in which they would work.

A great objection to the centralising of the mechanical transport was the extra work entailed on this Directorate. When operations were contemplated, the Corps or Division would be asked for their probable demands, and this appeared to be worked on the principle "so many men, so many rations." This was put into tons and multiplied by four Ford vans to the ton with 100 per cent. spare. The detail was, for the sake of argument, 600 vans. The demand would come through to G.H.Q. saying 600 Ford vans would be required for this specific operation. G.H.Q. had then to work out their actual requirements, taking into consideration the fact that they had other second-line transport. It would probably be found that their actual requirements would be somewhere nearer 300 vans than 600. They always asked for about double the number they actually required! On occasions when trying to obtain transport, it would be stated that 200 vans would be sufficient, a number which would, in the course of a day or two, be found to be totally inadequate.

The work of collecting these vehicles was very often like a game of chess. The chief drawback at times was the difficulty in obtaining complete units to send, though this was done when possible. It was advocated by Colonel Donohue that companies in the field should only be equipped with a first-aid staff of artificers with a few hand tools. This might work well in nine cases out of ten, but owing to the conditions in this country it would not have been a feasible proposition. Large workshops were not available for the concentration of all heavy repairs, and spare parts were so scarce throughout the whole campaign that companies were able to keep an enormous number of vehicles on the road simply and solely because they happened to have a mobile workshop on the spot and able to do the numerous jobs which would otherwise have had to be sent a hundred or two miles away to a heavy repair unit. I do not advocate that heavy overhauls should be done in the field, but the line of communication in Mesopotamia was a very difficult one, and the organisation for repairs was considered the best under the circumstances.

All Army Service Corps Mechanical Transport units kept in touch with the Directorate of Supplies and Transport by means of weekly reports, which contained information on the following lines:

Number of vehicles under repair.

Shortage of spare parts.

Number of vehicles worked during the week.

Any items of importance from a mechanical transport point of view which it was considered essential to bring to notice.

A copy of each unit's Army Form B.213 was necessary, so that shortages in personnel could be made up almost as soon as they occurred, authority being afterwards given by the D.A.G., 3rd Echelon. This Army form also showed a unit's strength, and was sent to the D.A.G., who dealt with reinforcements, and who issued the orders for the replacement of casualties.

The column commanders rendered weekly reports, and, in addition, a conference was held on the first Monday in each month, consisting of the Assistant Director of Mechanical Transport, Column Commanders, O.C. Advanced M.T. Depôt, Officer-in-Charge Advanced M.T. Stores, and the Inspector of Mechanical Transport, M.E.F. Various matters were discussed and settled on the spot. There was also a meeting each Monday in the A.D.T.'s office, consisting of the O.C. Advanced M.T. Depôt and the Officer-in-Charge of the Advanced M.T. Stores, and of course the A.D.T. These meetings saved endless writing, and numerous points which might have formed the subject of lengthy correspondence were thus settled amicably and expeditiously. The Mechanical Transport inspecting officers of Divisions also rendered a weekly report to their O.C. Divisional Train, who forwarded it to D. of S. and T.

The growth of mechanical transport out here necessitated the changing on one or two occasions of War Establishments, and the introduction of the Asiatic driver occasioned the constant changing of the Ford van company's war establishment. With regard to war establishments, G.H.Q. on the whole were very good to us, and the only difficulty experienced was the supply of the requisite number of artificers from England.

In addition to all the units previously mentioned, at the time of writing the following companies are in the country, though they have not taken part in any of the operations up to the signing of the Armistice. Actually they are at the Base, some waiting the arrival of their vehicles, while others are about to be dispatched up country.

*New Companies at the Base*

|  |  |
|---|---|
| No. 1093 | Ford van companies. |
| ,, 1094 | |
| ,, 1095 | |
| ,, 1096 | |
| ,, 1097 | |
| ,, 1098 | |
| ,, 1099 | |
| ,, 1110 | |
| ,, 1111 | |
| ,, 1114 | Peerless lorry companies. |
| ,, 1115 | |

It has often happened that on concentrations only a part of each company could be sent, chiefly because a large number of detached vans had to be employed. The object, however, was that on concentrations as many as possible complete Ford van companies should be sent.

It had been necessary in the past to split up certain units. For example, at one time half the Peerless company were employed at Basrah, and the other half at Baghdad. At the time of writing three-quarters of this unit are now employed in the forward area, the remaining quarter being left behind at the Base. The same applies to No. 23rd M.A.C. Vehicles built to carry eight passengers were originally concentrated at Basrah, but on the entry into Baghdad a certain number were sent to Amarah and also to the forward area. These vehicles, when detached, have always a parent workshop to look to for supervision and upkeep. It is much harder from the company's point of view to maintain these vehicles when they are split up, and it should always be avoided when possible.

Numerous cars and motor cycles allotted to various directorates spread all over Mesopotamia are all attached to some unit for supervision. A great number of these vehicles are embraced in the extra war establishments allowed for in the L. of C. Mechanical Transport companies, as mentioned on a previous page, but there are a number in the forward area which cannot be looked after by these units. Complete returns had to be rendered both to the War Office and to India with regard to the types of vehicles in the country, both available and under repair.

It is seen, therefore, that very careful records had to be kept to enable this Directorate to keep in touch and to be able to render complete returns. A card system for every car, lorry, and motor cycle was kept in the office of the D. of S. and T., and an officer was specially detailed to supervise this. This card was practically a medical history, so to speak, of the vehicle in question, and one could always, at a moment's notice, find out where any particular vehicle was situated.

In cases where vehicles were lost through accident, the result of enemy engagements, etc. etc., a Court of Inquiry was held. The proceedings were sent to the Director of Supplies and Transport, for his approval.

When it was necessary to publish suggestions, drawings, ideas, and improvements, or to bring any particular point to the notice of companies, these were sent out in the form of A.D.T.'s circulars. When suggestions and improvements came in from various officers, full credit was always given to them when the subject was sent round in the form of these circulars. Naturally, one or two points considered in

1916 to be rather valuable were found on exhaustive trials to be more or less valueless. This resulted in the cancellation of some previous order.

All M.T. formations had abbreviated telegraphic addresses which consisted of the number of the unit, followed by the word Backaxle. For instance, 976 Backaxle stood for No. 976 M.T. Company A.S.C. The Base M.T. Depôt's abbreviation was Magneto. The Advanced Store Section was Advanced Magneto. The Advanced M.T. Depôt was Advaxle.

As mechanical transport was practically unknown in this country, its limitations were certainly unknown, and in a way one had to guess the best procedure to counteract climatic conditions and roads, and also to deal with a large number of inexperienced drivers. Occasionally a few small mistakes were made, but they were never serious. I feel sure there was no loss of War Department money due to these mistakes.

The Mechanical Transport in this force as a rule worked from a fixed base, so they were able to have the headquarters of the company and the mobile workshops inside some building, which materially assisted in keeping vehicles on the road. Whenever operations were in progress, it was practically impossible to utilise the workshops, or in certain parts of the country to take these vehicles at all. The mobile workshops, as a rule, were brought close to the front in which their units were working, and spare parts and stores were dispatched to the nearest railhead. Broken-down vehicles were taken to the railhead and dispatched direct to the Advanced M.T. Depôt.

Towards the end of 1917 G.H.Q. decided that all formations should have distinguishing signs, instead of the designation of the Corps, Division, Unit, etc.; so the Mechanical Transport had what were known as company signs. Some of these signs were rather elaborate, but the majority of them were simple and, incidentally, remarkably useful. It could often be seen from a distance what unit a vehicle belonged to, and the word could thus be passed on to the company concerned if one of their vehicles was in trouble.

In addition to the Mechanical Transport inspecting officers of divisions, there is, of course, the Chief Inspector of Mechanical Transport. He is part and parcel of the D. of S. and T. Directorate, and acts as a travelling inspector, visiting all units and detachments of Mechanical Transport situated throughout the country.

I have said little or nothing about Light Armoured Motor Batteries. These were working under the officer commanding the Light Armoured Motor Brigade, and came under the heading of Army Troops. There is also the Locker-Lampson Armoured Car Brigade, which up to the present time has been working in Persia directly under the command of the G.O.C. Persian Force. As mentioned in other parts of this book, Ford vans were employed on numerous duties besides the actual carriage of supplies. It would therefore be more or less incorrect to call them supply columns.

The following is a list of the other units, the designations of which speak for themselves. Though they were not actually A.S.C. M.T. units, they would naturally require A.S.C. drivers to drive them.

6th Light Armoured Motor Battery
7th ,, ,, ,, ,,
8th ,, ,, ,, ,,
13th ,, ,, ,, ,,
14th ,, ,, ,, ,,
15th ,, ,, ,, ,,

*Locker-Lampson Armoured Car Brigade*

49th Anti-Aircraft Section
50th ,, ,, ,,
80th ,, ,, ,,
92nd ,, ,, ,,
93rd ,, ,, ,,
118th ,, ,, ,,

26th Ordnance Mobile Workshops
34th ,, ,, ,,
35th ,, ,, ,,
49th ,, ,, ,,
50th ,, ,, ,,
61st ,, ,, ,,

1st and 2nd Corps Signal Companies
13th Divisional Signal Companies
14th ,, ,, ,,
15th ,, ,, ,,
17th ,, ,, ,,
18th ,, ,, ,,
Army Signal Company.
2 Cavalry Combined Field Ambulances.
18 Combined Field Ambulances.
3 British Field Ambulances.
5 Combined Field Ambulances (modified).
21 Electric-light vehicles (lorries).

All the vehicles with the C.F.A.s were Fords, and they had what might best be described as a "mixed grill," i.e. three ambulances and two touring cars, the latter being chiefly employed for sitting-up cases. The Signal companies were equipped with two Star one-ton vans and their allotted number of motor cycles. These varied from fifteen to twenty-four, according to Divisional or Corps units. Toward the latter part of 1918, in addition to the "Stars," A.E.C., vehicles came out with a small electric-lighting plant on board. At the time of writing these have not been brought into use.

The A.D.T. M.T. also acted as the O.C. A.S.C., for practically all Mechanical Transport companies working under Army Troops, and this resulted in numerous circulars being sent out to units on questions dealing entirely with interior economy. It was necessary to issue orders with regard to company routine work; hot-weather precautions, economy, care of letters and postal instructions; the procedure regarding telegrams; guarding against sickness, wastage and care of petrol, how to open petrol tins; informing units that certain necessary items which were in constant demand were not available; instructions with regard to the employment of local labour, dress, correspondence, promotion, pay, iron rations, log books, drivers' orders. Special sanction was necessary for the issue of certain articles surplus to mobilisation store table.

All units on arrival at the Base were issued with copies of all A.D.T. circulars, extracts from G.R.O.s, L. of C. orders, Base orders, etc., to enable O.C.s to become acquainted with orders issued prior to their arrival. There was also a special letter of instruction to O.C. units informing where their camp would be; where they would draw their rations; and the situation of all depôts.

During the advance on Kut a Peerless lorry belonging to the 33rd M.A.C. went through the pontoon bridge into the River Hai, because the bridge proved incapable of taking a lorry of its size. The police on the bridge were unaware of the weight of the lorry when laden, and the driver was not apparently asked. This made it evident that some form of instructions would have to be drawn up to enable police posted on bridges to ascertain if the bridge was capable of carrying the vehicles which traversed it, and so a comprehensive circular illustrated with a diagram was drawn up by the Engineer-in-Chief, G.H.Q., demonstrating the various classes of pontoon bridges in use throughout the country, and giving a full description and silhouette diagram of different types of mechanical transport vehicles. A corresponding "class" number was painted on the dash. Thus, for example, a lorry fully laden, weighing not more than seven tons, could go over a Class III bridge and would have "Class III" painted on the dash; Class I and Class II the same. A notice would be posted at the entrance to the bridge showing the class of vehicle it could take, so that the police and drivers were at once able to see whether the bridge was capable of taking the vehicle.

While on the subject of the Peerless lorry which fell into the Hai, it might not be out of place to inform my readers that the River Hai as a rule is dry for four or five months during the year. The lorry in question fell in during the month of February 1917, and, unfortunately, the driver was drowned. The lorry disappeared, and even the top of the canopy could not be seen.

All hope of rescuing it was not given up, and the Political Officer at Kut was wired to some months later with regard to the possibility of getting it out. He replied that this might be done when the river was dry. As a matter of fact when this actually happened the bed of the river was thoroughly searched, but there was apparently nothing to show where the lorry had fallen in. The exact position was pointed out, and, after digging away in the mud, the lorry was unearthed. A delay ensued because the lorry could not be got away until sufficient water came down the Hai to float a boat capable of taking this vehicle. The actual date on which the vehicle was brought from the Hai was March 19, 1918, and was dispatched up to the Advanced M.T. Depôt, and notwithstanding the fact that it was about thirteen months in the bed of the river—the majority of that time under water—it was put on the road again after being overhauled, and is now hard at work.

While on the subject of organisation, I would like to bring out a few details with regard to the dispatch of Mechanical Transport stores, etc., up river, demonstrating what an increase there has been in the past year, and also the time taken to get these important articles from Basrah.

All stores arriving from England are off-loaded at Basrah, taken to the Stores Section, checked, etc., and brought on ledger charge.

Outstanding indents from the Advanced Section at Baghdad are then completed. The requisite amount of river tonnage is then demanded from the Director of Supplies and Transport for a week ahead. Sanction is accorded to this from the D.Q.M.G., and the I.G.C. is informed accordingly.

The stores are loaded at Basrah on to a barge, and remain on that, as a rule, until they arrive at Baghdad.

The railway is used on occasions, but only for small consignments, and is not nearly as expeditious a route as the through one, by river.

Barges can be brought alongside the stores wharf at Basrah, and also at Baghdad, and each of the sections is fitted with trolley lines and trolleys.

The following table is introduced to give you some idea of the growth of tonnage of M.T. spares sent from Basrah to Baghdad.

| Period of 6 months. | TONNAGE. | | |
|---|---|---|---|
| | Applied for. | Allotted. | Shipped. |
| July–December 1917 | 485 tons | 437 tons | 428 tons |
| January–June 1918 | 475 ,, | 417 ,, | 522 ,, |
| July–December 1918 * | 1077 ,, | 1077 ,, | 1022 ,, |

* Figures are up to and including December 10, 1918.

The tonnage sent up recently is :

| | | |
|---|---|---|
| September 1918 | . . . . . . | 176 tons 8 cwts. |
| October 1918 | . . . . . . | 187 ,, 10 ,, |
| November 1918 | . . . . . . | 175 ,, 10 ,, |
| December 1918 | . . . . . . | 172 ,, 12 ,, |

The following schedule shows the time it took for consignments to reach Baghdad after dispatch from Basrah.

| Barge No. | Date of leaving Base. | Date on which Receipt of Cases was acknowledged. | Time (days). |
|---|---|---|---|
| C. 607 | 11.11.18 | 5.12.18 | 24 |
| C. 273 | 8.11.18 | 28.11.18 | 20 |
| B. 124 | 24.10.18 | 25.11.18 | 32 |
| C. 91 | 22.10.18 | 15.11.18 | 24 |
| C. 271 | 19.10.18 | 15.11.18 | 27 |
| C. 460 | 17.10.18 | 10.11.18 | 24 |
| B. 507 | 29. 9.18 | 21.10.18 | 22 |
| B. 523 | 18. 9.18 | 9.10.18 | 21 |
| B. 209 | 7. 9.18 | 10.10.18 | 33 |
| B. 518 | 23. 8.18 | 21. 9.18 | 29 |
| C. 91 | 29. 8.18 | 21. 9.18 | 23 |
| B. 257 | 14. 8.18 | 13. 9.18 | 30 |

| Barge No. | Date of leaving Base. | Date on which Receipt of Cases was acknowledged. | Time (Days). |
|---|---|---|---|
| C. 472 | 13. 8.18 | 13. 9.18 | 31 |
| B. 312 | 5. 8.18 | 18. 8.18 | 13 |
| B. 532 | 31. 7.18 | 18. 8.18 | 19 |
| 529 | 25. 7.18 | 7. 8.18 | 13 |
| T. 47 | 21. 7.18 | 7. 8.18 | 17 |
| B. 313 | 19. 7.18 | 6. 8.18 | 18 |
| 286 | 16. 7.18 | 27. 7.18 | 11 |
| 321 | 14. 7.18 | 25. 7.18 | 11 |
| T. 41 | 10. 7.18 | 20. 7.18 | 10 |
| T. 42 | 11. 7.18 | 25. 7.18 | 14 |
| C. 625 | 30. 6.18 | 14. 7.18 | 14 |
| B. 507 | 21. 6.18 | 1. 7.18 | 11 |
| 646 | 13. 6.18 | 28. 6.18 | 15 |
| 268 | 8. 6.18 | 17. 6.18 | 9 |
| 514 | 21. 5.18 | 18. 6.18 | 28 |
| B. 163 | 30. 5.18 | 8. 6.18 | 9 |
| P.S. 59 | 29. 5.18 | 8. 6.18 | 10 |
| C. 443 | 11. 5.18 | 3. 6.18 | 24 |
| *Average*—19·53 *days* | | | |
| P.S. 58 | 27. 4.18 | 13. 5.18 | 17 |
| T. 40 | 19. 4.18 | 9. 5.18 | 21 |
| T. 44 | 8. 4.18 | 23. 4.18 | 16 |
| B. 124 | 3. 4.18 | 12. 4.18 | 10 |
| C. 74 | 29. 3.18 | 16. 4.18 | 19 |
| P.S. 87 | 21. 3.18 | 7. 4.18 | 18 |
| Per rail to Amarah | 15. 3.18 | 2. 4.18 | 19 |
| 278 | 13. 3.18 | 26. 3.18 | 14 |
| Per rail to Amarah | 6. 3.18 | 26. 3.18 | 21 |
| Do. | 3. 3.18 | 26. 3.18 | 24 |
| Do. | 5. 2.18 | 7. 3.18 | 31 |
| B. 277 | 6. 2.18 | 20. 2.18 | 15 |
| Per rail to Amarah | 16. 2.18 | 9. 3.18 | 22 |
| Do. | 25. 2.18 | 11. 3.18 | 15 |
| C. 631 | 3. 1.18 | 23. 1.18 | 21 |
| Z.A. 249 | 26. 1.18 | 22. 2.18 | 28 |
| 272 | 26. 1.18 | 4. 2.18 | 10 |
| 514 | 19. 1.18 | 26. 1.18 | 8 |
| 618 | 31. 1.18 | 20. 2.18 | 21 |
| C. 479 | 6.12.17 | 19. 1.18 | 45 |
| C. 423 | 14.12.17 | 7. 1.18 | 25 |
| B. 530 | 20.12.17 | 19. 1.18 | 31 |
| Kalika | 26.12.17 | 19. 1.18 | 25 |
| A. 317 | 21.11.17 | 11.12.17 | 21 |
| 124 | 29.11.17 | 19. 1.18 | 52 |
| C. 479 | 6.12.17 | 19. 1.18 | 45 |

Average by barge . . . . . 23·12 days.
Average by rail . . . . . 22·00 ,,
Average by barge over whole period . 20·96 ,,

The barges as a rule travelled one on either side of one of the numerous river-steamers.

It might be interesting to record here that during the year 1918, approximately 45,000 packages were received at the Base M.T. Depôt, mainly from England. The number dispatched by that unit totalled 50,000, most of which were consigned to the Advanced M.T. Stores, Baghdad. From the foregoing it will be seen that even after arrival of the stores from England, at least five weeks elapsed before units up the line could benefit, even under the most advantageous circumstances. The stores on arrival at Baghdad had to be unloaded; sorted out and units informed, in order that they could collect them. As a rule, it was two months after the arrival of a ship before a unit received the necessary spares.

It was a point for discussion whether M.T. spares from overseas should be off-loaded direct on to the barges and sent up to Baghdad, sorted and checked there, and the parts required for the L. of C. units sent down stream again. It was decided that there were undoubted advantages by this method, but the disadvantages outweighed these and were briefly as follows:

1. Delay in alteration of existing organisation, at a time of great pressure.
2. Lack of storage room in Baghdad
3. Lack of accommodation for personnel.
4. The off-loading, checking, and returning to Base of a large number of parts required for the L. of C. and for stock purposes.

It will be as well in this chapter to include a list showing the amount of spares which was considered should be carried by all Ford companies, but the spare part question practically never admitted of these being issued, and, as stated in another part of this book, it was a hand-to-mouth existence. The list, however, is published for information and possibly future guidance under similar conditions.

List of Spares for Ford Van Company of 130 Vans

| Cat. No. | Name of Part. | Quantity. |
|---|---|---|
| | **Front Axle** | |
| 2692 | Spindle body with arm, right | 2 |
| 2693 | ,, ,, ,, left | 2 |
| 2733 | Front radius rods | 6 |
| 2734 | ,, ,, ,, nuts | 12 |
| 2704 | Stationary cones | 2 |
| 2705 | Adjusting cones, left side | 6 |
| 2706 | ,, ,, right side | 6 |
| 2805 | Inner race | 6 |
| 2804 | Outer race | 6 |
| 2806 | Outer ball retainers | 6 |
| 2807 | Inner ball retainers | 6 |
| 2800 | Front wheels | 4 |
| 2803 | Front hub assembly, less flange | 4 |
| 2710 | Spindle bolt with oiler | 4 |
| 2713 | Spindle body bushing | 4 prs. |
| 2709 | Spindle washers | 6 |
| 2715 | ,, oilers | 24 |
| 2707 | ,, nut, left side | 6 |
| 2708 | ,, ,, right side | 6 |
| 3800 | Front spring | 12 |
| 3808 | ,, ,, clips | 12 |
| 3847 | ,, ,, retainer clip with bolt and nut | 12 |
| 3811 | ,, ,, tie bolt and nut | 12 |
| 2819 | Hub cap | 6 |
| 3813 | Front spring hanger | 6 |
| 2810 | Balls, large | 72 |
| 2811 | ,, small | 72 |
| 2809 | Felt washer, front or rear hub | 12 |
| | **Back Axle** | |
| 2814 | Rear wheels | 4 |
| 2815 | ,, hub tapered, less flange | 4 |
| 2500 | ,, axle assembly | 2 |
| 2818 | Diff. drive gear | 3 |
| 2505 | Axle shaft tapered | 4 |
| 2508 | ,, ,, roller bearing | 6 |
| 2509 | ,, ,, ,, ,, sleeve, right | 3 |
| 2509 B. | ,, ,, ,, ,, ,, left | 3 |
| 2597 B. | D.S. Pinion | 3 |
| 2566 | Hub brake shoe assembly | 12 |
| 2825 | Hub bolt and nut | 24 |
| 2545 B. | Rear axle grease cup | 6 |
| 2520 | Diff. gear | 3 |
| 3824 | Rear springs | 12 |
| 3833 | ,, ,, clip | 12 |
| 3848 | ,, ,, retainer clip with bolt and nut | 12 |
| 3837 | ,, ,, tie bolt and nut | 12 |
| 3840 | ,, ,, hanger | 6 |

| Cat. No. | Name of Part. | Quantity. |
|---|---|---|
| | ENGINE | |
| 3221 | Comm. case with fibre assem. | 2 |
| 3165 | ,, brush assembly | 4 |
| 3960 | Fan and pulley | 2 |
| 3002 | Cylinder head gasket | 1 |
| 3003 | ,, ,, cap screw | 12 |
| 3025 | Conn. rod cap bolt and nuts | 12 |
| 3034 | C.S. bearing bolt, centre and front | 6 |
| 3035 | ,, ,, ,, nuts | 6 |
| 3036 | ,, rear bearing bolt | 6 |
| 3052 | Valves | 100 |
| 3054 | Valve springs | 12 |
| 3056 | Valve spring seat | 12 |
| 3057 | ,, ,, ,, pin | 24 |
| 3024 | Connecting rods | 4 |
| 3020 | Piston complete | 4 |
| 3061 | Exhaust pipe pack nut | 3 |
| 3063 | Inlet and exhaust pipe gasket | 12 |
| 3005 | Cylinder head outlet conn. gasket | 6 |
| 3008 | ,, ,, ,, ,, screw | 6 |
| 3018 | ,, water inlet gasket | 6 |
| 3945 | ,, ,, ,, hose clip | 6 |
| 3007 | ,, head cutlet ,, ,, | 6 |
| 3077 | Crank-case front bearing cap | 6 |
| 3080 | ,, drain clip plug | 3 |
| 3079 | ,, oil cock | 2 |
| 3081 | ,, ,, tube | 1 |
| 3250 | Magneto coil assembly | 1 |
| 3041 | Camshaft | 1 |
| 3300 | Transmission assem. | 1 |
| 3320 | ,, driven gear sleeve bushing | 6 |
| 3413 | ,, band assem. | .6 |
| 3416 | ,, ,, linings | 72 ft. |
| 3422 | ,, ,, rivets, ½ inch | 72 |
| 3423 | ,, ,, ,, $\frac{5}{16}$ inch | 288 |
| 3536 | Ball and socket joint | 6 |
| 3534 B. | Commutator pull rod | 2 |
| 3535 | Carburettor pull rod | 2 |
| 2909 | Feed pipe | 2 |
| 3925 | Radiator | 3 |
| 3932 | ,, rods | 2 |
| | ,, hose rubber, 2 inch | 20 ft. |
| | ,, ,, ,, 1¼ inch | 10 ft. |
| 3970 | Fan grease cup | 3 |
| 4350 | Spark plug wire, No. 1 | 12 |
| 4351 | ,, ,, ,, No. 2 | 12 |
| 4353 | ,, ,, ,, Nos. 3 and 4 | 24 |
| 4355 | Commutator wire assembly | 12 |
| 4350 | Carburettor complete | 2 |
| 4451 | ,, float with lever assem. | 2 |
| 4732 | Coil unit | 4 |
| 4733 | K.W. vibrator with T.P. | 4 |
| 4734 | ,, ,, bridge with T.P. | 4 |
| 3260 | Magneto contact assem. | 2 |

| Cat. No. | Name of Part. | Quantity. |
|---|---|---|
| | CHASSIS | |
| 4025 | Silencer assembly . . . . . . . | 1 |
| 4030 | ,, rod only . . . . . . . | 12 |
| 4816 | Running board truss rod front . . . . . | 6 |
| 4817 | ,, ,, ,, ,, rear . . . . . | 6 |
| 2853 | Front cross member . . . . . . . | 3 |
| 2854 B. | Rear ,, ,, . . . . . . . | 3 |
| 6576 X. | Electric head lamp door lens . . . . . | 12 |
| 6572 X. | ,, ,, ,, bulb . . . . . . | 36 |

Attached also is a copy of the weekly report received from the officer commanding the Advanced Signal Park, with regard to the motor cycles on charge of all Signal units throughout the country. This report is rendered weekly to the office of the D. of S. and T. The M.T. inspecting officers with Divisions carried out weekly inspections of all Signal units. The Advanced Signal Park were authorised to do numerous minor repairs to motor cycles which were sent in from outlying units, but complete overhauls were carried out by the Floating Workshop. The Advanced Signal Park had got a certain amount of plant and machinery available, and had also a matter of about a dozen highly skilled motor-cycle experts. For this reason they were authorised to do these minor repairs—the results justified the concession.

As will be seen from the attached report, out of a total of 215 motor cycles on the War Establishments only four were non-effective. It happens I have picked upon a good report, but on going through them, the average number of non-effectives never exceeded eight to ten, and the units were at once made up to War Establishment immediately a cycle was non-effective, by the Advanced Signal Park, who had a floating stock of six cycles, and were thus enabled to supply units direct on receipt of a wire.

I think it will be interesting to record here that at the

## Report on Motor Cycles with Signal Units for the Week ended October 12, 1918

| | I. Corps Signal Co. | III. Corps Signal Co. | Army Signal Co. | No. 1 Sec. No. 1 L. of C.S.C. | No. 2 Sec. No. 1 L. of C.S.C. | No. 2 L. of C. Signal Co. | 13th Div. Sig. Co. | 14th Div. Sig. Co. | 15th Div. Sig. Co. | 17th Div. Sig. Co. | 18th Div. Sig. Co. | 6th Cav. Sig. Bde. Trp. | 7th Cav. Bde. Sig. Trp. | 11th Cav. Bde. Sig. Trp. | Aust. Wireless Sig. Sqd. | A. & C. Trps. No. 2 Wireless. | No. 4 Wireless Obsn. Grp. | Dunster Force Sig. Co. | Sch. of Sig. | Adv. Sig. Park. | TOTAL. |
|---|---|---|---|---|---|---|---|---|---|---|---|---|---|---|---|---|---|---|---|---|---|
| War Establishment | 25 | 23 | 22 | 28 | 2 | 6 | 15 | 13 | 13 | 15 | 13 | 6 | 6 | 6 | 11 | 4 | 2 | 2 | 1 | 2 | 215 |
| On charge . . | 25 | 23 | 22 | 28 | 2 | 6 | 15 | 13 | 13 | 15 | 13 | 6 | 6 | 6 | 11 | 4 | 2 | 2 | 1 | 2 | 215 |
| Non-effective . | 1 | 1 | 0 | 0 | 0 | 0 | 0 | 0 | 0 | 0 | 1 | 0 | 0 | 1 | 0 | 0 | 0 | 0 | 0 | 0 | 4 |
| To complete . | 0 | 0 | 0 | 0 | 0 | 0 | 0 | 0 | 0 | 0 | 0 | 0 | 0 | 0 | 0 | 0 | 0 | 0 | 0 | 0 | 0 |
| Received from units | 1 TMH. B516 | 0 | 0 | 0 | 0 | 0 | 0 | 0 | 0 | 0 | 1 TMH. B519 | 0 | 0 | 0 | 0 | 0 | 0 | 0 | 0 | 0 | 2 |
| Issued to units . | 1 TMH. 1096 | 2 TMH. 1069 1070 | 1 DGS. B646 | 0 | 0 | 0 | 0 | 0 | 0 | 0 | 1 TMH. B515 | 0 | 0 | 0 | 0 | 0 | 0 | 0 | 0 | 0 | 5 |
| In A.S.P. Workshop | 1 TMH. B518 | 1 DGS. B588 | 0 | 0 | 0 | 0 | 0 | 0 | 0 | 0 | 1 TMH. B936 | 0 | 0 | 0 | 0 | 0 | 0 | 0 | 0 | 0 | 3 |
| Returned to M.T. Depôt . . | 0 | 0 | 0 | [illegible] | 0 | 0 | 0 | 0 | 0 | 0 | 0 | 0 | 0 | 0 | 0 | 0 | 0 | 0 | 0 | 0 | 0 |

Machines held as spares at the Advanced Signal Park: "Douglas," Nos. B298 and 308; "Triumph" Nos. B1097, 1098, 1099, and 1277.

(*Signed*) E. W. P. Fulcher, *Lieutenant*,
O.C., Advanced Signal Park.

end of 1918 the following was the approximate strength of the A.S.C. M.T. in Mesopotamia :

| Officers. | B.O.R.s. | I.O.R.s. | Arabs, etc. |
|---|---|---|---|
| 360 | 8,500 | 3,000 | 800 |
| Lorries. 3-ton. | Lorries. 30-cwt. | Fords. All types. | Cars and Ambulances other than Fords. |
| 420 | 480 | 4,000 | 200 |
| Armoured Cars. | Caterpillar Tractors. | Motor Cycles. | Fire Engines. |
| 90 | 40 | 1,300 | 7 |

It will be seen, therefore, that approximately 7,000 motor vehicles, including cycles, had to be maintained.

# CHAPTER VIII

## OPERATIONS, NOVEMBER 1916 TO MAY 1917

**Operations around the Hai—Retreat of the Turks—The British advance —Crossing the Dialah—Capture of Baghdad—Two M.T. companies to join the Russians—Battle for Samarah.**

THE actual date on which the late Lieutenant-General Sir F. S. Maude took over command of the Mesopotamian Forces, or the I.E.F.D. as it was then called, was August 28, 1916. The months of September, October, and November saw the whole force being reorganised. The only operations of note prior to December were of a punitive nature by a force under Major-General Brooking, who tackled large numbers of irregulars north-east of Nasiriyeh, and put some 850 men out of action, in addition to destroying a large number of the enemy's towers.

In describing the work of the Mechanical Transport companies from now onwards, it will be necessary to give a brief account of the various operations which were in progress at the time, so that my readers can realise the reasons why the Mechanical Transport units were working on these particular lines of advance.

On December 13 an advance was made to the Shatt al-Hai, and a strong force sent across to secure the west bank.

Repairing break in bund, flood near Baghdad.

Other side of break in bund.

RESULT OF THE TURKS CUTTING THE BUND ON THE EUPHRATES. BAGHDAD IS IN THE DISTANCE.

THE PEERLESS CONVERTED TO RUN ON THE BROAD-GAUGE RAILWAY, BAGHDAD.

REPAIRING A BRIDGE WHICH, THOUGH FLIMSY LOOKING, IS CAPABLE OF TAKING THREE TONS.

December 14–18 the British advanced and occupied 2,200 yards of the right bank of the Tigris south-east of Kut al-Amarah; and on December 20 our Cavalry operated at Husaini Bend on the Tigris, thirteen miles west of Kut al-Amarah.

Between January 9 and 19 operations in the Muhammad Abdul Hasan loop resulted in the complete evacuation by the Turks of the right back of the Tigris down stream of a point due south of Kut. The Turks suffered enormous casualties in this engagement.

January 11–14 our Cavalry temporarily occupied Kut al-Hai, capturing large quantities of grain, sheep, cattle, arms, and ammunition.

January 25–28 the British attacked in the Hai salient up both banks of the Hai River, which resulted in the capture of two outer lines of Turkish trenches on the east bank. In this engagement the enemy lost heavily.

Between February 1 and 16 the enemy were driven out of their advanced position on the west bank of the Shatt al-Hai, which was followed by a Turkish withdrawal to a position flanked on the Liquorice Factory. The Turks were finally cleared from the Shumran and Dahirah Bends with very heavy casualties.

Between February 17 and 22 the Turkish position at Sannaiyat was bombarded, and during operations between February 18 and 23 the British bridged the Tigris in the Shumran Bend and crossed to the left bank, capturing the third- and fourth-line trenches. On the following day we captured the Sannaiyat, Nakhailat and Suwada positions, and the Turks were in full retreat, covered by a strong rearguard, which fought stubbornly in Dahirah peninsula.

The enemy retired on February 25-27 on and through Aziziyeh. The retreat was continued with the various minor operations up to the Dialah River, and between March 8 and 10 the British crossed the river after severe fighting, entering Baghdad on March 11.

The above résumé of the fighting between September and

the entry into Baghdad is related so that my readers can follow the work done by the Mechanical Transport companies and other similar Mechanical Transport units which took part in this advance over very difficult country, the roads in places being almost impassable.

As previously mentioned, No. 33 Motor Ambulance Convoy was the first to arrive at Sheikh Sa'ad and very soon got to work. No. 783 M.T. Company A.S.C. (Ford vans) arrived at the end of November, and were chiefly employed in carrying R.E. stores, such as barbed wire and pickets for same, water pumps and hose, picks and shovels, between their headquarters and Sinn. When this unit first came up, the road ran for a few miles only, i.e. about as far as the Twin Canals. After this the vans had to travel over the ordinary desert, and in some places had to traverse recently cultivated ground. When the rain fell, as it did about this time, the going was almost indescribable. Early in December some fifty odd vans of this unit were out all night, stuck in the mud up to their axles, and it was only with the greatest difficulty that they were eventually got back to camp.

On December 14 the company moved its headquarters to Sinn. It was still being employed on the carriage of R.E. stores, which were very urgently needed. A few of the vans also carried supplies, and others ammunition.

Towards the end of December No. 784 M.T. Company (Ford vans) arrived and camped at Arab Village. They were chiefly employed between that place and Sinn on the carriage of supplies. It must be remembered that neither of these companies at this time had workshops and were dependent entirely upon spares, a portable forge which each company possessed, and the assistance rendered by the floating workshops. Material was also extremely difficult to obtain, and spring steel was almost worth its weight in gold! Old springs from tongas (Indian carts) had to be "roped" in to try to keep these Ford vans on the road, owing to the enormous breakages. It is remarkable the way these two companies worked right up to the time of the arrival of their workshops in June 1917.

It was seen hereabouts that the roads would have to be repaired, and every week saw an improvement, but, even then, tremendous damage was done by A.T. carts (Indian transport carts). Captain Vallat, in charge of No. 773 M.T. Company attached to 33rd M.A.C., was instrumental in getting out a road plough made of wood. It was heavily built, triangular in shape, with cutting knives placed in echelons underneath, and when drawn by a tractor made a remarkably good surface. It assisted materially in keeping Mechanical Transport vehicles on the road. These ploughs were afterwards employed on numerous areas right up to and including the year 1918.

During all the operations around the Shatt al-Hai, No. 784 M.T. Company continued to work from Arab Village and No. 783 Company from Sinn up to the front line, carrying ammunition and bringing back the wounded. The vans of both units were constantly out all night.

On February 4, 1917, No. 783 Company moved up to Atab on the right bank of the Hai, and here eighty vans of No. 784 Company joined them. On the morning of February 23 a convoy of No. 783 Company's vans took up rowers for the pontoons required for bridging the Tigris, which, as already mentioned, was completed that day. On February 25 No. 783 Company crossed the Tigris by this bridge at Shumran Bend, and two or three days later No. 784 Company passed them and camped at Imam Mahdi. Both companies were then employed in carrying up supplies from the Shumran Bend to Imam Mahdi as the advance proceeded. During the advance right up to Aziziyeh both companies came in for some very hard work, on occasions taking water and ammunition to the troops.

On March 5 No. 783 Company had orders to move to Aziziyeh, and on the same date No. 784 Company moved from Imam Mahdi forward. During the journey a very severe sandstorm was encountered—one of the most severe sandstorms it has ever been my lot to be in. I happened to be returning from Aziziyeh and passed both companies, and informed the officers commanding the convoys that I did not think it possible to get through. No. 784 Company gave up the journey and No. 783 Company also did so within fifteen miles of Aziziyeh, where they were forced to stay the night.

No. 773 M.T. Company attached No. 33 M.A.C. did remarkably fine work on the whole way up in the advance, evacuating wounded from the front line. I also saw this unit at Aziziyeh on March 4. Their workshops, owing to their being the heavy Peerless vehicle, had been left behind at Sheikh Saad, where they remained for some considerable time and were eventually brought up by river to Baghdad. A few ambulances were, naturally enough, shed on the way up, but in view of the amount of spare parts available, the lack of repair facilities, and the rapidity of the advance, the number of casualties amongst the mechanical transport was remarkably few. All ranks of these three companies are to be congratulated on the way in which they worked to keep their vehicles on the road.

With regard to Nos. 783 and 784 Companies, their loads for the latter part of the journey up to Aziziyeh consisted of emergency rations and petrol, the latter being at that time and at that place, priceless; in fact a fair number of vehicles had to be abandoned on the march up simply and solely owing to the lack of petrol. On March 8 these companies had orders to move to Bawi, and Captain Gibbons was sent on reconnaissance duty to the right bank of the Tigris to ascertain if the ground was possible for motor traffic and to try to find a main road running into Baghdad. It was found impossible, however, owing to irrigation channels.

It was considered necessary, though, by the General Staff to have some thirty vans on this side of the river, so they were sent from No. 784 Company, under command of 2nd Lieutenant D. A. G. Brown. The main object of sending

M.T. CONVOY *EN ROUTE* TO JOIN THE RUSSIANS.
NOTE THE HILLS.

SAMARAH RAILWAY-STATION.
Showing damage done by Turks to engines on Baghdad line.

GROUP OF COSSACKS INTERESTED IN A FORD CAR.

FIRST FORD VAN COMPANY TO REACH BAGHDAD PARKED IN THE CITADEL ON MARCH 11, 1917.

these vans was for the purpose of carrying water, but when this was found unnecessary they were employed in carrying troops and machine guns. Both companies, viz. Nos. 783 and 784, continued their march, and on the 11th received orders to proceed to Baghdad. No. 783 Company were the first away and were the first over the bridge at the Dialah, chiefly owing to the fact that No. 784 Company were held up by numerous troops and prevented from crossing.

No. 783 Company entered Baghdad on March 11 and No. 784 Company the next day.

The detachment of thirty vans arrived at Baghdad railway-station on March 11, but did not join their company until a day or two later, the vans being ferried across the river to Hinaidi. On off-loading the vehicles at this place this unit (No. 784 Company) lost the services of one of its best men, Private Cattanach, and the whole company felt his loss keenly. He apparently tripped over a rope on the barge, and, falling into the river, was lost. This type of accident often happened on the Tigris, and it seems remarkable that even the best of swimmers failed to save themselves.

Both these units camped in Baghdad for a few days, occupying the Citadel and Cavalry Barracks. On March 18 and 19 a convoy of both companies, under command of Captain Gibbons, carried troops, the object of which was a surprise attack on Baqubah and the capture of the town and pontoon bridge. On arrival there it was found the bridge had been destroyed, so the troops were left at Baqubah and the vans returned to Baghdad. The following day the vans took more troops and supplies.

On March 18 the officer commanding No. 784 Company took over sixty vans of No. 783 Company. With 2nd Lieutenant Kirwan these were for work at and beyond Baqubah. Between March 14 and 25 operations for the protection of Baghdad were undertaken. This consisted in the advance to Mushaidie in the centre, the occupation of Baqubah on the right, and Felujah on the left.

The 13th Turkish Army Corps at Sharban, some fifteen

miles north of Baqubah, was attacked on March 25, and heavy losses inflicted on them. On March 29 they were driven across the Shatt al-Adhaim, sustaining heavy casualties; while on March 31 the Russians, who had been operating wide on our right flank, occupied Qasr-i-Shirin.

On April 2 the Turks evacuated Sharban and retreated northwards across the Dialah River, and the British established contact with the Russians at Kizil Robat.

A convoy of forty-six Ford vans, under command of Captain Pelly, left Baqubah on April 5 with one officer and sixteen other ranks and one Lewis gun. Kizil Robat was reached at noon, and the convoy came under heavy shell fire from three enemy guns. The first thirty-two vans of the convoy and the touring car went on to within 600 yards of the village, and then turned east across very rough ground, two ditches having to be filled in before the cars could pass. Two cars had to be abandoned here with bent front axles and radius rods.

The thirteen vans in the rear of the convoy were about one mile behind the main column when the shelling began, and halted at large intervals on the road, the personnel taking cover. Second Lieutenant Brown went in and brought back one car facing the rear. Sergeants Stewart and Ofield brought out one car each, and drove on to the main column, leaving ten cars under shell fire. Captain Pelly went back from the main column to collect the men. Officers and men all deserve the greatest credit for their coolness, the discipline being excellent.

A start was made at 3 p.m. towards Khaniquin, and on getting clear of Kizil Robat the convoy of thirty-one vans was again shelled, but without damage. They eventually reached Qasr-i-Shirin at 10.30 p.m., where a great welcome was accorded them by the Russians and General Radatz, who inspected the detachment on April 7, 1917.

The convoy left Qasr-i-Shirin at 4 p.m. on April 9, and practically took the same cross-country journey as on the outward journey, picking up all the cars which had been abandoned on the way up, with the exception of one car which had been left five miles north of Kizil Robat.

I can scarcely do better than include here an extract from the "Order of the Day, No. 71," dated April 20, 1917:

"AWARDED THE MILITARY CROSS

"Captain Edmund Godfrey Pelly, Army Service Corps.—For gallant conduct and resource when in charge of a Motor Transport convoy which was heavily shelled, fourteen lorries being temporarily put out of action. It was largely due to his determination and fine example that the convoy, though seriously checked, succeeded in reaching its destination.

"AWARDED THE MILITARY MEDAL

"No. M/20 34581 Acting Sergeant James Ofield, Army Service Corps.

"No. M/2 200886 Acting Sergeant Donald Rosling Stewart, Army Service Corps."

While this most important action, from a Mechanical Transport point of view, was taking place, the major operations of the Mesopotamian forces were in full swing. On April 8 the British captured Balad railway-station, with numerous prisoners; and between April 11 and 15 the Turks retreated into the Jebel Hamrin range behind Deli Abbas. The British forced a passage of Shatt al-Adhaim held by a detachment of the Turkish 18th Army Corps, and completely routed the enemy, many prisoners being taken. On April 23 the British captured Samarah. This was the most important capture after Baghdad, as the main Berlin-Baghdad line ran from Samarah to Baghdad.

I have previously mentioned in this chapter the question of the abandonment of vehicles on the march up from the Shumran Bend to Baghdad. The chief offenders, if I might call them offenders, were the Field Ambulances. The three causes for having to abandon vehicles on the road up were as follows :

(1) Lack of petrol.
(2) Lack of spares.
(3) Ignorance.

The latter would appear to require some explanation, but it was apparently not known by the officers unaccustomed to mechanical transport vehicles that one Ford ambulance or car, as the case may be, was quite capable of towing another one.

On March 4 I went to Aziziyeh from Sheikh Sa'ad by road and saw a number of vehicles which had been abandoned. On my next journey up from Sheikh Sa'ad to Baghdad a few days later a further number were counted between Aziziyeh and the Dialah. These vehicles had to remain out some time, as there were no facilities, in view of the rapid advance, for getting them up to Baghdad. Captain Vallat, A.S.C., was later sent down with a few spare wheels and spare axles and a Ford car to retrieve all he possibly could and bring them to the posts along the river, in order that they could be got up to Baghdad. Twenty-five ambulances and cars were altogether rescued, to say nothing of a few captured Turkish lorries. While on the subject of these Turkish lorries, I might mention that two of them were towed with two Ford cars a distance of two or three miles across the desert, although the solid rubber tyres on the cars had been completely stripped off the wheels. None of the Turkish vehicles captured on the advance on Baghdad were ever worth repairing.

The practice of stripping vehicles at this time was lamentable, and yet was not to be wondered at in view of the shortage of spares. General routine orders were published on the subject which had a beneficial effect afterwards. I am glad to say that the stripping of vehicles except by the unit concerned is not now often done.

I have previously mentioned that the work done by the

33rd Motor Ambulance Convoy all through the advance and right up to the capture of Samarah was excellent. This unit had been at work night and day, and was also handicapped by the fact that no Army Service Corps officer was present with it at this time, and as previously mentioned, its workshops were far behind. With the exception of the Star Ambulance Convoy at the Base, No. 23 M.A.C. and a few ambulances with Field Ambulances with Divisions, it was the only convoy that formations could depend on for the rapid evacuation of sick and wounded. It had been working practically without rest right through the advance on the Hai up to the capture of Samarah. Colonel Donohue, who at this time was out here, and myself took the opportunity on April 21 of inspecting the various Mechanical Transport units on the line, and on the night of April 21 we stayed with No. 784 M.T. Company, camped at Sindiyah.

On April 22 we were present at the battle of Istabulat, and were up with the guns on this occasion. We spent the night with No. 33 M.A.C., and left early next morning to try to get into Samarah with the advancing troops. This was accomplished, and on looking back it must have been rather an amusing spectacle to see two little Fords trekking along about 250 yards behind the advancing line of scouts. The railway-station had been set on fire by the Turks, and was still burning when we arrived there. It contained one long stream of engines, the cylinders of which had been blown out by the Turks the night before. One or two anti-aircraft sections were also seen, and Colonel Donohue was able to form a very good idea of the country over which Mechanical Transport would have to work, though at this period it was seen at its best.

Before completing this chapter I should like to mention that it was found necessary to send a second convoy of Fords up to the Russians at Kizil Robat, with Captain Gibbons in command. Colonel Donohue and myself took advantage of this convoy to inspect the kind of country in this part of the world, though a fairly accurate idea of it could be formed from reports which had been furnished us by Captain Pelly, who had been up with the previous convoy.

The convoy left on or about May 8, 1917, with an escort of one armoured car, a Lewis gun, and some twenty Indian other ranks. When we were nearing Sharban we were informed that the convoy would probably be shelled after getting through the Jabal Hamrin. A section of guns and some cavalry had already been sent up to safeguard the flank of the convoy, but these had orders not to move beyond Sharban. It seemed rather amusing at the time that the escort for a fast-moving convoy was not allowed to proceed more than half-way, but the unfortunate convoy, with little means of defence, had to go the rest of the way more or less unprotected. The Jabal Hamrin was negotiated easily, the only trouble experienced being boiling radiators, and a halt was made on the north side of this range of hills to collect all the vans prior to striking the open stretch of country towards Kizil Robat. Everybody expected to be heavily shelled, but we eventually arrived safely, and camped near the spot where the detachment of Russians were situated.

From what I saw of the Russians one could hardly imagine they were soldiers. They looked more like brigands. However, they could dance well, and entertained us in no small way for several hours during the evening. We thought we might be able to salve the Ford van which had been left behind on the previous convoy, so a first-aid party was sent out at daybreak. The Turkish guns were still active, and we were awakened early with the sound of shells whizzing over our heads. The van was again left behind, and the first-aid party returned. Soon afterwards a start was made for home, and the foot of the Jabal Hamrin was reached in safety. The Turks were apparently expecting the convoy to go north and were not on the look-out for us on the other side of the village. I have many times since been over this road, which has been considerably improved, and, indeed, the country after the occupation by the 14th Division in this area is almost unrecognisable.

There were several Anti-Aircraft sections and "Caterpillar" companies which also took part in this advance to Baghdad. The "Caterpillars," however, were unable to move owing to the fact that no bridges were able to carry their weight at the time, and they were eventually brought up by river. The Anti-Aircraft sections, notwithstanding the extraordinary heavy going over deep sand, managed to get through to the Dialah by dint of pushing and towing, etc. Most of them suffered a fair amount of damage, the dumb-iron and Cardan shafts being a source of trouble. With regard to the frame, it was considered that the position of the towing hook was too low down, and these were afterwards placed at the bend of the dumb-iron, in a straight line with the rest of the frame.

It was a very interesting trip on March 4, passing through the marching Infantry divisions and getting up with the Cavalry as far as Aziziyeh, though on this date one Infantry division was established there. One could judge the hurried manner of the Turkish retreat. Abandoned vehicles and ammunition breathed of chaos, while their dead were left unburied.

This chapter now brings us, from the M.T. point of view, well into the year 1917.

# CHAPTER IX

## OPERATIONS, MAY TO OCTOBER 1917

Capture of Ramadie—First and second efforts—Deli Abbas—Arrival up country of extra Ford van companies—Hot-weather operations—Night march on Hit with M.T.—Concentrations of M.T. companies—Remarks.

In May 1917 it was necessary for me to proceed to the Base, as the main operations had ceased, owing to the hot weather, which was premature. I do not wish my readers to think that the work of the Mechanical Transport was at an end, for both Nos. 783 and 784 Companies were still hard at work. They had a large number of vehicles on detached duties; they were also trying to get numerous repairs carried out after the hard work in the advance and other minor operations in which they participated. A number of men were sick, and a shortage of drivers was being felt.

The Advanced M.T. workshops and floating workshops at this time were busily employed on the overhauling of vehicles which lasted through the hot weather, and the conversion of four Peerless lorries for use on the Baghdad Railway was also put in hand. Numerous vehicles were arriving at the Base, and it was anticipated that Nos. 729 and 730 Companies could shortly be dispatched up country.

On looking up the official record for May 1917, the chief item of importance was the completion of the railway line from Baghdad to Samarah, and the first British train ran from Baghdad to the latter place on May 6, 1917.

June, so far as operations are concerned, was a dead letter, but even in Mesopotamia, with an average temperature of 118 in the shade, the Mechanical Transport never rested, being busily employed all this time.

No. 729 Company was ready for the road at the end of June, and a consignment of Star vans for the use of Signal units were also ready about this time.

I spent more than a month at Basrah on this visit, and left at the end of June to come up by road with No. 729 Company, under command of Major Snepp, A.S.C. The convoy consisted of 136 vehicles, including the Star vans, and we arrived at the Dialah on the evening of July 3, 1917, and camped on the right bank.

No. 784 Company was also busily engaged in carrying supplies from Baqubah to Beled Ruz, prior to the advance against the Turks in the region of Mendali. This was a very difficult run for mechanical transport at this time of the year. Certain stretches of the road were in a very bad condition, and while no road maintenance was possible, naturally enough, the Ford soon turned what was termed a road into a very bad track.

Convoys used to go out about 5 a.m. and run practically the whole of the day. The last vans as a rule got into camp between 4 and 5 in the afternoon. This does not sound very dreadful, but it should be borne in mind that the heat was intense and that few, if any, of the drivers had ever experienced such weather. The dust was excessive ; the breakage of springs numerous ; and punctures and coil trouble had to be contended with,—yet the work was carried out.

On July 11 a British force of all arms after a night march attacked the Turks covering Ramadie on the right bank of the Euphrates. The failure to capture the position was attributed to lack of water and the intense heat, which necessitated a withdrawal to Felujah.

When one considers the Mesopotamian Campaign, where little or no fighting is done throughout the hot weather, it was questionable whether any such operation should have been attempted in the month of July, especially when the maximum shade temperature reached 124.

It was apparently rendered necessary for the following reason. Shortly after the entry of the British garrison into Baghdad, the Turks had cut the Serriyeh Bund on the Euphrates, above Felujah. The cutting of this bund had the effect of flooding Lake Akkar Kuf, which lies a few miles W.N.W. of Baghdad. The lake overflowed and the tract of country between the lake and Baghdad was flooded. It was presumably intended by the Turks to flood a large area between Nuktah and Baghdad, and possibly break up the railway bund of the main Baghdad-Samarah line. Strenuous damming operations took place, and a possible flood averted.

It was evident, however, that it would be necessary to make an advance from Felujah, for it was apparent that a bund might be cut further up, which, when the Euphrates rose, would result in considerable damage, to say nothing of the possibility of isolating, more or less, that portion of the country. Hence the advance on Ramadie, with a view to stopping the Turks from doing any more damage to the bunds along the Euphrates.

A small concentration of mechanical transport was necessary on these operations, for supplies had to be got up to Felujah. The line from Baghdad was not completed, and they were dependent on supplies by road transport from Baghdad and by river transport from Mufraz.

Major Snepp was placed in command of the concentration. He had practically his own Company, No. 729, also fifteen Star vans, in addition to a dozen Fiat lorries under the command of Lieutenant Vlasto. This officer and his Fiat lorries became a well-known detachment throughout Mesopotamia. Wherever he and his Fiats were seen, moving from one flank to another, it was always recognised that some operations were in progress! This detachment from the middle of 1916 took part practically in every operation in this country, and did some brilliant work.

There is very little to remark about these operations beyond the fact that the Mechanical Transport earned very high praise for the way in which they carried out the work, in spite of the intense heat. The vehicles were chiefly used for the carriage of supplies, including water. On one occasion 2nd Lieutenant Martin, who afterwards received the Military Cross, took a detachment of Fords carrying water for the troops up to within 500 yards of the Turkish trenches. Sixteen of the vans were hit by machine-gun fire, but luckily none of the drivers, who showed remarkable coolness, were hit.

When vans were employed on the carriage of supplies up to the fighting line, advantage was always taken on the return journey for the purpose of carrying wounded. No. 729 Company took their baptismal fire splendidly, and showed that they were quite capable of tackling the very difficult country over which they had to work.

When all of these minor operations are over, there is always a lot of clearing up to be done from a Mechanical Transport point of view. Abandoned vans have to be got into workshops; vehicles require a complete overhauling; casualties among the drivers have to be replaced; and there is always a general clear-up with regard to the evacuation of dumps. Therefore, when operations are shown officially as being in progress from six to ten days, this means three weeks' hard work, if not longer, for the Mechanical Transport.

If the operations are successful, the line of supply has to be extended, and it means, in all probability, that the Mechanical Transport vehicles employed on the concentration cannot be released at all.

No. 730 M.T. Company left Basrah on the morning of August 27 for Baghdad, although the actual journey was not begun until August 29, the two days being spent in ferrying the vehicles across the Euphrates at Gurmat Ali in barges. This was a very tedious and heartbreaking job. The company was up to full strength, and in addition had approximately fifty odd vehicles tacked on to it for the journey up. The barges were only capable of taking approximately twenty vehicles at a time, and all had to be man-handled into position. The heat was most intense. There were several casualties from heat-stroke while this work was being carried out.

There is no need to mention the details of the run up of this unit to Baghdad, which, on the whole, was very satisfactory. There were two vehicle casualties. A van was run into by a train while attempting to cross the railway-line between Kut and Baghdad, and completely smashed up, and another caught fire, but luckily only the woodwork of this was destroyed. The company was rather unfortunate during the journey, having numerous admissions to hospital, but the conditions under which the run was carried out were exceedingly trying.

While on the subject of trying conditions during the hot weather, I always considered—and I think most M.T. officers will agree—that it was much better to run convoys through the heat of the day instead of halting. The chief drawback to running was the question of punctures or other small mechanical defects on the road, which necessitated the men having to get out of their vans and work in the sun.

On the whole, the men preferred starting off at six or seven in the morning, and getting back to camp about half-past three in the afternoon. After a rest, they were able to look round their vehicles in the cool of the evening.

In the neighbourhood of Baghdad there were now four complete companies available for any future operations, though at the time work could have been found for at least another four.

Although in July it was necessary to withdraw the fighting troops from this line to Felujah, it was the intention of the G.O.C.-in-Chief to take Ramadie at the first opportunity, and the 15th Division, under the command of General Brooking, was again entrusted with this operation.

On September 28 and 29 a British force, advancing from

Dhibban, again attacked the Turkish position at Ramadie, with Cavalry astride their line of retreat along the Aleppo road. The Turkish garrison capitulated on September 29. The captures included the Euphrates Group Commander and his staff, 145 officers, 3,240 other ranks, and eleven guns, together with much war material.

The force employed at this time was stronger, and the concentration of mechanical transport was on a far larger scale than in the previous attack. Major Snepp, A.S.C., was again placed in command of this concentration. The total number of vans collected amounted to 350, with the addition of ten Fiats under the command of Lieutenant Vlasto.

The composition of this concentration was Nos. 729, 730, 783, and 784 Companies, though the latter two companies had detachments only. Before the actual operations began most of the vehicles were employed in getting a reserve of rations from Felujah to Madhij, and also moving the ammunition dumps from Dhibban to Madhij. There was only one bridge at Felujah, over which all troops and transport had to cross, and convoys were constantly held up for hours at a time to allow guns and Cavalry to cross.

There was one very bad stretch of road, a few miles outside Felujah, which was responsible for practically all vans sticking when attempting to cross. It meant that all these had to be pushed through. Large gangs of Arabs were employed under the Engineer officers, and this particular part was soon made passable. The vans on this concentration were chiefly employed in taking forward supplies, ammunition, water, and, as previously mentioned, on all occasions brought back sitting-up wounded cases on the return journey from the forward dressing-stations.

The capture of Ramadie was an entirely successful operation, and it was thought possible at the time that Hit might also be captured. One hundred Ford vans were ordered out for this duty, carrying up Infantry and Lewis guns. This column, accompanied by ambulances and armoured cars, moved off at about 7.30 p.m. Orders were issued that no lights were to be used, so it is left to the imagination of my readers who have not experienced this, what the feelings of officers and men must have been proceeding over an unknown country on a dark night without lights. I say unknown country because nobody with the column had ever been over this part before.

Captain Sykes, A.S.C., who at this time was in command of the floating workshops, had had five years' experience in Mesopotamia. He knew the country in and around Ramadie, and was generally lent to the 15th Division for these operations. On this occasion he accompanied the vehicles on the road to Hit.

It is possible that running might have been successful had all the men and vehicles been in first-class order, but the vehicles had been doing a considerable amount of work, day in and day out, during the operations and little time had been allowed for even ordinary running repairs. The men had all done an exceptionally hard day's work, and, in fact, the officer commanding the column had to stop and warn the drivers of ambulances that drastic action would be taken if any man fell asleep at the wheel.

At a point about five miles outside Hit, which the column reached about 5 a.m., orders were given for its return, and a start was made about an hour and a half afterwards. One ambulance was abandoned on this night march and two vans had to be towed back on the return journey, owing to a broken back axle and a damaged radiator.

During the operations which ended in the capture of Ramadie, there were numerous cases of sickness among the drivers, and officers, N.C.O.s, batmen, and cooks, all had to lend a hand in driving the cars. I believe the trouble was caused through irregular meals and the drinking of unchlorinated water. The heat was also intense during this period. If men are thirsty, and there is no chlorinated water available, they will naturally drink water which has not been chlorinated. It is only human, and I have myself been guilty on several occasions. I am sure a great number of my readers have, too !

The work done by the Mechanical Transport on these operations earned great praise from the General Officer Commanding 15th Division. In my first chapter on Operations, it was necessary to go into more detail than perhaps the occasion warranted, but this was merely to show my readers the sort of work the Mechanical Transport units had to do in this country. Since the number of units were few, their work stands out rather more prominently than later, when a number of them got grouped together. Up to this time mechanical transport was in its first stage of usefulness in this campaign, so to speak.

As the number of Mechanical Transport units increased and the concentrations from a fighting point of view got larger, small details will have to be omitted, and a lot must be left to the imagination of my readers.

In the operations just concluded, four companies were concerned, but this is really from a Mechanical Transport point of view a minor operation compared with the majority of those coming afterwards. The only other operation of note which occurred during this month was on September 29 —the occupation of Mendali and the flight of the Turkish garrison, ending with the capture of a convoy of 300 camels loaded with grain.

After Ramadie and Mendali had been captured, both Nos. 784 and 729 Companies were employed in filling up the latter place with supplies. They continued to do this while a force was in occupation there.

The month of September 1917 might be considered the beginning of the winter operations in Mesopotamia which proved so successful. It was apparently the intention of the G.O.C.-in-Chief to clear the Turks farther away from his right flank, and also in the centre beyond Samarah. A short official account states that between October 18 and 20 Deli Abbas and Jabal Hamrin astride the Dialah River were occupied. The Turkish detachment at Kizil Robat withdrew across the Dialah and destroyed the boat-bridge there. These small operations, like all others, necessitated a large concentration of mechanical transport, which was now possible on account of the recent arrival of a number of Ford van companies from home.

The number of Ford vans which took part in this concentration was approximately 800 ; practically eight complete companies, as follows : Nos. 729, 730, 783, 784, 815, 818, 971, and 954. Five hundred of these vans were under the command of Major Pelly, and worked from Baqubah, the remainder under Major Gibbons worked from Tuwair. They were chiefly employed on the carriage of supplies, etc., right forward and also returned with the minor wounded cases.

There is very little to report with regard to these operations from a Mechanical Transport point of view. New country was traversed, but the type was very similar to that over which they had been previously working. Generally the runs were long. Taking day in and day out, it is considered that for two years,while employed on the carriage of supplies, the average daily mileage per car was about sixty miles. Some days it would reach as much as 110 miles ; it was seldom less that fifty ; and the average of sixty included, of course, the time during which the cars were in the workshops. When it is considered that the M.T. seldom had a day's rest except when it was raining, it is easy to realise the hard work performed during these two years.

An amusing incident in this operation occurred when a Ford van of No. 783 Company was left behind. The driver happened to be of small stature. He had some engine trouble, and had just put things right and was about to step into his van when he saw an enormous Turk running down the road towards him. He immediately jumped into his car and drove away. Apparently he had not rectified the engine trouble, as the car appeared to be going on two cylinders, so very slowly. On looking behind, the driver saw the Turk following him. His car stopped suddenly, and, snatching up a rifle, he waited the oncoming Turk. As the latter approached, it was noticed that he was holding up his hands and was most anxious to be made a prisoner. Perhaps the Turk wanted a free ride into the British lines! The subsequent arrival of this tiny driver with one of the few prisoners captured in this operation—a man who stood about 6 feet 3 inches—must have been a very amusing spectacle.

In this operation, with four new companies at work, it was natural to expect that there would be numerous breakages of springs, and this proved to be the case. Those of my readers who have never been in this country should never criticise the large amount of breakages without seeing the places over which mechanical transport had to work.

Prior to the capture of Deli Abbas, there is one small incident worth recalling, which happened with the vans of No. 730 Company. The unit was on a run from Tuwair to Bint-al-Hassan, and after arriving back at Tuwair it was found that a van was missing. Although it was dark, it was decided to send two vans to look for it. The search-party had been some time on the road, and going in the wrong direction, passed Bint-al-Hassan and almost went into the Turkish lines at Deli Abbas.

I mention this in order to show how easy it was for transport to go through our outpost line without apparently being discovered. The van and the search-party returned safely back without coming under fire.

The chief point emphasised in this concentration was the necessity for senior and experienced M.T. officers being placed in command of a specific number of vans. They were in communication with the G.O.C. Corps or Division undertaking the operations, and also with the Directorate of Supplies and Transport. It has been found throughout a great help having an experienced officer to act as Mechanical Transport Adviser during the time operations are in progress.

The clearing-up after these operations took some time,

and all repairs had to be carried out. None of the companies in these operations were able to take their workshops with them, but No. 784 Company was in the satisfactory position of having its workshops at Baqubah, and was within easy reach of its vehicles most of the time.

# CHAPTER X

## OPERATIONS, OCTOBER 1917 TO FEBRUARY 1918

Peerless lorries sent up from the Base—Operations round Tekrit—Death of General Maude—General Marshall appointed G.O.C.—Operations over the Sakaltutan Pass and occupation of Qarah Tappah—Work of the M.T. during the operations—Dispatch of supplies to Sharban—The M.T. concentration for the Cavalry up the Adhaim—Occupation of Qasr-i-Shirin—The Pai Tak Outpost—The Dunsterville Mission—Arrival of extra M.T. companies

In a previous chapter, so far as operations are concerned, we had got as far as Deli Abbas. While these operations were in progress, mechanical transport was also employed on the left flank, between Baghdad and Felujah. It would appear, judging from the number of vans which were employed on the concentration between October 18 and 20, that there would be a shortage of vehicles to carry out any work on this flank, but No. 953 Company arrived, and forty Peerless lorries were ordered from the Base. The first detachment of these actually left on September 8, 1917. These heavy lorries were brought by barge from Basrah to Kurna, and there off-loaded.

One lorry was dropped into the Tigris at Amarah, and was under water for two or three hours. It was salved and was running again within two hours of its immersion.

All vehicles soon after arrival were put to work between Baghdad and Felujah, but the number was afterwards reduced to twelve. Numerous Ford van companies were employed on this run from time to time, and when any detachment of other companies could be spared they were also brought into use.

It is now necessary to go back to the main operations. After the capture of Deli Abbas, a number of vans still remained to clear up the situation, working from Tuwair. Others had been withdrawn, and had been employed on the Felujah run at the end of October.

The official account of these operations is as follows :

Between November 2 and 5, a strong Turkish rearguard was driven out of its entrenched position at Mashshad-ad-Daur. Eighty-nine prisoners and four ammunition dumps remained in our hands.

November 5.—The British attacked the trench system of nine-mile perimeter encircling Tekrit. Two brilliant assaults gained all objectives and heavy loss was inflicted on the retiring Turks. Three hundred and nineteen prisoners were captured, and the enemy was forced to blow up three ammunition dumps and to abandon much material, including a repairable aeroplane.

To avoid possibility of recapture, the Turks fired the *Julnar*, which was aground near Fathah. (This steamer was captured while attempting to reach Kut with provisions in April 1916.)

As usual, such operations began with a concentration of Ford vans, and orders were issued on October 28 to Captain Sellwood, O.C. 971 M.T. Company, to proceed the next day to Bint-al-Hassan, and from there to Sadiyeh, the place chosen for the concentration on October 31, 1918. Approximately 210 vans, under the command of Major Gibbons, were to join him, and about 180 would proceed from Baghdad. All companies included on previous concentrations were also included in this one, though several were not up to full strength. The total number of vans for this concentration was approximately 500, in addition to the Fiats under command of Lieutenant Vlasto.

It was intended that the march up of the Ford

vans from Sadiyeh to Samarah was to be kept secret, so orders were issued that the 510 vans, plus the ten Fiats, were not to start from Sadiyeh until 5 p.m on November 1. It was necessary, too, that the road should be reconnoitred, and a couple of officers with Ford vans were sent out for this purpose. From a Mechanical Transport point of view the march was a very successful one, and also the work which was done by all the units.

During this concentration there were several defects brought to light which were remedied in future operations. It is essential that Corps and Divisional commanders should always give the fullest possible scope to the officer commanding a Mechanical Transport formation. In these operations I was informed by the officer in command that he was detailed to accompany columns on the road. He also informed me that he was not consulted about the main requirements from a Mechanical Transport point of view, but merely told to detail so many vans for the different jobs. Under Corps Orders supply columns also worked from the front line back to the base and out again, spending the night away from camp, which gave no opportunity for the systematic detailing of vans, or knowing how many vans were available for duty. They were never in camp for more than two hours at a time, while they refilled with petrol and reloaded.

Numerous vans were also detailed to individual officers doing intelligence work or other important duties. An amount of damage was done to vehicles through being detached in this way. Naturally the duty is very important, and if the officer has to get to a certain place, he attempts to make the driver do all sorts of things that he should not do. To quote an instance, a driver explained he could go no farther without water, as his radiator was boiling. He was told to go on, with the result that the engine seized up and could not complete the journey. Infantry officers, too, were placed in command of water columns. So long as they got the majority of vans in and out, these officers did not worry much if one or two vans were left out in the desert, and the unfortunate M.T. officer had to go out and get them in, generally at night. There were a number of accidents, too, due entirely to the fact that the drivers did not get sufficient sleep. A strong report was sent in to G.H.Q. on the numerous points brought forward,

There is no doubt that the general idea among officers unused to mechanical transport was, that it is a very easy job, and that drivers should be capable of working twenty-three hours out of the twenty-four. I say this *was* the opinion, but I now think that most officers who have seen the Mechanical Transport working day in and day out for the past two and half years, in this climate, and who have on a number of occasions experienced the hardships of a 500-mile journey under trying conditions, do not consider the lot of the M.T. driver one to be envied.

A number of these vehicles, after being withdrawn from the preceding operations, were put to work again on the line from Baghdad to Felujah, Major Snepp being still in command of the Mechanical Transport in that section.

At this time it was necessary to concentrate on this line for the following reasons:

(1) To put in maintenance of the 15th Division.

(2) To complete reserves ordered by the G.O.C.-in-Chief.

(3) To carry to Felujah the balance of clothing, ordnance stores, ammunition, etc., required by the 15th Division.

As previously stated, there was no railway, and the tonnage required by the 15th Division was approximately 150 tons a day, the river being only available between a place called Mufraz, on the Euphrates, up to Felujah and Ramadie. No more than twenty-five tons a day could be calculated for this, all of which had to be dispatched by rail to Mufraz from Baghdad. The Local Resources were also responsible for certain supplies. Every effort was being made to hasten on the railway, but pending that being completed, mechanical transport was to be utilised to the fullest extent along this line.

THE LATE LIEUT.-GENERAL SIR FREDERICK STANLEY MAUDE, K.C.B., C.M.G., D.S.O.

The Peerless lorries on the Felujah run wore themselves and the roads out, to a considerable extent. After a short time it was only possible to work these vehicles from a place called Nuktah, A.T. carts carrying out the supplies from Baghdad, which were then transhipped on to the lorries at a point about a mile and half on the Felujah side of Nuktah. The railway (broad gauge) from Baghdad to Felujah reached Nuktah on November 15, and a small railhead depôt was at once established. This eased the transport difficulties from Baghdad enormously. The road, however, between Nuktah and Felujah became worse, and it was found impossible to work the Peerless lorries on this run after December 12, 1917. Consequently they were all recalled to Baghdad, the majority of them requiring considerable attention in the workshops.

The date, December 12, 1917, is a little ahead of the main operations, but with the exception of the Persian L. of C., of which more anon, the Peerless lorries as a whole did not take part in any of the major concentrations.

These lorries might be considered to have saved the situation on this flank at a time when light moving transport was employed in other operations. The officer in command of the Peerless detachment was Lieutenant Williams, and both he and all ranks were congratulated by the D.Q.M.G. on their splendid work during October and November over exceptionally difficult roads. The vehicles suffered considerably, and the constant ploughing over heavy sand had a very bad effect indeed upon the engines.

November is a month which I will always look upon with sad memories. It was on the 18th that Lieutenant-General Sir Stanley Maude, K.C.B., D.S.O., died. It is not my intention to talk about our late beloved Chief, as he has already been eulogised, and rightly so, in practically every newspaper and magazine published in the English language. One can only say that he was loved and respected by every officer and man throughout the whole of the Mesopotamian Expeditionary Force, and his sudden death came as a bitter blow to all. His name will live for ever among those of our great soldiers.

It was fitting that a man and a soldier of his capabilities should have made his name, so to speak, in a country where, centuries before, great soldiers had also made their mark. Sir Stanley Maude recognised the value of mechanical transport, and always took an exceptionally keen interest in the work it did. A photograph of this great soldier faces page 128. It was left to the Mechanical Transport Branch to pay its last respect to our beloved Chief through the medium of a motor ambulance, on which his remains were carried to rest.

Lieutenant-General Sir W. R. Marshall, K.C.B., took over command of the Mesopotamian Expeditionary Force on the death of Sir Stanley Maude.

The next operations of any note in which the Mechanical Transport were involved did not take place until December 3, when the British advanced. The Turkish 13th Army Corps were holding a line along the Jabal Hamrin (on the Dialah right bank) to a point opposite Kizil Robat. By nightfall the enemy had been cleared from the area south of Qarah Tappah, with the exception of the Sakaltutan Pass. The British Cavalry force operating up the River Adhaim threatened the enemy's right flank, but was unable to advance further than Abu Ghuraib.

On December 4 the British continued to advance, occupying the Sakaltutan Pass, the enemy falling back on a position just north of Qarah Tappah. The latter place was occupied after a lively engagement on December 5. The Turks retired slowly on Kifri, where the coal dumps were fired. During these three days, six Turkish officers, including a regimental commander, 221 other ranks, and two guns were captured.

A small Russian force of Cossacks under Lieutenant-Colonel Bicharakhov, co-operated with the British right flank throughout these operations and rendered valuable service. When pursuit was discontinued on December 6,

LIEUT.-GENERAL SIR WILLIAM RAINE MARSHALL, G.C.M.G., K.C.B., K.C.S.I.

the British withdrew to new positions at Kizil Robat and the Sakaltutan Pass.

After the Tekrit operations the majority of vehicles were put on to what was known as the Felujah run, but a certain number, under Major Pelly, M.C., were working from Baqubah up to Sharban. These vehicles were employed in putting reserves into Sharban and Abu Jisra, and, in addition to Ford vans, thirty light Packard lorries and the first detachment of No. 976 Company were employed. Supplies for the Cavalry operating up the River Adhaim had also to be obtained.

With regard to the Cavalry, the original order was that reserves of ten days' supplies at operation scale for the Cavalry Division were to be available on the evening of November 30 at a depôt on the left bank of the River Adhaim. The bulk of the supplies was sent up from Baghdad to Beled, and was then carried by mechanical transport from Beled to Akab, where the depôt was situated. The number of Ford vans utilised for this was approximately 400, and fifteen Fiats, the whole under command of Major Carty, M.C. The actual orders were given to Major Carty on November 23, and he took over approximately 200 vans from Major Gibbons, who had been in charge of a convoy up as far as Sharban. The vans were handed over at Baqubah, and the balance to complete 400 proceeded from Baghdad.

The actual distance from Beled to Akab is not far, but the road soon became bad with the 400 vans constantly passing to and fro. On several days two complete journeys were made, and the Cavalry's rations were in the depôt on the evening of the 30th.

As soon as the operations began, the vans detailed were utilised for carrying the supplies from the supply depôt, twenty-five miles up the left bank of the Adhaim, from which place the Cavalry were refilled. For the two days following the supplies were taken up the left bank of this river to a distance of forty-five miles. Owing to the Cavalry not being able to advance beyond Abu Ghuraib, the Mechanical Transport were not required any more on this side of operations, and returned to headquarters on December 8, 1918. While these operations were in progress practically no mechanical transport was in use on the Felujah run with the exception of the Peerless lorries and about a dozen Ford vans.

It might be interesting to mention the companies which were employed on the Divisional concentration :

| | | | |
|---|---|---|---|
| No. | 783 | M.T. | Company |
| ,, | 815 | ,, | ,, |
| ,, | 729 | ,, | ,, |
| ,, | 818 | ,, | ,, |
| ,, | 954 | ,, | ,, |
| ,, | 730 | ,, | ,, |

The Mechanical Transport with the Infantry force which was operating up towards the Sakaltutan Pass contained vehicles from the following companies :

| | | | |
|---|---|---|---|
| No. | 729 | M.T. | Company |
| ,, | 730 | ,, | ,, |
| ,, | 784 | ,, | ,, |
| ,, | 954 | ,, | ,, |
| ,, | 971 | ,, | ,, |

All the above represented roughly 800 vehicles.

It will be seen that on some of these concentrations referred to, two columns may possibly have vans from the same company. This was due to the exigencies of the service ; for to make up the requisite number, companies had sometimes to be split up. The Mechanical Transport for the force which was operating up the Dialah River was practically based on Qalet Mufti for their supplies, though, on the morning of December 3, 1917, a battalion of Infantry had to be taken up to a point opposite the Sakaltutan Pass through the Jabal Hamrin. The forward dump of supplies formed by the Mechanical Transport during this operation

THE SALKALTUTAN PASS OVER THE JABAL HAMRIN.

HOW THE FORDS HAD TO GET OVER.

was just at the base of the Sakaltutan, though this was purely a provisional one.

Exceptionally long runs were experienced and the going was very difficult indeed, especially over the Sakaltutan Pass. Several of the companies had been continuously on the road without rest for thirty-five hours in these operations. The road up and over the Sakaltutan Pass was an extraordinarily difficult one—a succession of soft and irregular stretches, sharp bends, and very short and steep inclines. Owing to the giving nature of the soil, it was not possible to drive loaded vans up the Pass. They had to be towed by mules, and the photograph facing page 132 depicts this operation in progress.

It was expeditiously done, however, for the time taken to get the vans over was little longer than if they had gone over under their own power. As will be seen, three mules were harnessed to each van. The breakage of springs, too, on this run was rather abnormal, and it was found necessary to reduce all loads from 7 to 6 maunds, i.e. 560 to 480 lb.

The Mechanical Transport in these operations showed that they were almost capable of going anywhere, though the country over which they had to work was exceptionally difficult.

The Transport working with the Cavalry had an exciting time, being constantly attacked by Arabs. On one occasion Lieutenant Smith, No. 818 Company, swore that the Arabs were using explosive bullets, and the convoys after that were protected by a small escort with a Lewis gun. These operations on the whole might be considered fairly successful. All ranks earned the highest praise for the way in which they carried out their work.

There is little doubt but that at this time the Turks were beginning to get all they wanted. It will be seen that the British forces operating in Palestine occupied Jerusalem on December 9, and on this date, too, Khanikin was occupied by our troops without opposition.

Often we advanced, not actually beyond our objective,

but beyond the position in which it would be possible to constantly supply the troops. We have halted there for several days, received local supplies, and made friends with people in the vicinity. On the first and second occasions we were welcomed with open arms, but after a few days' occupation a retirement would take place a few miles farther back; presumably this was in order to ease the supply and transport situation. This policy, no doubt, had a bad effect upon the inhabitants, for when the Turks reoccupied the different places, they at once enforced penalties upon those people who had been friendly to the British. The penalty, as a rule, was death.

This brings us now to the end of 1917.

On January 2, 1918, Qasr-i-Shirin was occupied by the British forces without opposition. At this time railway extensions were proceeding apace, and the Ford van companies were constantly in use filling up the various supply dumps to assist troops in the forward area. The month of January 1918 was not a rainy one, and the vehicles were seldom off the road during this period. The Ford van companies were employed both on the right and left flanks, practically all those in the centre, in the neighbourhood of Samarah and Tekrit, having been withdrawn. The columns had also been formed, and all ranks were settling down to conditions in Mesopotamia.

The next operation of importance was the departure of what was known as the Dunsterville Mission to Hamadan and beyond. It fell to the lot of the Mechanical Transport to take General Dunsterville and his advanced party to their destination, and the preliminary arrangements necessitated a lot of work. Everything was limited—officers, B.O.R.s, and vehicles. The mission was going to travel at a bad time of the year over very difficult country, through numerous valleys which for certain months during the winter were impassable; and very little indeed was known about the kind of roads to be encountered. The distance from Baghdad to Hamadan is 356 miles.

As Ford vans were being used, everything had to be cut fine. Each van had to be equipped with a spade, pick-axe, and towing-rope, and each vehicle was fitted out with new tyres and tubes, one spare cover, one spare tube both front and rear, and also the Stepney. A special list of spare parts which had to be carried was made out. Two good fitters had to be provided. Each man had to carry his rifle and 100 rounds of ammunition; rations for all ranks not to exceed 20 lb. per head. The weight allowed for each officer was 2 maunds (160 lb.), which included a small tent. The men had to be warmly clothed and the drivers had to be specially selected and picked men. No. 730 M.T. Company A.S.C. was chosen to supply the personnel, etc., and Captain Aldham, A.S.C., was placed in charge of thirty-six vans and six cars.

I have mentioned a few of the details with regard to this convoy for the simple reason that it was a most important one. It was essential that General Dunsterville should get through quickly, and everything possible was done. The petrol question was the burning one, owing to road conditions being practically unknown. The petrol consumption for Ford vans in Mesopotamia generally averaged about eleven miles per gallon. An estimate was made out which allowed seven miles per gallon for Persia. It was hoped that a certain amount of this useful commodity could be obtained at Hamadan, but little could be purchased, and then at an exorbitant price.

The distance from Surkhadiza Khan to Hamadan is approximately 200 miles. As mentioned, an estimate was drawn up at seven miles per gallon of petrol per car, or, in other words, every van had approximately to carry from just beyond Pai Tak Pass thirty gallons to enable each vehicle to get through to Hamadan. Each van, therefore, had to carry about 300 lb. weight of its own necessaries before personnel could be considered.

My readers will appreciate at once the difficulty of a transport problem such as this, where no supplies were obtainable *en route.* There was no railhead where this small column could come in and draw its petrol of an evening, and it was, of course, not possible for all the petrol to be carried from Baghdad. A convoy, therefore, had to be dispatched in advance with the necessary quantity, and take it as far as Surkhadiza Khan. This was done the day before the Dunsterville Mission started, and as a matter of fact the convoy actually got there, dumped its petrol, and returned as far as the bottom of the pass, where they met the head of the Dunsterville column.

The photographs on the opposite page will give those of my readers who have not been over this pass some idea of it, but those who are not used to the desert of Mesopotamia cannot realise what an awe-inspiring sight this must have been to drivers who for over a year hardly knew what a gradient on a road meant, except the approaches to bridges. Since the time this first convoy went up, this pass has been considerably improved, and one can now go up in a Ford car a considerable distance on top speed.

Formerly it was a good pull of about three and a half miles of low gear work all the way. In addition to it being a steady climb, the surface was bad, and there was a drop of anything up to 1,000 feet on one side. No vans, however, experienced any difficulty in getting up, and to the column carrying up the mission it was child's play, for they were all picked vehicles. I have been up and down this pass myself on several occasions, and can quite imagine how these drivers felt before going up and coming down, with the roads in a treacherous, greasy state. These Persian hills presented a lovely picture, all covered with snow.

It is not my intention to go into a long report with regard to the journey of the Dunsterville Mission. Numerous troubles were met with on the road and delays occurred here and there, owing to rain and snow. The journey must have been a very disheartening one, as the districts through which the mission travelled were suffering from starvation, and numerous dead and dying were seen lying about. The

Alexander's Arch, half-way up the Pass.

A view showing a bend in the Pass.

Another view on the way up.

PAI-TAK PASS ON THE ROAD TO KERMANSHAH.

road from Pai Tak Pass right through to Enzeli will be mentioned again in the chapter which concerns the work done on the Persian L. of C., and it is not intended to talk about it here.

I went over most of these roads myself under good conditions during the month of July, and when up at Kasvin I saw Captain Aldham. Practically all the vehicles he had taken up in January were in good running order, which speaks highly for the way in which they had been looked after. How Captain Aldham managed to keep his vehicles in running order with the small stock of spare parts which he took up with him is hard to say. There was some mechanical transport in use with the Russian force, which included a few Fords, and no doubt a small supply was obtained from this source. Even later on, when the roads were opened through from Kasvin to Baghdad, the supply of spare parts was always a great difficulty. There were practically no operations during the month of February 1918, but the M.T. was still fully employed wherever it was being used.

The months of January and February, however, saw the following new companies arriving at the Base: Nos. 1013, 1014, 1015, 1016, 1017, 1018, 1019, and 1020. Steps were at once taken to make these units fit for the journey to Baghdad. No. 1023 M.T. Company was the first Burmese company to be formed. The officers, N.C.O.s, and men were all recruited in Burma, and the company came over under the command of Major Marris. Their vehicles were issued at the Base. The other companies came out with 60 per cent. British drivers. On arrival at Basrah they had to be issued with their full complement of Indians, and it fell to the lot of No. 1014 Company to be the first to receive the new type of driver, No. 971 Company, stationed at Felujah, being the second. All the other companies in the country were issued in turn, giving up a proportion of British drivers, and by this means all the companies which had just arrived at the Base were made up to full war establishment.

# CHAPTER XI

## OPERATIONS, JANUARY AND FEBRUARY TO MAY 1918

The number of M.T. vehicles under repair—Occupation of Hit—The advance to Anah—The M.T. concentration—A water column—British advance to Kirkuk—Large M.T. concentration—Work of the Cavalry and the M.T. with that force—Charge of L. of C. during operations—Remarks.

IN January, although no particular operations were in progress, a considerable number of Ford vans were employed in what was known as the 3rd Corps Area. In fact, the bulk of Mechanical Transport was working on the right flank through Baqubah, Sharban, Kizil Robat, and also up to Deli Abbas. One company was employed between Ramadie and Felujah.

On looking up an official return, taken at random, I find that on January 6, out of a total of 1,130 Ford vans which were employed on transport, 151 were under repair, 140 were segregated, the remainder all being available for use. One or two companies had smallpox or some other virulent disease, and had to be worked independently, whenever permission could be granted them to work. The number under repair varied at this time, and increased to 259 by the end of January.

The work was undoubtedly hard, and the roads around Qasr-i-Shirin and Khanikin were in a very bad state, as this particular part of country had just recently been captured. Efforts were made to improve the roads, but it took some time.

When dry weather is experienced in the winter, the going as a rule is good, but in the summer time, over the small foothills, these roads crack up badly under transport, and there is no water available to assist in maintaining them. The great trouble in the winter, when formations are dependent on mechanical transport for the carriage of their supplies, is that when rain falls mechanical transport is immobile for the most part. Advantage, therefore, has to be taken of the dry days to get in all the tonnage possible. One day, late in January or the early part of February, I went up this line in wet weather, and it was extraordinary to see some of the roads over which the little Ford van was able to proceed.

During January and February of this year the Ford van companies employed throughout Mesopotamia were having an extraordinary hard time of it.

It was thought that the arrival of new companies would ease the situation, but such was not the case. The more companies that came out, the greater was the radius of action given to the forces engaged, and the mechanical transport had to be employed to a greater extent than ever. Towards the end of February it was apparently decided by G.H.Q. that another advance should be made up on the left flank, and this was carried out by the 15th Division. It might be as well to quote a short official account from March 7 to 31. This embraces the capture of Hit and the advance as far as Anah.

March 7.—British occupied Hit. The Turks retiring up the Euphrates to Sahiliyeh and Khan Baghdadi. On night of 9/10 Turks evacuated Sahiliyeh, abandoning two mountain guns and some ammunition.

March 26.—British attacked Turkish 50th Division at Khan Baghdadi. Cavalry succeeded in making a wide détour and establishing themselves on the Aleppo road in rear of the Turks, whose attempts to break through this cordon during the night were defeated with heavy loss.

March 27.—Surrender of the Turkish 50th Division with its commander. British pursued column. Captured 500 men attempting to escape north of Haditha. A very large ammunition dump was discovered at Haditha.

March 28.—Pursuit of the remaining Turks continued, Anah being occupied without opposition. British pursuit column reached a point seventy-three miles above Anah, capturing more prisoners.

March 31.—British force withdrew from Anah, having destroyed the ammunition dump there, which was estimated to contain :

3,500,000–4,000,000 S.A.A.,
1,200 rounds mountain-gun ammunition,
30,000 rounds field-gun ammunition,
Large quantities of bombs.

Total captures during period March 26–29 amounted to :

18 Germans, including 2 officers,
5,236 Turks, including 212 officers,
12 guns,
57 machine guns and much material, including two German wireless stations.

A concentration of Mechanical Transport was, as usual, necessary, and Colonel Snepp was sent out to the 15th Division as O.C. M.T. for the operations.

No. 971 Company was employed at this time between Ramadie and Felujah, and the whole force was augmented by Nos. 1013, 1014, and 1016 Companies. There were also detachments of Nos. 1023 Burmese Company and 818 Company. A few vans of No. 729 were also engaged on this line, and the total number of vans employed was approximately 500.

Previous to the actual fighting, reserves of supplies had

to be pushed as far forward as possible. The Inland Water Transport were able to put approximately 180 tons daily into Ramadie. On or about March 6 this figure was increased to 200, on the 10th to 225, and by the 15th to 250 tons.

While on the subject of supplies, it might be interesting to note that the total weight for one day's supplies for Brooking's Column came to 215 tons. Posts along the line took 25 tons, so that a two days' reserve meant 480 tons.

Mechanical Transport, when employed in sufficient numbers, is to all intents and purposes a railway train. At the latter end of February, No. 1 M.T. Column, with Colonel Snepp in command, was removed from Baghdad to Ramadie. The M.T. companies were employed on convoys from Felujah to Ramadie, and forward as far as Uqbah. As the advance proceeded, so the companies moved forward.

The roads on these operations at the beginning were very good, but gradually broke up under the constant stream of traffic. Every effort was made to improve them at the time, and while the operations were in progress, endeavours were made to find an alternative route, from Uqbah to Hit. I notice in some of the reports which I have just been reading that the road from Dhibban to Ramadie was still in perfect condition on or about March 10.

These operations were a very good test for the Indian drivers, since this was the first occasion on which they were employed in any numbers. Beyond constant hard work and trying conditions due to bad roads, dust-storms, etc., there is little to report regarding the operations up to and including the capture of Sahiliyeh. The M.T. earned very great praise indeed from General Brooking. Mechanical transport was, however, still retained on these operations, as it was determined to make a further advance, and the supplies were pushed forward as far as possible. A further concentration of Ford vans took place on March 25 at Sahiliyeh.

It was now intended to use the majority of vans employed

with the 15th Division for something other than the carrying of supplies, and 300 vans, composed of :

75 from 971 Company
75 ,, 1013 ,,
75 ,, 1014 ,,
75 ,, 1016 ,,

formed the basis for what was known as Hogg's Group. Major Sellwood, A.S.C., was placed in command of the Mechanical Transport.

The object of the vans was to carry troops and machine guns. The column, under the command of Colonel Hogg, consisted of thirty-four machine guns, 800 troops and R.E. personnel, together with water, rations, ammunition, etc. It went into action on the 26th at 3 p.m., when other troops were tired, and on the 27th and 28th pursued the retreating Turks for seventy miles up to Anah. There were practically no casualties and numerous captures were made.

I understand that the captured Turks seemed pleased to be prisoners, since in this district they were not very popular with the Arabs. This column started from Sahiliyeh with full petrol tanks, i.e. approximately eight gallons, and four gallons of spare petrol. Some petrol was found both at Haditha and Anah, and all tanks were refilled from captured stock. Approximately 150 vans on arrival at Anah had to be sent back to bring up supplies for this force.

The workshop officer of No. 1014 Company, Lieutenant Christmas, also did very good work during these operations, and it was largely due to him that all vans arrived intact at Anah. This officer was also instrumental in salving derelict vehicles on the return journey, and got them safely back to their respective company's headquarters.

There was a large ammunition dump at Anah which was blown up on the morning of March 29, ten Ford vans being employed for the purpose of carrying the demolition party. The British force withdrew on this day. From reports which one can gather, the Turks must have been surprised at the rapidity of the British advance, and could hardly have been aware of the possibility of employing such an amount of rapid-moving transport for the carriage of troops. During these operations rain and sand-storms considerably interfered with progress, and the drivers, on the whole, had a very tough time of it.

Ford vans were again employed for the carriage of water, a special water column of fifty vans belonging to No. 1023 (Burma) M.T. Company being formed under the command of 2nd Lieutenant Cockman. The column carried water to the Brigade Headquarters during the operations.

During March 27, 28, and 29, while Hogg's Column was on the move and the Burmese detachment acted as a special water column, the remainder of the vans in action, approximately 150, were employed on the carriage of supplies and ammunition. The percentage of casualties was heavy. The best drivers had already been picked out for Hogg's Column, and work not so far forward was more difficult, because the roads had been so badly cut up by transport. Distances, too, were very long. On looking up records it is seen that on April 30 the vans were working from Hit to Hadithah and back, and from Ramadie to Hit and back. In the case of those convoys which went from Hit to Hadithah, only a single journey was possible in one day. On April 6 orders were sent out to the 15th Division to begin returning the Ford van companies which would be surplus for "clearing up" after the operations.

Before bringing the account of these operations to a close, I should like to mention that General Brooking, Commanding 15th Division, sent in a very strong letter of appreciation of the work done by the Mechanical Transport.

As there appeared to be no further likelihood of anything occurring on the left flank, it was apparently decided by G.H.Q. that another advance should be made on the right flank, and the orders for the withdrawal of the Ford van companies from the 15th Division was only the prelude to a further concentration, which was about to take place under the orders of the 3rd Corps. The actual operations did not begin until April 27, and concluded on May 10. I append a short official account of that:

April 27–29.—Qarah Tappah, Kifri, and Abu Ghuraib occupied. Seventy prisoners captured near Kifri.

The enemy retreated rapidly northwards.

A Cavalry column intercepted and charged a body of Turks retiring towards Tuz Khurmatli, killing over 100 and taking 538 prisoners.

British troops entered Tuz on the morning of the 29th, and continued the pursuit towards Tauq. Seventy-eight officers and 1,000 other ranks were captured on the 29th.

April 30.—Pursuit continued to the Tauq Chai.

Total captures from April 27–30 were 1,950 prisoners, twelve field guns, three mountain guns, and twenty-five machine guns. Enemy's losses estimated at 400 killed.

May 7.—Operations were renewed against the enemy, who had retired to Altun Kupri.

Kirkuk occupied without opposition; 610 sick and hospital staff, abandoned by the Turks, were captured.

May 10.—Enemy in Altun Kupri area had been reinforced, and on the 10th numbered nearly 3,000 rifles, 360 Cavalry, eighteen serviceable guns, and fifty machine guns. Enemy withdrew to right bank Lesser Zab. Further prisoners found in Kirkuk amounted to 173.

Lieutenant-Colonel Gibbons, M.C., O.C. No. 3 M.T. Column, was placed in command of the M.T. concentration, and left Baghdad early in April to work with the 13th Division, who were under the 3rd Corps. The companies at once placed at his disposal were:

No. 1017 M.T. Company, A.S.C.
,, 784 ,, ,,
,, 1016 ,, ,,
,, 954 ,, ,,

All of these companies had approximately 100 vans available.

HORSCH LORRIES CAPTURED FROM THE TURKS, MAY 1918, AT KIRKUK.

Though badly smashed up, all these were put on the road later on in the year.

A FIRE WHICH BURNT UP EIGHT FORD VANS AT BAQUBAH.

Nos. 1016 and 1017 Companies were stationed at Abu Saida and worked to Ain Laila, carrying supplies. Abu Saida is on the River Dialah, and the rations had been brought to this place previously by the M.T. and A.T. carts. The two Ford van companies, i.e. Nos. 784 and 954, were commanded by Major Gray. They were stationed at Longridge Hill, where there was a supply depôt, and worked from there to Ain Laila. This supply depôt at Longridge Hill had been in use for some time, and reserves had been placed there by means of A.T. carts working from the railhead, which at that time was at Table Mountain. The A.T. cart is a small two-wheeled vehicle drawn by two mules and driven by an Indian, which is the General Service transport cart of the Indian Army.

Two companies stationed at Abu Saida had to move their camp on April 11 to a place called Qalet Mufti, because the River Dialah had risen considerably. Qalet Mufti had previously been filled with a good reserve of supplies, so there was no difficulty in loading the Ford vans with the necessary commodities. It was seen, however, that sufficient supplies could not be got up in time, and on or about April 14 No. 1014 Company was dispatched to work under Colonel Gibbons.

On April 22, so far as could be seen, sufficient supplies had been moved to Ain Lailah, and the column headquarters and all the companies which, up to this, had been employed moved to Ain Lailah. They were all required for work forward from that place, as soon as the main advance began.

No. 2 Column, which was working forward from Khanikin, had practically been stripped of all its M.T., and it was expected that the balance still due from the 15th Division would be shortly available. As a matter of fact, on or about the 24th of this month, the total number of vans employed on this concentration reached 1,200. In addition to the companies already mentioned, the following had by that time joined: Nos. 1015, 1018, 815, and 818, and a detachment of 783. Nos. 815, 818, and 783 Companies were stationed at Table Mountain, and ran from there to Ain Lailah, carrying supplies. On April 24 it was decided to change the L. of C., which then ran from Ain Lailah to Table Mountain. The new L. of C. was Table Mountain, Chaman Kupri, and then to Tuz. No hitch whatsoever in the carriage of supplies occurred while this change was taking place.

The vans in this concentration might be considered to have worked practically in echelon. Six hundred under Major Player were stationed at Table Mountain, and worked from there to Chaman Kupri. Four hundred vans, with Major Plews as O.C., were stationed at Chaman Kupri and ran to Tuz. Two hundred vans at Tuz, where the column headquarters were, went forward with the troops during the advance. Rain considerably hampered operations. In addition to rain, the stages over which the M.T. had to work were very long—all of them being over eighty miles—and the roads were in very bad condition.

When advancing into the enemy's country it was not possible to form dumps of supplies, and there was insufficient transport to carry supplies for two days. This meant that practically no supplies were on hand with the fighting troops, beyond what the vans brought up each day, and on one occasion, owing to rain, it was not possible to run the convoys for two days on end. The unfortunate troops in the forward area received quarter rations. The roads, or tracks, in this locality took longer to dry up than is usual in Mesopotamia after rain, and even on the third day they were not much better.

A special effort was required to get some supplies forward, and 200 vans were sent out. They took thirteen hours to do thirty-six miles. Practically every van had to be manhandled through a number of nullahs, and three rivers in flood had to be crossed.

When Kirkuk was captured, the vans ran from Tuz to that place with supplies, returning with Turkish prisoners and refugees.

I understand that the return of these Turkish prisoners

was also very amusing. They all assisted in getting vans out of difficult places, and the last thing they seemed to wish was to stray very far away from camp. I use the word " stray " as it appeared that little or no guard was required to look after these men. They seemed only too pleased to be in good hands.

The difficulty of maintaining troops so far forward as Kirkuk was foreseen. The troops up beyond Khanikin were on half rations, owing to the lack of transport, so Kirkuk was evacuated about the middle of May and the troops all began to come back.

While the main operations which ended in the capture of Kirkuk were in progress, another smaller concentration was taking place, composed of nineteen Fiats and eighty Ford vans, under command of Captain Dickinson. The vans in question came from Nos. 729, 730, and 1020 Companies, and the Fiats were practically one section of No. 976 Company, the light Packard company, which at that time was under Dickinson's command. On April 4 this officer received orders to proceed to Tuwair to get instructions from the G.O.C. 7th Cavalry Brigade, under whose orders he would work. The Brigade in question was preparing for operations in the Jabal Hamrin, in the neighbourhood of Satha.

Captain Dickinson was instructed to make a road reconnaissance and render a report to the G.O.C. the Brigade. On April 20, after the above-mentioned transport had been sent to him, he proceeded to Tuwair, where the first portion of his transport due for this minor concentration joined him, consisting of thirty Fords and nineteen Fiat lorries.

Second Lieutenant Medlycott was in charge of the Fords, and 2nd Lieutenant Baskett in charge of the Fiats; the balance of fifty Fords of No. 1020 Company under 2nd Lieutenant Crombie did not arrive until April 22.

On April 23 the 7th Cavalry Brigade left Tuwair, and, marching in a north-westerly direction, reached Dojmanah at night. The M.T. column left at mid-day, and delivered its supplies at Dojmanah. The road conditions were extremely bad, and some very swampy ground was encountered in the neighbourhood of the Nahrwan Canal. The majority of Ford vans had a rough passage, so it was decided to leave them at Dojmanah, and the Fiats and a few Fords returned to Tuwair.

There was no need for any more supplies to be sent to the Brigade until the 25th, and owing to the bad state of the roads it was decided to give the vehicles one day's rest. A road reconnaissance was made in a northerly direction towards Satha. An excellent road was found, and was at once nicknamed the "Brighton Road." This road did not figure on any map, and was apparently the remains of some ancient highway. A number of the places mentioned in this small concentration are not marked on the map, but it will be sufficient for my readers to know that the 7th Cavalry Brigade marched right up the Adhaim, their object being to protect the Band-i-Adhaim Pass, in case the Turks, who were being engaged by the 3rd Corps from the direction of Kifri, should attempt to break back, the road through Tekrit and Fathah being open to them.

The M.T. practically worked in echelon, the Fiats going to the supply depôt; the Fords met them and went from that to the refilling point of the Cavalry Brigade.

On April 26 the Brigade moved up and attempted to drive the Turks out of the pass. During the action a heavy storm took place, and the Turks cleared out of the position, which was at once occupied by the Cavalry. As the troops working under the 3rd Corps were successful and the Turks had been driven back, the 7th Cavalry Brigade received orders to proceed to Ain Nukailah to watch the Tuz Khurmatli—Fathah road, the Turks being strongly entrenched at the latter place. It was most important that they should be prevented from joining forces.

Owing to the want of water facilities, the Cavalry had to return down the Adhaim the way they advanced, and keeping on the left bank of the Tigris went to Samarah, thence on to Daur, and finally reached Ain Nukailah in the evening of May 7. This brigade, having been reinforced, now became known as Norton's Column, but the M.T. still accompanied it. All the Ford vans were taken off the supply work at Samarah, and formed into what is known as a "mobile column," carrying machine guns with the necessary ammunition and personnel intended to act as advance and flank guards to the Cavalry.

The Fiats still continued on supplies, and one day's work is specially worthy of notice.

This detachment of Fiats left Samarah on the morning of May 6, proceeding to Daur to pick up supplies. They went on to Tekrit, the last two miles across soft, open, and recently cultivated ground, the "going" of which can only be described as atrocious. They left their loads there, and returned to Daur, reloading ready for an early start on the following morning. Great praise is due to 2nd Lieutenant Baskett and Sergeant Mason and in fact every man in the convoy for the manner in which they tackled a very strenuous programme. The Fiat detachment have often come in for praise, but never more so, I think, than on this occasion.

One remarkable fact about the men forming this detachment was that they were always smiling, which was remarked upon by more than one General.

From May 7 to 14 this detachment fed the column from Tekrit to 'Ain Nukailah Springs, and on one occasion, after it had been suggested that the column might have to operate on the north side of the Jabal Hamrin towards Fathah, a small convoy of Fiats went right over the pass and on to the road in question to demonstrate the possibility of the Fiats still feeding the column, should such a move be undertaken. In the meantime, the "Mobile Column" put in a considerable amount of work, both in road reconnaissance and carrying sappers, etc., to and fro on the road towards Fathah.

On May 15 Norton's Column moved back, reaching Samarah on the evening of the 16th. This ended a small though strenuous concentration so far as M.T. was concerned. Out of a total of ninety-nine vehicles which composed the M.T. column at the end of the operations, only four of them were out of action.

There is one amusing incident worthy of relating, viz. on April 28 Captain Dickinson was leading the column by a new and shorter road to the Fiat rendezvous, and seeing some gazelle in the distance stopped the car and had a couple of shots at them, but missed. It might have been due to the vibration of the car or else to an unsteady hand that the gazelle escaped. On the report of the rifle, however, up jumped three figures from the long grass with their hands extended above their heads. These proved to be three Turkish soldiers who had attempted to get through this way when left behind by their comrades, and the British were occupying the pass. They were at once taken to Brigade Headquarters, and I understand they proved to be the only prisoners which were captured in these operations, with the exception of one half-witted Armenian bâtman. The detachment returned to Baghdad on May 18.

There is another point of interest which I should like to mention with regard to the M.T. During the operations, ending in the capture of Kirkuk, some thirty-six Fords were formed into a small "mobile column" armed with machine guns. I understand they did very good work. Unfortunately some of the vans were not quite up to the mark, and a number of the drivers were Indians—who were not experts in the handling of their vehicles. Interest, however, was aroused in this by G.H.Q., and a War Establishment was afterwards sanctioned and called "Lewis Gun Company in Ford Vans."

This unit never actually came into force, but was intended to be organised should the necessity arise. Its strength was eighty Ford vans, two Clement Talbot lorries, two motor cycles, eight officers, and 266 other ranks. I feel sure that this kind of unit would have done wonderfully good work had it been available on the advance to Baghdad, especially after the advance from Aziziyeh. They would no doubt have performed what the Cavalry were unable to do, owing to the lack of water. The idea should not be lost sight of.

As the troops returned to their allotted positions, so the M.T. was released ; and on May 25, the operations were considered closed, and the last echelon of troops moved to their summer quarters.

Two Ford van companies were left to supply the line, Table Mountain to Tuz. The companies were Nos. 1014 (based at Kifri) and 1017 (at Qarah Tappah).

As on previous occasions, the M.T. earned the highest praise for their work during these operations.

# CHAPTER XII

## OPERATIONS, MAY TO AUGUST 1918

Mobile column ordered for Persia—Concentration of the necessary M.T. —The Persian line of communication—General remarks—Dispatch of Infantry Brigade to Persia—Occupation of Resht and Enzeli—British in Baku—Difficulties of supply.

At the end of April 1918, Colonel Donohue, accompanied by Captain Waterlow, started on a tour in Persia, originally with the intention of valuing the workshops and mechanical transport of the Russians, which appeared to be strewn all over Persia. On reaching Kermanshah, however, notification was received from General Dunsterville that the Russians did not wish to part, so Colonel Donohue was recalled. His reports on his return were very interesting regarding the road conditions in Persia.

During the latter part of May orders were received that a mobile column was to be formed of five Ford van companies and dispatched to Persia. They were to be based on Hamadan, and were to be utilised for the carriage of troops, Lewis guns, etc. It was pointed out that the petrol supply for these, to say nothing of the spare parts, would render such an object impossible for some time to come, unless petrol could be found in Persia, or that a sufficient quantity could be brought down from Enzeli. Transport difficulties and the question of getting five Ford van companies ready

UP-HILL WORK IN PERSIA FOR THE FORD, COMBINED WITH MAN-POWER.

A ROAD IN PERSIA, JUST NORTH OF TEHERAN.

and completing each of them up to full War Establishment were also other obstacles.

The original strength of this mobile column was approximately 1,000 rifles, with Lieutenant-Colonel Matthews, D.L.I., in command. After some discussion with G.H.Q., and the difficulties of the arrangements pointed out, it was decided that three companies were to be concentrated at Ruz by June 5, 1918, and were to be ready to move off on the following day. The remaining two companies were to be ready to move from Ruz on or about June 11.

It was necessary at that time that some troops were to reach Hamadan as soon as possible. It was made clear that when this column reached Hamadan they would be immobile for the want of petrol, but this did not affect the situation. Apparently orders had come through that every effort was to be made to get troops into Persia, and the fact of hanging up Ford vans did not appear to be taken into consideration. At this period some good reports had reached us with regard to road conditions, yet at the same time only one convoy of any size had gone up, with the exception of the vehicles with the Locker-Lampson Armoured Car Brigade, so it was not known whether the vehicles were going to be sorely tried. It was reported that one or two bridges on the road would not stand the weight of Peerless lorries, which proved to be unfounded, for this heavy type of vehicle has gone over these bridges, both laden and unladen, without doing the slightest damage. I believe the bridges would have taken a " caterpillar."

When an expedition such as this is concocted, it would seem essential that every detail should be thoroughly gone into, but this was not the case with regard to this Persian Mission.

Little more than generalising was done, and it savoured more of the old British method : " I expect we will muddle through somehow." However, when a force is sent into a country it has to be maintained, and this means rations, clothing, ammunition, arms, equipment, hospital arrangements, postal arrangements, etc., etc.; also telegraphic communication has to be established between that force and main headquarters. There is also the question of getting reinforcements up to the force, and evacuating sick men.

As a matter of fact, these points were all raised, but were airily dismissed as minor obstacles. It was also pointed out that to keep five Ford van companies effective and at work in and around Hamadan as regards petrol, oil, etc., 360 tons per month would alone be required, spare parts not even being considered. There was also the question of rations for the M.T. personnel, which, at $2\frac{3}{4}$ lb. per man per diem, came to 75 tons per month.

What actually did happen was this. When the mobile column was sent up an amount of petrol was put in at Kermanshah to take the column to Hamadan. At the time, however, petrol was worth its weight in silver. Numerous cars and lorries of the Locker-Lampson Armoured Car unit were passing through, and by the time the first 300 vans of the mobile column came along there was little or no petrol to be had. More had to be sent up urgently, both for the first 300 vans and the second batch. The petrol was just sufficient to get these vehicles to Hamadan, after which for some weeks they did little or no work owing to lack of petrol. The mobile column became a stationary one, and the War Department lost the use of 500 vans in Mesopotamia, in order that somebody might be appeased by the fact that there was a column in Persia, whether it was mobile or immobile.

On June 3 orders were issued to Lieutenant-Colonel Gibbons, M.C., that the following five Ford van companies were to be placed at his disposal:

| | | | |
|---|---|---|---|
| No. | 818 | M.T. Company | A.S.C. |
| ,, | 1015 | ,, | ,, |
| ,, | 1020 | ,, | ,, |
| ,, | 1018 | ,, | ,, |
| ,, | 1013 | ,, | ,, |

Three of the companies were to be concentrated at Ruz on the evening of June 5, and were to set off for Hamadan on the morning of the 6th, Colonel Gibbons with the first three companies, and Captain Brown, Adjutant of the column, was to take charge of the remaining two companies to leave a few days later. All the Headquarters vehicles, workshops, store lorries, etc., were also to go. In estimating the transport to carry up the tonnage, it was necessary to further denude the Base of Peerless lorries, and some of the vehicles which were to be employed on maintenance were still at work with the 13th Division. They had not yet been set free from the Kirkuk operations. So from the beginning there was a drawback from a transport point of view. Had the mobile column been delayed for three or four weeks the matter would have been, to all intents and purposes, a fairly easy proposition. When one started with a deficiency of about 200 tons in the first fortnight, it was practically impossible to overtake it.

The question of transport up this Persian line for maintenance was always a difficult one. The Dunsterforce, as it was known, used to send down messages stating that the following priority stores were required, with the result that these stores had to be dispatched, usually at the expense of the M.T. maintenance.

With the arrival of the Peerless lorries from the Base things began to look more promising. In addition to the Ford van companies employed between Ruz and Pai Tak and No. 596 Company's Peerless lorries, there were approximately ten 30-cwt. lorries withdrawn from each of the eight "caterpillar" companies attached to heavy and siege batteries. These were all employed on the transporting of supplies up to Hamadan. The companies concerned were: 788, 789, 901, 902, 903, 968, 969, and 1028, and to keep these vehicles in a fairly good state of repair, three mobile workshops complete with staff were stationed along the line.

The great source of trouble on the line Ruz to Hamadan

was the supply of petrol. Petrol in Mesopotamia, put up in tins by the Anglo-Persian Oil Company under the supervision of the Inland Water Transport, was packed in wooden cases. Each case contained two tins—eight gallons. The constant vibration in Ford vans set up a rubbing action in the tins, with the result that 20 to 40 per cent. of the petrol had leaked out by the time it reached its destination.

Very little useful information could be obtained at the time of the dispatch of this mobile column with regard to the wear and tear of M.T. vehicles in this country. It was known that the Russians had between two and three hundred derelict vehicles strewn all over the roads, but this need not necessarily have been caused through an actual breakdown, since a lot of these Russians were careless drivers.

At one time efforts were made by General Dunsterville to try to reorganise what was left by the Russians. Captain Evans, Sergeant Honor, and Sergeant Stewart were sent up for this purpose. While on the subject I might mention that the whole proposition fell through. The Russians apparently did not want to be reorganised, neither did they desire to hand over any of their transport to the British Government.

The whole question of transport up this line, allotment of tonnage, etc., was worked through G.H.Q., and at the time the line was very disorganised. There was no control from Pai Tak Pass to Hamadan, a distance of 200 odd miles.

Lieutenant-Colonel Pelly, D.S.O., M.C., had a very busy time all through the hot weather. The M.T. were doing all kinds of jobs: acting as forwarding officers, transport officers, supply officers, road police, and in a number of cases as engineers, in addition to numerous other duties they had to perform. Convoys, too, were often arranged to take up commodities, and at the last moment a priority wire would be received and these articles would consequently have to be off-loaded to make way for others.

During July all the lorries were working between Ruz and

Kermanshah. The Pai Tak Pass was found to be a big obstacle to the Daimlers and Napiers, and they were eventually allotted the section Ruz to Pai Tak, the Peerless lorries finishing the journey. With regard to the latter, the tyre trouble began to assert itself. The road conditions were bad, the heat, although not so great as that experienced in Mesopotamia, was still obnoxious, and the tyres began to give out. Those of my readers who are used to running mechanical transport over beautiful macadamised roads with the maker's guarantee of 10,000 miles per tyre, would scarcely like tackling transport problems when the rear wheels did about 600 miles, and the front double that mileage.

The maintenance of M.T. on this Persian L. of C. had not been thought out a few months ahead. It came, one might almost say, as a bombshell, and we had to make the best of a hard job. Prior to the using of M.T. vehicles on this line, there were available in Mesopotamia 100 per cent. spare tyres for this type of lorry. As the rate of consumption has been given it seems hardly necessary to inform my readers that practically all the tyres in Mesopotamia were exhausted at the end of August. Some were obtained from India and one or two other fronts, but it was not until October or November that the first really good supply of tyres was available. By this time winter conditions had practically set in, and the heavy lorries had to be more or less taken off and brought down to headquarters at Khaniquin. With the exception of one or two isolated companies, they do not work into Northern Persia.

I deeply regret if I have gone ahead with regard to the remarks about the transport of this Persian L. of C., but it was galling to one deeply interested in the welfare of M.T. to see an almost impossible problem being attempted. It was economically unsound, and it was apparent from the general remarks which one gathered from various Generals and other officers that it was not a feasible proposition.

I will now try to enumerate, as far as possible, the work

done on this line during the months of June, July, August, and September; but before doing so I think it would be as well if my readers would study the small table of distances and read them in conjunction with the map.

| | | Miles. |
|---|---|---|
| From Ruz to | Kizil Robat | 12 |
| ,, ,, | Khaniquin | 34 |
| ,, ,, | Qasr-i-Shirin | 55 |
| ,, ,, | Karind | 105 |
| ,, ,, | Harunabad | 125 |
| ,, ,, | Kermanshah | 173 |
| ,, ,, | Bisitun | 197 |
| ,, ,, | Kangavar | 235 |
| ,, ,, | Hamadan | 290 |
| ,, ,, | Kasvin | 435 |
| ,, ,, | Enzeli | 556 |

Taking Ruz *as the starting-point*, the distance to each place from that point is approximately shown herewith.

Pai Tak Pass is not mentioned here, but it is about twenty-eight miles from Qasr-i-Shirin.

With the exception of certain parts of the grocery ration and hospital comforts, it was possible to maintain in Persia a force consisting roughly of a Division by means of local supplies. These were very expensive indeed. I think at one time tea cost about 15*s*. a pound, and other commodities in similar proportion. The country had been thinned by the Russians, and even where there were supplies of grain, etc., a vast amount was locked up by the inhabitants, and until they were certain of British methods, they kept it concealed. The country from the top of Pai Tak Pass to Hamadan was in an unsettled state. Military posts were placed along the road, and had to be fed.

I now wish to introduce the following transport problem for the benefit of my readers.

The distance from the then railhead, Ruz to Hamadan, was 290 miles, so that the return journey for a vehicle going to and from railhead would be 580 miles. The consumption of petrol in Persia where the roads were good was considerably better than that of Mesopotamia, but at the same time, for working out a problem such as this, ten miles per gallon was the consumption of a Ford van. The load for one of these vehicles was fifty-six gallons of petrol, plus eight in the tank, or in other words, a mileage which a Ford van could do with a load of petrol plus its tank was 640 miles.

Allowing for wastage, the following is arrived at, i.e. one Ford van could go from railhead to Hamadan and back carrying nothing but its own maintenance in the shape of petrol and oil, so even if you multiply this number by 100 or 1,000 the result is the same. No supplies could be carried from railhead, which meant that vehicles, sent on such a journey, could do no useful work. By making various stages on the road, it was possible by using a large number of Ford vans to get a small amount of tonnage into Hamadan.

As the railhead was pushed forward from Ruz, the situation eased, but not enough to make the carriage of supplies at all a commercial proposition. The following example will show my readers the difficulties of such a transport problem, which faced this force at a time when practically no other transport but mechanical was available on this line.

Let us assume the railhead is at Kizil Robat, and it is necessary to get supplies as far as Hamadan. The distance is about 275 miles, the return journey being 550. One hundred vans travelling from railhead (Kizil Robat) to Hamadan on a straight run could only carry maintenance for driver and vehicle.

The most important place on the route is Kermanshah, and for the sake of explanation of the problem, this will be taken as the half-way house. A few miles either way do not affect the main issue.

As already stated, 100 vans can go from Ruz to Hamadan and back without carrying a useful load; so, if fifty of these vehicles are based at Kermanshah, the fifty vans which leave railhead can only carry up petrol to take the other fifty on to Hamadan and back, as well as sufficient of this commodity to get themselves back to railhead.

The fifty vehicles, however, which are based at Kermanshah require only half the petrol. Therefore they get twenty-five vehicles available for carrying supplies, but as no supplies were available at Kermanshah, these had to be brought up. A further fifty vans, therefore, leave railhead, twenty-five of which are loaded with petrol to get themselves back and twenty-five are loaded with supplies.

These loads are taken on by twenty-five of the fifty which are based at Kermanshah. It is seen, therefore, by following these figures closely, that to put twenty-five Ford van loads of supplies into Hamadan, it requires 150 vans to do it, 100 of which have to leave the railhead, the other fifty being based, as previously stated, at the half-way house.

It must not be forgotten, however, that it takes two days for the vans to get from railhead to Kermanshah and two days for the return journey. The same applies to the vans from Kermanshah to Hamadan and back.

It will be seen that twenty-five van loads are only put into Hamadan once in four days, and allowing one day for the vehicles to remain in camp after their return journey, the supplies only reach Hamadan once in five days ; thus, to get a constant daily delivery of twenty-five van loads or approximately six tons a distance of 275 miles from railhead, the figures 150 must be multiplied by five, equalling 750.

If you allow 20 per cent. spare vehicles, it gives a grand total of 900 vans to carry six tons. Of course, whenever the roads were passable, Peerless lorries were used for the carriage of petrol, and later on, when the pack transport became organised, mules, camels, etc., were also utilised. This eased the situation considerably.

Had petrol been available at Hamadan, it would probably have not been so difficult a matter. These Ford vans were also extremely useful in bringing back sick and wounded men from Hamadan, and at the same time local supplies which could be utilised further down the line.

No. 596 Company (Peerless), with the exception of twenty-five vehicles at the Base and twelve in use in Baghdad, were employed on the line Pai Tak to Kermanshah. On occasions they went up to Hamadan, and sometimes as far as Enzeli.

It was seen in June that the Persian situation was likely to develop, and it appeared that the mobile column of 500 vans would be inadequate for the troops forming the column. It was then decided that an infantry brigade should be dispatched.

It will be remembered that the maintenance of the small mobile column alone was 360 tons a month, but this included all the M.T. employed on the line being worked to its fullest capacity. The brigade had to be dispatched, hence the maintenance suffered. This was another handicap, and the situation became almost impossible from a supply point of view. Maintenance had to go by the board. Troops had to be taken forward, and to do so Peerless lorries were requisitioned.

On July 6 orders were dispatched from the G.O.C.-in-Chief, Baghdad, stating that the 39th Infantry Brigade was to proceed to Persia, and that lorry convoys would convey the dismounted troops in three echelons from Ruz, each echelon taking 1,100 personnel, reserve rations, etc., for the journey. The troops were to be conveyed as far as Hamadan. The mounted troops and transport were to leave in echelons, leaving Ruz on alternate days, and starting from that place on July 13. Apparently it was intended that British troops should be sent up as far as Baku, and would join the Armenians and Russians in resisting the Turks, who, urged on by the Germans, intended to take this important city.

In the neighbourhood of Resht, a place some twenty odd miles from Enzeli, a port on the Caspian Sea, a person named Kushi Khan, commanding a big tribe of Jungalis, was in arms against the British. Therefore the road beyond Menjil Bridge to Resht was not what one could describe as a safe one for touring.

The British troops entered Resht on June 29, after a slight resistance by this tribe of Jungalis about twenty miles outside the town. The actual entry into Resht, however, was unopposed.

Notwithstanding what one might almost describe as the paucity of troops in Persia at the time, it was decided to send a force to Baku, and on August 6 British troops actually began to land there. At the end of that month troops from Enzeli arrived at Krasnovodsk. The arrival of the 39th Brigade naturally made a considerable difference to the fighting force available, but I am not in a position to say whether the game was actually worth the candle.

The Peerless lorries which were employed in conveying this brigade as far as Hamadan were knocked about tremendously, especially with regard to tyres. There was no petrol available all the way up, so in addition to carrying troops and petrol for the journey, they had also to take sufficient to bring them back. The consumption over this road from Hamadan worked out at about four miles per gallon. I travelled along this line at the time the first echelon was *en route*, and it was really wonderful that these lorries got even as far as Hamadan with the loads that some of them had to carry. Lorries were shed at various places on the way up owing to the fact that the tyres were worn through, or else that most of the rubber had been torn off in large strips.

The lorries on this line during July, August, and September were only capable of doing six hundred miles on the rear wheels. In a great number of instances they did not do this. It must be remembered that these Peerless lorries had done two years hard slogging in Mesopotamia, and the wood in the wheels had suffered to a great extent from the intense heat. These wheels, even when retyred, were not altogether satisfactory. They should all have been rebuilt. There were not sufficient spare wheels in the country to replace every one ; time, of course, was the great object.

The Locker-Lampson Armoured Car Brigade had brought

out a fair number of spare wheels, and these were all roped in, retyred, and sent up the line. Notwithstanding this, it was only with great difficulty that the brigade got as far as Hamadan, and other lorries had to render help owing to the enormous number of breakdowns. This factor again tended to reduce the maintenance tonnage which could be dispatched from Ruz. The actual feeding of the military posts along this line was carried out by Ford van companies.

The majority of the latter were based on Khanikin. No. 815 Company were stationed at Chasmah Safed, No. 730 Company at Kermanshah, with No. 976 Packard Company. Together with the Peerless, these were responsible for the carriage of all the supplies, troops, ammunition, ordnance stores, medical stores, telegraphic material, mails, etc., up as far as Hamadan. At the time of my visit there, this is about as far as they reached, as there were no vehicles or petrol for vehicles to carry the stores from Hamadan up as far as Kasvin. Three of the five Ford van companies forming the mobile column were situated here, while the two remaining companies went forward in the vicinity of Resht.

Incidentally, while the Peerless were employed on the carriage of troops, they could not be employed on the carriage of supplies, so there was no great tonnage lying at Hamadan in the way of stores. A number of the Peerless with the Duncar Armoured Car Brigade were also taken and worked from Kermanshah up to Hamadan.

They were really loaned for supply work, for the reason that this armoured car brigade had brought out its own transport, the maintenance of which was 100 tons per month. The carriage of this as far as Hamadan was guaranteed, provided they loaned fourteen Peerless. What actually happened in practice was that we obtained the use of the lorries, but the Duncar Armoured Car Brigade never got the 100 tons a month, all owing to the dispatch of this brigade up as far as Hamadan.

I do not wish my readers to think that too much stress has been laid on the dispatch of this Brigade into Persia, and the consequent disorganisation of transport along the line. I merely want to point out how difficult it is to maintain mechanical transport which had been sent into Persia on what one might almost describe as a false pretence, i.e. that maintenance had been guaranteed for the force, which was there, yet the move of the brigade took all the vehicles responsible for the maintenance.

Hereabouts efforts were being made to reorganise all pack transport along the road, and Captain Lloyd, S. and T. Corps, was sent forward. This took some time, and pack transport, as my readers are aware, is only suitable for a certain class of goods.

As an instance of what I mean, it would be a difficult matter to send up M.T. spares by pack. I am sure the ordinary Eastern donkey or mule would certainly resent being asked to carry up a Peerless wheel, or even the back axle of a Ford! Spare parts are mentioned because very few were able to be taken up even as far as Hamadan.

When petrol became available, wires came down from the Dunsterforce requesting M.T. spares to be sent up. It then became a question of dispatching men or M.T. spares. Of course the men took precedence, so in addition to supplies and necessary medical comforts, clothing, etc., for the troops, the dispatch of M.T. spares had to take a back seat.

One often wonders how much or how little was known by the authorities at home with regard to the conditions in enemy countries about July or August 1918. Surely some authentic information ought to have been forthcoming regarding the possibility of the Turks and Bulgarians asking for an armistice. If so, it would appear from the events which happened in Mesopotamia, and which one understands were conducted under orders from home, that Germany and Turkey were fit to go on fighting for years. Baku was, and is, undoubtedly the goose that can lay, and has laid, the golden egg or eggs. Yet one wonders at the policy behind this—an isolated effort to take hold of a large city with a handful of troops, with no visible means of support, beyond some doubtful Russians, and some even more doubtful Armenians ; when communication consisted of an inland sea, the control of which was in the hands of an unfriendly Government, the Bolsheviks.

I have digressed. I should be speaking about the mechanical transport situation, but this Persian L. of C. from the beginning has been a very difficult problem. It has cost thousands and thousands of pounds for the upkeep of vehicles ; hundreds of lives have been lost ; and it is really necessary to ask the question : "Was it worth it ?"

After this brigade had reached Hamadan, the lorries, in the condition they were, gradually drifted back, and the numbers available to take the road by the end of August were very few indeed.

The tyre press both at Baghdad and the one at Kermanshah had been working night and day in order to keep the wheels retyred. The headquarters of No. 596 Company, stationed at Chasmah Safed, was a most depressing sight, all the available wheels of workshop and store lorries having to be taken to keep vehicles on the road. More trouble was also experienced with the gudgeon pins, and the vehicles on the whole were showing considerable signs of wear, after two years' strenuous work.

The dispatch of the brigade already mentioned having upset all calculations, it can only be said that the best had to be made of a bad job. Urgent demands were sent to all fronts and home with a view to getting tyres to keep both Peerless and Fords on the road. The Mesopotamian scale for which a reserve was held, and which was ample for all vehicles in that country, was of little use in Persia. To get a supply from home took time, and in the month of August an appreciation of the situation was drawn up. It was made clear that practically every Peerless would have to come off the road about the second or third week in September. A few tyres were raised in India ; a few were found at Basrah and Baghdad, and it was found possible to get a fair number of these lorries on the road right up to October.

# CHAPTER XIII

## OPERATIONS, AUGUST TO OCTOBER 1918

Retreat of British from Baku—The Jelu refugees—Accounts of the convoys through Persia—The British advance and capture of Mosul—The M.T. concentration necessary for the operations—The Armistice—Remarks.

At the end of August the Turks attacked the British defending Baku, and also began an advance from Tabriz. On August 28 a strong enemy attack on Baku was successfully frustrated. On September 5, 1918, a small British force at Tikmadash, about forty-three miles E.S.E. of Tabriz, began to withdraw to Zinjan under pressure of an overwhelming Turkish force. Retirement was carried out in good order, the British Cavalry on the flanks greatly hindering the enemy.

A few days later, i.e. September 14, 1918, the Turks delivered another determined attack against the Allies defending Baku. The British bore the brunt of the fighting and were forced back to a ridge a mile in rear of their original position, but, holding the enemy, inflicted heavy casualties on them. During the evening, when the enemy had been fought to a standstill, the British withdrew by sea to Enzeli, more or less unmolested, although some of the boats were fired on by Bolshevik gun-boats during the passage.

The M.T. was working at full pressure along this line. The damage done to vehicles was enormous on some of the roads, and sickness was considerable among all ranks.

On August 14, 1918, Colonel Moens, D.S.O., was appointed Commandant Persian L. of C. Headquarters, at Kermanshah, and things showed signs of improvement. Roads were in process of construction throughout, and at the time of writing there is a light road now running from Pai Tak Pass to Hamadan available for Ford vans during all weathers.

Lieutenant-Colonel Pelly, D.S.O., M.C., was in charge of the M.T. on this route, and at the time of writing he is acting as O.C. Mechanical Transport Persian L. of C., Headquarters, Kermanshah. There is little more to be said with regard to the work done on this line, the wear and tear of tyres being abnormal. During October orders were issued that the Peerless and Packard companies would have to be brought down to the plains for the winter, as it would not be possible to work the heavy lorries along this road.

There are one or two very important convoys, though, which are worthy of special mention.

The first was a convoy of twenty-five Peerless lorries belonging to No. 596 M.T. Company A.S.C., sent from Pai Tak to Kasvin, a distance of 354 miles. They did this journey in four days. From Hamadan to Kasvin the convoy travelled day and night, a distance of 142 miles, and three drivers per lorry had to be provided.

The sickness *en route* was considerable. It began on arrival at Kasvin, where there was practically no hospital accommodation—either there or at Hamadan. Thirteen men, who were too ill to travel, were placed in a half-built hut belonging to the M.T. Depôt, and the medical officer in charge was asked to give all the attention he could. When I said there was no hospital accommodation at Hamadan on the 29th I should justify this remark by stating that there was no accommodation for the number of men who required admittance. Before the convoy reached Kermanshah on the return journey 46 per cent. of the drivers were ill, and two men died at Hamadan before the convoy got back.

As I have said, No. 596 Company was stationed during

the summer at Chasmah Safed, and a few lines taken from the weekly report from the O.C. of that unit will no doubt give my readers some idea of the difficulty of keeping tyres on the wheels of Peerless :

"It is found essential that each lorry proceeding to Hamadan should take a spare pair of rear wheels from the tyre press at Kermanshah. If a vehicle proceeds to Enzeli, a spare pair does not always suffice."

It is unnecessary to add that the M.T. Stores as a rule do not stock 100 per cent. or over of spare wheels for any type of vehicle.

During the months of August and September the Jelu refugees were brought back on the M.T.'s return journeys.

These people were a mixed tribe of Armenians and gypsies, and had put up a very strong and determined defence against the Turks, in the neighbourhood of Lake Urumieh. Owing to the shortage of ammunition and to the fact that the British had to evacuate Baku, these people were forced to retire. They had some transport with them, but as they numbered fifty to sixty thousand, the majority of them had to walk. The route lay along the road to Hamadan through Bijar, striking the main Kasvin—Kermanshah road, at Hamadan.

Arrangements had been made that these refugees were to be tãken under the wing of this force, and it was decided to form a large concentration camp at Baqubah sufficient to accommodate fifty thousand.

The scenes on the march down along the Hamadan—Kermanshah road beggar description. The men had no respect for their women-folk, or even for their children. It was entirely a case of who could hold out the longest. The M.T. were commanded to take back a tremendous number, and occasionally men were seen throwing women and children out of lorries in order that they could get in. This was the only time in which these men seemed to be able to summon up any energy to do any work.

The M.T. drivers employed on this work had a very tough

time. In addition to acting as drivers they were also acting as nurses to new-born babies and to invalid women. Arrangements had also to be made by the authorities on the Persian L. of C. for feeding, and it is wonderful that these fifty thousand refugees eventually reached Baqubah.

What might be described as a small concentration of Ford vans took place on the Persian L. of C., under command of Major Sykes, O.C. 730 Company. The total number of vans was 200, and came from the following three companies—954, 1054, and 1055. The main object of the convoy was to take Russian refugees as far as Enzeli, and to bring back petrol which was needed at Kasvin.

The outstanding feature was the work performed by 102 vans of No. 1055 Company, under the command of 2nd Lieutenant Kirwan. Proceeding from Khanikin to Kasvin, Enzeli, and Zinjan, it left Khanikin on September 14, and reached Surkhadiza, just above Pai Tak Pass, a distance of fifty-three miles in fourteen hours. This was entirely due to the fact that this company had recently arrived, and none of the drivers had experienced hilly country or rough roads. The negotiating of Pai Tak Pass always proved a considerable difficulty to the Indian drivers, one of whom drove his car over the Pass at Pai Tak, smashing it to pieces. The Indian, luckily, escaped unhurt.

On September 15 the convoy reached Kermanshah between the hours of 5.30 p.m. and 1 a.m. on the 16th. The next two days were spent on the road between Kermanshah and Hamadan.

The chief cause of trouble on this particular road was the Asadabad Pass, where the up-going convoy had to pass several returning convoys, both mule as well as M.T. On this pass, too, another Indian driver drove his car over the side, completely smashing the vehicle, and had to be taken to hospital, injured. The convoy left Hamadan at 9 a.m. on the 18th, and the tail arrived at Kasvin at 9 p.m. on the 19th.

Maintenance petrol and lubricating oil had to be carried

from Kermanshah. On the 20th cars were off-loaded, and sufficient petrol was drawn to take the convoy to Enzeli—a distance of 160 miles—where they arrived on the evening of the 22nd. They loaded up with 5,000 gallons of petrol, which was badly wanted and which came from Baku, and began the return journey to Kasvin on the morning of the 23rd. The tail of the convoy, however, did not arrive at Kasvin until 11 a.m. on the 26th. Most of the vehicles were in a bad way for transmission band linings, owing to very steep gradients and the continual use of the brakes on the forward journey and the use of the first speed on the return.

On the 27th the convoy had orders to proceed from Kasvin to Zinjan, a distance of 120 miles, with all available vans loaded with troops. The road was fairly good, and little difficulty was experienced, the convoy returning to Kasvin on the evening of the 30th.

October 1 was spent doing repairs at Kasvin and preparing for the return trip to Hamadan. It was loaded up with numerous sick officers and men, and left Kasvin at 9.30 a.m. on October 2, arriving Hamadan on the morning of the 4th.

It left the latter place on the morning of the 5th ; arrived Kermanshah mid-day on the 7th, and reached Khanikin on the 9th. The total distance covered by this convoy was approximately 1,600 miles, and the following spares were used :

Eight hundred new tubes (250 of which were repaired by vulcanisers and a further 250 repaired with Patchquik outfits, making a total of 1,300 punctures in all). In addition 278 covers, 35 front springs, 100 feet of transmission band lining, 14 radius rods, 15 connecting rods, 25 rear wheels, 16 front wheels, and 10 rear springs. Ninety per cent. of the vehicles required new transmission band linings.

Three cars, however, were completely wrecked, while twenty B.O.R.'s and nineteen I.O.R.'s were admitted to hospital at various stages of the journey. These are the chief points in connection with what can be termed a good performance.

A third convoy, which I should like to mention, was in charge of Lieutenant Stribling, No. 596 Company, carrying naval guns from Ruz to Enzeli. The convoy left Ruz on October 21, 1918, and there were minor troubles which delayed the convoy, such as carburettor, magneto, etc. One vehicle had to be exchanged, and Qasr-i-Shirin was reached at 8.30 p.m. the same night. Chasmah Safed was passed at 5.30 p.m. the following day, and Kermanshah on the 23rd. Two front springs were broken—an extraordinary thing in this country to happen to a Peerless lorry—and two new wheels had to be put on other lorries. All repairs being carried out, the convoy left on the morning of the 24th, but owing to minor troubles it had to camp three miles south of Kangavar for the night. It negotiated the Asadabad Pass by the evening of the 26th. Much delay was caused through the issue of petrol in seventy-five-gallon drums, and the tanks had to be filled from these.

The convoy passed through Hamadan and reached Kasvin on the afternoon of the 29th. On looking up the report of this convoy, I find that the drop of the temperature began to show its effect on the carburettors, most of them being frozen in the morning.

Next day the convoy left Kasvin at 8 a.m., having first loaded rations which they took to the post at Menjil. Resht was reached at 5.30 p.m. on the 31st, and Enzeli at 2 p.m. on November 1. This convoy had considerable difficulty through the frost, snow, and rain, in fact when the convoy was ordered some doubt was expressed if these vehicles would ever get back to Khanikin.

It is not intended to go into further detail with regard to the return journey of this convoy. It left Enzeli on November 2, 1918, and what with weather and road conditions and mechanical troubles, it did not get back to Khanikin until November 22, 1918.

As will be seen from the date, the forward journey occupied eleven and a half days, and the journey back took nearly three weeks. The weather and roads were bad, and the O.C. convoy stated the road south of Hamadan was absolutely unsuited for heavy traffic of any kind, once the rains had started. The new road across the Asadabad Plain was not ready for use; even if it had been it would not have been suitable for heavy lorries. Out of ten spare wheels carried, eight were used, notwithstanding that all the lorries had been retyred prior to the journey.

I have made special reference to these three convoys, as they are outstanding features in a way. Still, all the work of the Mechanical Transport on this line was good, and it is unfair to single out any particular convoy. That is one reason why I have devoted a short chapter to putting in the honours and awards earned by M.T. officers and men in this country, and also copies of appreciations which have been written by General officers and others with regard to the work done.

At the time of writing, the Persian L. of C. is still going strong. The war is over, yet the work of the Army Service Corps still goes on.

Demobilisation has started, but with a working corps like the A.S.C. it will be one of the last corps affected to any great extent. I hope and trust that by the time this book is in print it will be possible to carry out the transport of supplies from Pai Tak Pass to Hamadan by means of mule or pack transport, which will set free a number of M.T. units and so enable the men to get home.

The bulk of the M.T. is used on this line. During July I took a trip up to Kasvin to see the M.T. units at work, and the road conditions, and also to see if it was possible to get as far as Enzeli.

Arriving at Kasvin, I found No. 1013 Company encamped in the middle of the Jungali country and a detachment of No. 818 Company at Resht. It was impossible to get through to No. 1013 Company, though an attempt was made, but on the morning in question the Jungalis had been active, and had destroyed a bridge, two or three miles ahead of the point reached. The escort due to arrive from Resht could not get through, so I had to return to Kasvin. It was then found that the Jungalis had also made a determined attack on Resht, and had captured a large portion of the town. They were, however, driven out.

No. 1013 Company while in this camp did some fine work in addition to acting as a transport company. They acted as rearguard to any of the mobile columns which they carried about the country. A detachment of thirty or forty vans of this unit would go out with so many Gurkhas. Usually they were attacked along the road, and the vans would have to be left unattended and the country in the immediate vicinity scoured. It was on these occasions that all ranks behaved well and earned high praise.

Since it has been on the Persian L. of C. the unit has been transferred to Baku, after numerous journeys to and fro between Kasvin and Enzeli. It is now, at the time of writing, working under the command of the General Officer Commanding the Salonika Expeditionary Force.

In the late autumn it was decided that an advance should be made towards Mosul. The Turks were being very heavily hit in Palestine, and on September 30 we occupied Damascus. On October 3 Bulgaria capitulated, and between the 7th and 20th the British occupied the four following places: Beirut, Homs, Tripoli, and Hama.

So far as Mechanical Transport for the Mosul operations was concerned, their duty began early in October, and on the 7th of that month the following vehicles were detailed to proceed from Baghdad to the 1st Corps Area, i.e. Tekrit:

| | | | | |
|---|---|---|---|---|
| No. | 971 | Company, | 79 | vans |
| ,, | 783 | ,, | 33 | ,, |
| ,, | 729 | ,, | 28 | ,, |
| ,, | 1,023 | ,, | 36 | ,, |
| ,, | 953 | ,, | 8 | ,, |
| ,, | 784 | ,, | 36 | ,, |

These were under the command of Major Sellwood, acting as O.C. M.T. for the 1st Corps, as the operations were about to begin.

Totalling 220, these vans were dispatched. The drivers were equipped with the full winter scale of kit, and began work on October 9. It was found, however, that more vans were necessary, and between October 16 and 18 two more companies were sent up, Nos. 1014 and 1019.

The first company had to be withdrawn off the Persian L. of C., and the other from Kifri, where they had been employed all through the spell of hot weather. Approximately a week after these companies joined, No. 953 Company had to detail forty-five vans and No. 784 Company thirty-three vans, making a grand total of 514 vans.

The railhead at the beginning of these operations was at Tekrit, and the Ford vans were employed, under the 17th Division, carrying supplies from this railhead to Jift, on the right bank of the Tigris, where a supply dump was made. The distance from railhead to Jift was approximately twenty-six miles; the journey there and back was completed in a day. The headquarters of the M.T. was for the time being at Tekrit. On October 14 it was found that the supplies were not being brought up quick enough, and the vans for the next two days made a double journey. The roads not being first-class, this was a good performance.

The dump at Jift was completed on the 17th, when the vans were allotted to the 18th Division to enable it to form dumps at Jift, left bank of Tigris, and 'Ain Nakhailah. The M.T. also moved the headquarters of their camp from the right bank to the left, because the road between the railway and the bridge-head was in such a fearful condition, and it was impossible to work transport over it. The supplies were taken from the right to the left bank by means of A.T. carts, and were then loaded on to Ford vans, to be taken from that place to the dumps at Jift and 'Ain Nakhailah.

On the 22nd all vans had orders to move to 'Ain Nakhailah,

A CATERPILLAR COMPANY *EN ROUTE* TO TAKE PART IN THE MOSUL OPERATIONS.

Loaded up near Ramadie and off-loaded at Tekrit

VIEW OF THE ASADABAD PASS.

It is very hard to form any idea of the gradient. The top of the Pass is on the right of photo, near the highest point.

and so far as they were concerned this was the point from which the important advance was commenced.

Unlike other operations here, the advance was made from both sides of the River Tigris towards Mosul, the 18th Division on the left bank and the 17th Division on the right. The 7th and 11th Cavalry Brigades were at first employed on the right bank.

In addition to the advance up the Tigris, an advance was made on Kirkuk and Altun Kupri between October 24 and 31. Tuz Khurmatli was captured without opposition on October 23, 1918. Compared with the main operations, this can only be considered as a minor one. After various other minor successes the British occupied Altun Kupri on October 31, the enemy having withdrawn. Only one M.T. Co., No. 1017, was employed on this minor operation, and did very good work.

To return to the main concentration, the British force on October 24 advanced up the Tigris and compelled the enemy to withdraw from his position astride the Fathah Gorge, taking up a reserve position along the line Bilalij—'Ain Dibs—Mushak. The British Cavalry crossed the Lesser Zab at Uthmaniyeh, fourteen miles up-stream of the Tigris—Zab confluence. On October 25 the enemy moved three battalions from reserve across the Tigris seven to eight miles up-stream of the mouth of the Lesser Zab. British infantry and artillery forced a passage of the Lesser Zab near its mouth, and co-operated in an encircling movement against the enemy of the left bank of the Tigris. Vigorous pressure from three sides, combined with a strong aerial offensive, forced the enemy to again retire to the right bank of the Tigris. On the right bank of the Tigris the enemy continued to hold his defensive position along the line Bilalij—'Ain Dibs—Mushak. On October 26 the enemy still held his Bilalij position. Our Cavalry forded the Tigris, fourteen miles north of Shargat, and established themselves astride the Mosul road, seven miles farther south.

These movements affected the M.T. to a great extent.

The 7th and 11th Cavalry Brigades started from 'Ain Nakhailah, and each of these formations was allotted 100 Ford vans. Those with the 7th Cavalry Brigade took the road to the north of the Jabal Hamrin, which was in a bad condition, deep sand and deep nullahs necessitating much pushing and towing of vehicles. This resulted in vans being left out at night, and having to start out again immediately they got back to camp.

The work on which the vans of the 7th Cavalry Brigade was first employed was the forming of a water-dump, as there was no water available. This completed, they were then required for rations. For three or four days the vehicles and men were going practically night and day over appalling roads. Broken chassis, springs, and various other parts of the vehicles, were numerous.

The 11th Cavalry Brigade marched from 'Ain Nakhailah, N.N.W., accompanied by 100 Ford vans, which were utilised for water and rations. They went out on the morning of October 24, and none of these vehicles was seen again for a matter of about four days. They eventually crossed the Lesser Zab, joining the Tigris at Ferry Bridge, and came down again to Fathah, after the main advance had got beyond them.

During the night of October 26/27 the enemy evacuated the Bilalij position, and began entrenching on a line covering Shargat from the south-west. A British column moved up the left bank of the Tigris to prevent any enemy attempt to cross. On October 28 our Cavalry, astride the Mosul road, under continuous pressure withdrew their right flank back to the Tigris to meet an attack, and carried the first line of the position three and a half miles south of Shargat.

On October 29 part of the Cavalry holding the Mosul road effected a sweeping movement to the north-west and captured 1,000 prisoners and much material. The British southern force continued its advance, and established contact with the northern force, completing the cordon round the Turks, who were strongly entrenched on a two-mile front

RESULT OF AN INDIAN DRIVER TAKING A SHORT CUT TO CAMP DURING THE MOSUL OPERATIONS.

west of the Mosul road. An assault was launched at 4 p.m., and by nightfall had penetrated well into the Turkish trenches.

On October 30 Isma'il Haqqi Bey, commanding the Turkish force, surrendered in the morning with his whole force.

Qaiyarah was occupied, and a further 1,000 prisoners, one gun, and ten machine guns were captured. Up to the night of October 30 the total captures amounted to 643 officers, 10,679 other ranks, 50 guns, and 2,085 animals. The following river-steamers fell into our hands, *Tekrit*, *Bourhaniyah*, *Hamidiyah*, *Khalifah*, and *Baghdad*.

While these movements were actually in progress, the remainder of the vans were ordered away from 'Ain Nakhailah and went to Jift, right bank, working up the desert road towards Shargat.

On October 30 practically all the M.T. was moved over to Fathah on the right bank, when the 100 Fords previously mentioned, which had been at work with the 11th Cavalry Brigade, rejoined them.

The following announcement was made to the Army in Mesopotamia on November 1, by the General Officer Commanding-in-Chief:

"An Armistice has been signed between the British and Turkish Governments, as from 12 noon on October 31.

"In making this announcement to the Army in Mesopotamia, the General Officer Commanding-in-Chief wishes to convey his most hearty and sincere thanks to all ranks of the force, and to congratulate them on the final and happy results so largely contributed to by their devoted courage, endurance, and hard work."

Needless to say, all ranks were thoroughly pleased with the announcement.

On November 3 all vans again moved back to Shargat and were employed carrying supplies for Fanshawe's Column advancing towards Mosul. The first M.T. convoy arrived at Mosul on November 5, and from that date all available vans were run between the railhead at Abu Rijash and Mosul.

No. 1014 Company, which was complete, moved back to Fathah, and were responsible for bringing up all the ordnance and canteen stores to Shargat. Their loads were taken on by No. 1019 Company as far as Mosul.

The remaining detachments, of which a list has already been given, were used for supplies for Fanshawe's Column between Shargat and Mosul.

It will be seen from the foregoing account that the base from which vans were worked was constantly being moved. This necessitated continual movement of workshops and the leaving behind of derelict vans with personnel to look after them in each camp.

Convoys have repeatedly gone out in the morning from headquarters and have not returned. No definite information could be obtained as to their probable movements. Needless to say, this made the work of repairs and bringing in of derelicts and unserviceable vehicles extremely difficult. Owing to the advance being on both sides of the Tigris, the crossing of this for certain vehicles was a difficult procedure.

The bridge at Fathah was only a light one, and consequently it was unable to take even first-aid Talbot lorries belonging to companies. These and also the workshops had to go right down to Tekrit when it was desired to cross the river. This meant that companies and detachments were without their repair lorries, sometimes for two or three days on end, and that vans were temporarily off the road longer than they should have been.

At the time of writing, approximately two hundred vans were employed under the 18th Division, and were working between Shargat and Hammam Ali, about fifteen miles south of Mosul. The railhead had got as far as Baiji, and A.T. carts were employed between Baiji and the M.T. camp at Shargat.

The only other item of importance from an M.T. point

of view carried out in these operations was a reconnaissance by a light armoured motor battery on the left bank of the Tigris. Eighteen vans of No. 971 Company, under command of 2nd Lieutenant Spencer, accompanied it, and did very good work.

One amusing incident occurred during these operations. A detachment of No. 1023 Burma M.T. Company, under Lieutenant Bayley, was sent out as a water convoy. As they had some distance to traverse and the road was unknown, a guide was furnished by Headquarters. The guide, as is usually the way with most guides, led the convoy almost up to the Turkish position, where they came under heavy rifle fire. Lieutenant Bayley managed to get his convoy back without any casualties, and proceeded towards Headquarters to report the inefficiency of the guide. On his way he was met by a staff officer, who congratulated him heartily on the very good piece of reconnaissance work which he had performed!

One or two points of interest were brought out in these operations: for instance, the Ford vans being sent out into the "blue" with the 11th Cavalry Brigade, and not seen again for several days; the difficulty of supplying a force such as a cavalry brigade when water is not available; and also the employment of M.T. over roads which are absolutely unsuited for it was not only an interesting point, but also a very serious one, and one which has constantly hampered the use of Mechanical Transport throughout the whole of the Mesopotamian Campaign.

# CHAPTER XIV

## SO-CALLED IMPROVEMENTS

Labour-saving devices—Hints and helps for M.T. companies—Description of improvised machinery and time-saving appliances, etc.

I HAVE mentioned in the chapter on Organisation that during the years 1916–1918 various circulars were issued by the Office of the Director of Supplies and Transport for the benefit of O.C. M.T. companies and other units having mechanical transport on their charge. These circulars contained useful information with regard to the care and maintenance of self-propelled vehicles in Mesopotamia. The information was the result of experience in this and other countries with mechanical transport, and any fresh ideas or inventions sent in by O.C.s M.T. companies were fixed on as being of general practical use. All O.C.s companies were asked to forward anything in the nature of an improvement for keeping vehicles on the road—any labour- and time-saving devices, or any fresh ideas on the subject of convoy running which would be for the benefit of the Mechanical Transport in general.

Numerous troubles were encountered in this country on convoy work, and with individual vehicles. Spare parts were always difficult to obtain, and in order to keep vehicles running, it was absolutely necessary to depend upon the ingenuity and resource of Mechanical Transport officers, more especially the workshop officers and staffs.

The following list will show my readers the various headings under which inventions and so-called devices were issued, and the remedy for coping with same, mainly for Fords:

1. The draining of oil sumps.
2. Prevention of over-lubrication of cylinders.
3. Seizing of the spindle of the hand-brake lever. A greaser was fitted to remedy this.
4. Lubrication of the swivel pin which carries the stub axle.
5. Correct registering of the centre bolts in cross members, and with regard to the rear spring a hole was cut in the floor boards of Ford vans, so that the head of the bolt could be seen. The bolt itself was fitted with a taper head for tightening purposes.
6. Insertion of sheet rubber packing between the radiator lugs and the frame, also between the engine lugs and the frame.
7. Adjusting of the tye rod to try to preserve radiators.
8. Lengthening the life of trans-band liners by packing out with a strip or two of tin when the bands were worn.
9. Protection of woodwork of the wheels from the heat of the sun when vehicles were stationary.
10. Care of rear wheels on Fords—keeping bolts tight.
11. Instructions with regard to the method of rebuilding wheels when spokes were loose, due to wood shrinking.
12. Use of the "Stepney" spare wheel. As far as possible these were not used, and were only issued by companies to detached vehicles.
13. Care of shock absorbers.
14. Care of spring clips.
15. Making of rebound leaf for the springs of 30-cwt. lorries.
16. Leather spring pads on Fords found unsatisfactory owing to hardening, wrinkling up, and loss of resiliency due to climatic conditions. Canvas pads of same shape and thickened at the ends were made out of old and unserviceable outer covers.

17. Trouble with the Apollo sparking-plug, due to shorting. This was due to the current jumping the space between the flange of the central electrode and the inside of the shell of the plug. A remedy was effected by boring the plug out $\frac{1}{32}$ inch all round, thus increasing the air-gap.
18. Use of points made from rupee silver in lieu of platinum. A small hand-punching machine was made, and at one time, when platinum was short, this was most successful.
19. Prevention of dust trouble in coils by the addition of rubber sheeting between the dash and the coil-box. Two-inch projection all round the coil-box. This also assisted in keeping out rain-water, which used to run down the inside of the dash.
20. Doing away with ignition switches altogether.
21. Strengthening of Ford van bodies and the method of doing so.
22. An easy method of securing oil-filler caps on Douglas motor cycles.
23. Adjustment of Vauxhall carburettors.
24. One or two methods of repairing Douglas motor-cycle springs.
25. Instructions for the general running of Mechanical Transport convoys and companies.
26. Frost precautions.
27. Care of motor cycles.
28. Economy to be practised when ordering spares.
29. Salving of all derelict vehicles, worn spare parts, etc.
30. Care of tools and tool kits.
31. Description of a complete overhaul, and what it comprised.
32. Issue of special forms used when returning damaged and worn-out vehicles to the Advanced M.T. Depôt.
33. Provision and use of bonnet covers and non-skid chains.
34. How to make fan belts from canvas of old outer covers.

35. Return of unserviceable spare parts.
36. Method of reinforcing springs for Fords.
37. Method of reinforcing side members for Fords.
38. Repair of tyre valve plungers.
39. Fitting of bolt valve plates.
40. Substitute used for Saflux.
41. Fitting of rear mud-guard bracket on the top side instead of underneath the wing, thus preventing the cutting of tyres by the bracket when the vehicle is loaded, due to excessive deflection on rough roads.
42. Manufacture of rear hubs (bronze) from old Turkish guns, by the Advanced M.T. Depôt. These were made with a thickened flange.

In addition to the foregoing there were various other makes of vehicles out here, most of which were slightly improved one way and another.

### Thornycroft Anti-aircraft Gun Lorries

The front towing hooks of these were altered and placed higher up just on the bend of the dumb-iron, so that a straight pull could be obtained instead of the original position, which was inclined to have a lifting action. This was found necessary in view of the number of dumb-irons which were smashed in towing these heavy vehicles over almost impassable stretches of desert.

### Daimler

These vehicles gave a lot of trouble in this country, owing to the breaking of the engine suspension bolts, and, in some cases, the cross suspension members. The three-point suspension was tried, found to be successful, and was taken into universal use on all these vehicles. It was composed of the trunnion type of connection. The swivel-pin block was bolted to the engine crank-case by the front suspension bolts. The engine front suspension member was cut, drilled, and suitably strengthened, and distance pieces and pins fitted, on which the trunnion swivels. The side suspension was fixed. At one time it was thought that the difficulty might be overcome by making stronger suspension bolts. These were successful, but it was considered the three-point suspension was the better method.

## Peerless Lorries

As mentioned in a previous chapter, the first and chief source of trouble with these vehicles was the gudgeon pins, which had a habit of working loose. There were one or two devices thought out. The first was by means of grinding the gudgeon pin at each end and fitting copper discs. These discs acted as distance pieces between the pins and the cylinder walls.

A locking device for set screws to prevent them coming loose was also tried. Another device was to continue the set screw through the gudgeon by the softening down of the gudgeon pins for drilling, and tempering them again without disturbing the case-hardening. This was done successfully, but not with the same finish as previously, owing to lack of facilities. New set screws had to be made, but owing to the pins being distorted when tempered, a new gudgeon pin bushing had also to be made. This is a lengthy process, and the copper-disc idea was chiefly adopted.

Another method was to soften the pin locally in the neighbourhood of the pin-hole by standing the pin in water up to a point about a quarter-inch below the hole, and heating the exposed part. It is only necessary, therefore, to take a few threads off the set screw and drill a pin-hole near the point in addition to enlarging the hole on the gudgeon pin. The existing lock-nut can be used. Another method was to soften the pin and put the set screw right through into the gudgeon and secure by means of a split pin.

### Non-skid Chains for Solid Tyres

After constant use on the concrete road at Basrah the non-skid chains caused grooves across the tread of the back tyres. In order to economise in tyre consumption, the tyres were taken off and turned a few inches, so that the grooves did not come opposite each other. Extra mileage was the result.

### Peerless Wheels

The wooden wheels of Peerless also gave trouble, as they shrank considerably in the heat. Practically all of them had to be rebuilt in Mesopotamia. A certain number of steel wheels were obtained and proved themselves to be the right type of wheel for this country.

### Talbot

The ground clearance of this car was insufficient to be of any use out here, and to raise this, blocks were fitted under the front springs, thus increasing the clearance about 3 inches. The blocks in question were made of bronze, and were cast by the Advanced M.T. Depôt.

### Fiat Lorries

It was found necessary to put a Stauffer lubricator to the propeller shaft bearing, immediately behind the universal joint, as it was discovered, when these vehicles came to be overhauled, that the bearing had at some time been seized, due to lack of lubrication. A three-point suspension was also tried on these vehicles, but it was not a mechanically sound job, as the front and one side suspension were fixed, while the other could roll.

It was also found that in the timing wheels of these lorries the white metal keys were unsatisfactory, owing to the white metal becoming loose. Steel keys were substituted. The timing wheels were fixed solid in the shaft, doing away with the spring drive which had given a lot of trouble. Experiments were made to reduce the load on the valve springs, as it was believed that the strength of these springs was the cause of the timing wheels wearing in two places. After a good test with lightened springs, the timing case was taken off and the gun-metal timing wheels showed no signs of wear. This method was universally adopted afterwards.

### Packard Lorries (Water-jackets)

In a country such as Mesopotamia this would appear to be a weak part of the design; there is not enough room for water to circulate freely. This probably causes a steam pocket, the point of fracture being in the cylinder top in the central walls of Nos. 2 and 3 cylinders. Up to the present no crack has been found in the jacket or cylinder walls of Nos. 1 and 4 cylinders. There is no doubt that the water-space is too small, possibly accentuated out here through dirty water having on occasions to be used. This causes sediment to lodge inside. It is most important, therefore, that there should be a good water-space.

Considerable trouble has also been experienced with the Packard differential gear by the fracture of the teeth. This is due to the fracture of a tooth on the pinion wheels, resulting in the stripping of the others. The metal at the point of fracture was in every case sound and correctly formed, and made of a grade of steel suitably hardened. The differential gear is on the light side, and a redesigning and increase of metal in this particular direction will probably eliminate further trouble. It will also make this car more suitable for the conditions prevailing in this country.

At the Advanced M.T. Depôt a large number of improvised tools, machines, and jigs were made, all of a labour-saving character.

The following is a summary of the machinery, etc. To meet the requirements of the various crucible and temporary furnaces in use, the necessary blast was supplied by means of a worn-out Ford engine adapted as an air compressor.

The alterations and additions to the engine were as follows:

The half time shaft and its gearing were removed. The whole of the planatory transmission, also the coil assembly, were removed, leaving the magnet assembly only for the purpose of utilising the Ford system of lubricating.

The exhaust valves were then screwed at the sides and bolted down, permanently closing them. The inlet valves were lightened by recessing the tops, and fitted with a very light spring, making them suitable for automatic induction without any mechanical lift. Aluminium plates were then fitted to the piston tops with the object of reducing the compression space to a minimum. The sparking-plug holes were bored out, and a spring-operated outlet valve fitted to each. These four valves are coupled up to a manifold, made up from standard steel pipe fittings, and the extension taken to a large cylindrical tank fitted with an improvised regulating safety valve and an outlet pipe for discharge to service pipes feeding the various crude-oil burners. The timing-case end was blanked up, and a 6-inch extension screwed to the standard Ford crankshaft for the accommodation of a driving pulley.

For the purpose of ensuring the lubrication of the pistons and the cylinder walls, which were only definitely lubricated by crankshaft throw at speeds possibly greater than that required for air supply, each cylinder head was drilled through the water-jacket, and the copper oil-duct fitted over the top of each piston. These oil-ducts were fed by two non-return ball-valve automatic lubricators of special design, one feeding Nos. 1 and 4 cylinders and the other Nos. 2 and 3. The whole was mounted in a frame comprised of wooden blocks, shaped at each end to conform with the base chamber outline, and secured on the top by means of clamping plates.

The machines can be run at any speed between, say, 100 and 700, and give a proportionate output of compressed air at a reasonably high-efficiency figure. At the higher speeds, the supplementary piston and cylinder lubrication device might be found unnecessary. At the Advanced M.T. Depôt two of these machines are running, one off line shafting at 200 r.p.m., and the other is fitted on a self-contained bed with an electric motor drive, speed reduction being made by a countershaft, at 300 r.p.m. The engines were very old—too worn for further service as an I.C. unit.

### Piston Ring Lapping Machine

This consisted of a main shaft, with an old engine fly-wheel at each end, and a driving pulley in the centre. Both fly-wheels were fitted with crank-pins, giving a 2-inch throw. Above the main shaft was a table for the reception of Ford cylinder blocks, fitted with dowel pins for registering and locating exact position. At the sides of the table were two vertical guides, and on these were fitted cross-heads with a horizontal spindle carrying four connecting rods, specially designed clamps for attaching to the skirts of Ford pistons. Cylinder blocks were brought to the table with pistons and rings fitted. The connecting rods were clamped to the end or skirts of the pistons, and the horizontal bar and cross-heads were moved up and down the cylinder in their correct position. A fine abrasive is fed in from the top. This machine, constructed of old and scrap materials, enabled piston rings to be lapped into their own cylinder until they fitted perfectly and had a finely polished surface. This operation obviates the necessity of a running in process of the motor under its own power.

### Planishing Machine for Coil Contacts

All coil contacts received for repair were more or less badly pitted and unevenly worn on the face. To bring these square and face them, an old electric-fan motor was fixed in a frame in a horizontal position, and the spindle fitted with a 6-inch brass disc. On this was fixed a disc of very fine emery cloth. This device is fitted up at right angles to a surface plate, and the spring contact blades are placed in a jig with the platinum tip protruding through a hardened steel plate (which limits the amount to be faced off to a minimum), and thereby brought into contact with the grinding disc. Points can be faced off dead square and perfectly smooth and polished at the rate of two per minute.

### Bench Testing Set for Magneto

This consisted of an old electric-fan motor fitted horizontally in a frame, with a 4-inch grooved pulley on the end of the spindle in lieu of the fan blades. In front of this was fitted a simple form of magneto plant. A magneto for test was fixed therein, with a small grooved pulley, coupled up to the motor by round belting. By means of the fan rheostat, the magneto was revolved at variable speeds and the intensity of its spark ascertained at all ranges of speeds before it was passed for issue or fitting.

### Plug Testing Device

This was an addition to the above set and worked with it. A rack for, say, six plugs was made from iron flat bar, earthed to the magneto. Plugs were dropped in the holes provided for them, and by means of leads from the distributor terminals tested at practically all ranges of engine speeds.

### Trembler Coil Testing Device

This consisted of a rectangular box fitted with interior terminals connected with a twelve-volt accumulator. Coils for testing are slipped inside until the terminals meet. By means of a simple switch, the current is put on, and breaks across a variable gap, fitted on top of the box. This is a simple and extremely effective method of testing Ford coils.

### Remagnetising Apparatus for Ford Magnet Assembly en bloc

This consisted of a resistance frame run off the 110-volt circuit and giving 30 amps. From this frame two insulated handles with steel contact points were carried on flexible leads. After the polarity of the magnets had been ascertained by means of a compass or a pole-finder, intermittent and instantaneous contact was made. About forty contacts resulted in a considerable increase in the strength of the magnet. This was sometimes as much as 100 per cent. When a magnet will support in suspension a 2-pound weight, it is passed for use. This recharging can be carried out either with the magnet and coil assembly built up in the engine, or dismantled.

### Engine Trolley

From two old Ford front axles and wheels a very convenient and handy form of truck was made. The track of both wheels was first reduced to 3 feet by cutting the axles in the middle, shortening and rejoining with bar-iron plates fitted in the "H" section, and either bolted or riveted. The two axles were bolted up to an angle-iron frame member by the hole provided in their design, and the wooden platform fitted to suit the requirements with a top adjustable iron rails "L" section to accommodate the various engine bearers at one end. The stub axle steering arms were bolted solid to the frame with the wheels in line with same, and at the steering end a stud was fitted in the centre of the axle. From this a handle was fitted to the radius rod by means of a pin with a slotted hole engaging same. The handle was extended to the front for pulling, and by using the axle as a fulcrum a very simple form of steering was obtained. This large wheeled type of trolley is particularly suited for the uneven mud roadways in and around workshops, and can be made from parts beyond service in their original capacity.

### Rotary Blowers

For forced draught to the thirty-seven forge fires in the Advanced M.T. Depôt, which are built running in two parallel lines, two home-made blowers of the four-bladed centrifugal type were manufactured. The casing was made from ¼-inch iron plate, and a gun-metal centre, bored, split, and clamped to a 1⅜-inch shaft. The shaft rotates in Hyatt roller bearings which are carried on two "A" frames, fixed independent from the blower casing, and are driven at 1,250 r.p.m. by means of whittle belt drive to a motor mounted on a frame. One blower, feeding twenty-four fires, takes only two kilowatts, and gives an ample supply of air throughout the range.

### High-speed Grinder

For the purpose of grinding cutters, tools, and work in general, an old home-made milling machine was converted into a high-speed grinder, capable of doing excellent work with a grinder up to 6-inch diameter. It was made with a counter-shaft and grinding stone spindle, clamped to the steady bar, and by means of a whittle belt and rope belt, the grinder revolved at 6,000 r.p.m., both counter-shaft and spindle being mounted in radial and thrust ball bearings.

### Home-made Milling Machine

This machine started life as a horizontal wood-turning machine, and was left behind by the enemy (when they evacuated the town) in a broken condition. A milling machine was badly wanted, so a steady arm carrying a back centre was fitted, and collets and mandrels made to suit. Various cutters were manufactured, and the machine was successful for many months in all classes of work, until the arrival of a larger and better milling machine enabled it to be converted into a high-speed grinding machine.

### Lathe Grinder

A ⅓-h.p. motor was obtained and fitted with a countershaft mounted on ballraces, and carrying on one end a 6-inch emery wheel. The necessary brackets and slides were made to make it attachable to the lathe saddle of a 6-inch lathe. The work held in the lathe centres revolves against the direction of the stone. With this attachment more than 100 Ford gudgeon pins alone have been ground weekly as well as other work, and another long-felt want was successfully met. The motor revolved at 1,100 r.p.m. The stone revolved at 3,850 r.p.m.

### Disc Grinder

The major portion of an old disc grinder was found; supplies of discs were obtained, but no adhesive could be got suitable for sticking emery cloth to steel. After some experimenting a method of "cold vulcanising" was successfully tried, and the machine is now in daily use and doing excellent work.

### Rotary Blowers

Before the Ford type of air compressor was introduced, the crude-oil burners were supplied with air by home-made rotary positive blowers, of orthodox design. Two of these were successfully made, and ran with fairly satisfactory results for many months.

### Wood-planing Machine

There was an old-fashioned band saw with a table, of dimensions far in excess of requirements. It was consequently utilised—or, to be more correct, a portion of it was used—in the construction of a planing machine for wood. The cutter blades were 10 inches long. Three of them were fitted in a holder mounted on ball bearings, driven at required speed by a small motor fitted underneath the table, and coupled up by whittle belting.

### Jigs and Tools

In the machine shop all work dealt with in quantities was jigged to the fullest extent, ensuring standardisation, speed, and accuracy. The following attachments for machine tools were also made :

Dividing head for milling machine ; hollow dividing head for milling splines on axle shafts ; and a complete set of jigs for remetalling and finally reaming out Ford main bearings.

### Spring Leaf Shaping Press

The hand shaping of a Ford rear spring assembly is, owing to its shape, a difficult matter, and not only requires an experienced smith but takes a long time. Each leaf has to be bent and exactly mated to its fellows. Consequently a machine for doing the work was designed and made, which has worked with the excellent results of saving much labour.

From 2-inch square section iron bar (made from A.T. cart axles) nine pairs of spring dies were made, each pair of dies making a different leaf numbered from 1 to 9. One ¾-inch steel plate was fitted to a worm nut with a four-start worm (1½-inch pitch) working in same, one end fitted with a handle for turning, and the other a block with connecting plates for the male die. The nine pairs of spring dies were all fitted with studs, which register the holes drilled in the base plate of the press. Assuming that 100 sets of rear spring assemblies were required, spring steel would be cut off the required length for each leaf.

The bottom die plate for No. 1 leaf would then be fitted into its locating holes, and the top one coupled to the end of the worm by loose connecting plates. Leaves properly heated were tonged from the furnace and dropped into a registered position between the top and bottom die plates and the worm was immediately screwed down, thereby pressing the hot metal to shape between the two. Immediately it was set, the screw pressure was withdrawn, and the operation repeated. When all No. 1 plates were pressed, No. 2 leaf-die plates were fitted in their located holes, and the operation repeated in this size, and so on, until the whole of the 100 sets of plates were completed.

### Piston-cleaning Machine

An apparatus was also made by means of which pistons were cleaned. This operation formerly required four Arab boys. It is now a more satisfactory job and a saving of two boys.

### Main-bearing Remetalling Jigs

Formerly, short mandrils were used, and only two engines could be remetalled per day, in addition to other remetalling work. With present jigs fixed on plates and located by existing bolt holes in cylinder block, four engines could be remetalled per day in addition to other remetalling work.

### Remetalling Jigs for Ball Cups (Universal Joint)

Ball cups were formerly remetalled singly. With a jig consisting of a plate with a fixed hollow mandril and four locating studs, four ball cups could be remetalled in one setting.

### Main-bearing Reamer

Formerly, main bearings were finished completely by hand scraping, after the cylinder block left the remetalling bench. Later a reamer bar, with three cutters, and located by bearings on machined face of cylinder block, reamed out all three bearings at once and thus saved a great deal of time at the bearing bench.

### Big-end Jig and Reamer

Big ends were formerly reamed out singly. Latterly a plate on which was fixed a bracket for holding four connecting rods, in addition to two bearings through which passed a mandril (fitted with a reamer), enabled the operator to ream out four rods in one setting.

### Front- and Rear-spring Spreader Bar

(To fit front and rear springs to chassis in erecting shop.) Previously it required four men to stand on the chassis, in order to compress the spring sufficiently to fit shackles. A spreader bar has been made, having a right- and left-hand thread with a turn buckle. The ends of the bar are placed in the neck of both spring eyes, and with a few turns at the turnbuckle it is now possible for one man alone to fit any spring.

## Forging Tools

(Tools for making Ford front and rear cross members.) Apart from the repair of broken members, new members had to be made to replace those lost or badly damaged. For this tools have been forged to the shape of the members, hinged at one end, and the top member has a long leverage to give the necessary pressure. When in position the flanges of the cross member are hammered into shape.

## Ford Crankcase Suspension Arms

Owing to so many of these being broken and not being procurable, a jig was made and new arms forged. This proved very satisfactory, the metal used being 3-inch by $\frac{3}{8}$-inch mild steel.

The Ford crankcases coming in for overhaul were found to be twisted badly, but this was overcome by making a jig of two "H" iron girders coupled together, with studs inserted on the face, so that after repair the pans could be laid on the jig and tested before being bolted up to the engine block.

This saved a lot of time in the erection of an engine.

## Repair to Ford Axle Shafts

To meet the demand for Ford rear axle shafts, two serviceable ones were made from three scrap axles. This was achieved by cutting off the tapered end of each shaft and welding another piece on the differential end of same. These axles have been tested under all road conditions and proved sound.

## Arab Labour

In order that Arab labour could be employed to a greater extent, various jigs and templates have been made, so as to ensure the necessary standard of work being turned out and thus increase the output. This refers in particular to the making of Ford stock parts; also the lengthening and altering of spring clips, spring hangers, etc.

## Spring Heating Furnace

In the manufacture of laminated springs, it is essential that uniform heat be obtained, especially for hardening and tempering of the leaves. Previous to the building of this furnace, the only method of heating springs was by means of smith's hearth fire, or a prepared wood fire. This was unsatisfactory, for these various reasons:

1. The uncertainty of the uniform heat.
2. The waste of time.
3. The maintenance of fire. In the case of a wood fire, fuel was scarce.

An oil-fired furnace was therefore designed with a heat chamber 7 feet 6 inches long, 2 feet wide, and 15 inches deep, fire-brick lined, and reinforced with steel work. Fuel was gravity fed to jet, and sprayed into the furnace under compressed-air blast. The fuel itself was ordinary crude oil, and the compressors converted Ford engines.

The flame passes over the work-floor of furnace, and, travelling the whole length of heat-chamber, passes up the stack. The furnace door was operated by means of a weight attached to a cable passing over pulleys and down the sides of the furnace.

Very little time is expended in getting the furnace to working heat, when a continuous cycle of work could be maintained, with first-class results and creditable output. All that is necessary to start the furnace is a piece of waste soaked in paraffin and thrown lighted into the heat-chamber. When the furnace was up, a clear vision of the work inside was obtained.

### Tinsmiths

To eradicate faulty work being turned out in the repair of radiators, a system was in vogue for testing, by means of a large square tank partly filled with water. After a radiator had been repaired, the bottom outlet was sealed, and the filler cap was connected to a tyre pump. When screwed down, the radiator was submerged and air pumped in at about 6 lb. pressure. If leaking, the exact spot can be located immediately, thereby saving much valuable time. Owing to the entire lack of a supply of tubes for the repair of radiators at one time, unserviceable radiators were dissected, all unserviceable tubes removed, and these were used to make serviceable radiators. This enabled every radiator to be given its full cooling capacity.

### Vulcanising Department

To enable repairs to large outer covers to be undertaken when the canvas casing was burst, a mandril was made, suitable for taking 880 by 120 and 895 by 135 covers. This mandril had to stand a working steam pressure of 100 lb., which meant that covers could be repaired which otherwise would have been scrapped. Jointless joints, inside and outside, have been made suitable for all sizes of tubes. Good sections were cut from scrap tubes, and these jointed together made serviceable ones. To meet the demand for rubber hose water joints, of which 30 feet to 40 feet were required weekly, rubber from scrap tubes and canvas from scrap covers were utilised, the canvas being laid between two surfaces of rubber.

### Saflux

This solution was unavailable for some considerable time, and to meet the situation all the plastene cuttings were saved, and to every pound was added one gallon of petrol, which makes excellent substitute, and was sufficient to repair 400 to 500 tubes, or 15 to 20 covers, according to condition.

### Foundry Oil-fired Crucible Furnace

This furnace was designed to meet the requirements of the foundry, whose previous means of melting was by the coke fire. It was a brick-built structure, reinforced by steel work, and accommodated two crucible pots. The crucible chambers were connected by flues. It was oil-fired by means of two jets, which were gravity fed, the oil being carried into the furnace in a spray by compressed air supplied by an air compressor, converted from a Ford engine.

The flame, after encircling the crucible, passed from one chamber into the other, and rising to the top of the furnace again passed through the flue which surrounded an oven in which cores were dried. The drying of cores had previously been a source of trouble, and this oven obviated this.

The crucibles are of 60, 90, and 120 lb., and six per day—three heats—could be obtained.

The furnace itself stood only 1 foot out of the ground, enabling a safe and speedy removal of the crucibles and an easy loading and examination of these under heat.

Front radius rods of Fords were giving great trouble, through the splitting of the tube when the latter was bent as a result of a collision, etc., and it was found that, owing to the tube being of the lapped welded type, it was not possible to repair it. In order to overcome this, steel barrels, taken from the rifles captured from the enemy, were used in lieu of the tubes on the front radius rod. This substitution was quite successful.

### Description of New Type of Ford Front Spring as manufactured at the Advanced M.T. Depôt

This spring has been designed to eliminate the use of the centre bolt, it being estimated that 75 per cent. of front spring breakages occurred at the centre bolt hole, the weakest part of the spring.

Each leaf of the new type of spring is rippled or curved

⅜ inch in the centre, and the special designed pad, or distance piece, is fitted between the top of the spring and the front cross member. When the spring is bolted into position by means of spring "U" clips, the ripple in the leaves prevents the leaves getting out of alignment.

### Bronze Emergency Bearings

It was necessary to manufacture these for Ford front wheels, owing to the failure of the ball races and the shortage of the necessary replacements. These bronze bearings are used in substitution of the outer race and the balls, and are inserted into the hub and adjusted by the inner cone. If well lubricated they will answer quite satisfactorily for a time, if used only for emergency purposes.

It was essential, in view of the output required from the Advanced M.T. Depôt, to save time and labour in every possible way. Ideas and improvements proved to be sound were taken into use at once. A number of these could not be undertaken in the small mobile workshops of M.T. companies, yet at the same time various officers were able to turn out a limited number of different articles for the use of their own units, and send in samples for inspection. All worked hard to keep their vehicles on the road. When the latter were eventually sent into Baghdad, they were completely overhauled, and all the latest improvements embraced. In this way O.C. units would have the up-to-date sample of what the vehicle should be like, and when time permitted they took the matter in hand themselves. I think this chapter will give my readers some slight idea of the resourcefulness of the O.C. Advanced M.T. Depôt, Lieutenant-Colonel Carty, O.B.E., M.C., and the numerous workshop officers employed under him, in addition to that of the workshop officers, etc., of the mobile units, who were responsible for some of the ideas.

## CHAPTER XV

### SOME LESSONS FROM THE CAMPAIGN

General policy—Provision of men—Type of vehicle—Labour—Salvage.

One could almost write a book upon the subject-matter of this chapter alone. It is not my intention, however, to go into very great detail, but merely to point out what should be considered as outstanding points which require attention in conducting such a campaign.

It is not for me to start to lay down hard-and-fast rules: this, in any case, would be almost impossible. Situations have had to be met as they arose and difficulties unforeseen had to be overcome. I do not wish my readers to run away with the idea that this book is written with the object of making destructive criticism on various points. Such is not the case. It is merely intended as a narrative of the doings of Mechanical Transport in a country the difficulties of which were unknown from that point of view. It is necessary in places to point out the shortage of spare parts, but this was equally well known to the authorities at home. It also showed how the M.T. overcame such difficulties.

We in our little corner of this great world-war naturally thought that the fate of the world hung on the result of the Mesopotamian campaign, and could not understand why various delays occurred with regard to delivery of vehicles and spares.

It is essential to look at this from a broad and central point of view. In a war such as this, and where mechanical transport was so universally employed, it was absolutely necessary to control supplies from one central head. This central power is alone capable of knowing which of the various battle-fronts is the most important. It is quite possible, and, as a matter of fact, it happened on more than one occasion, that vehicles, etc., intended for Mesopotamia, even after being loaded, had to be transferred to another front. The shipping difficulty was also known to be great.

It must, therefore, be thoroughly realised that though I make certain remarks which doubtless are open to criticism, I was fully aware of the difficulties which the home authorities were up against, and that it was not possible at the time to send out what was apparently required, nor was it the wisest course to pursue. Had all our demands been met at once, irrespective of other Fronts and shipping difficulties, we should have been better off. But a serious disaster might have befallen our army or armies in another theatre of war.

My readers must remember that though relating facts about this campaign from my own point of view, I was fully aware of the reasons why certain things were not forthcoming. The War Office were also aware of our needs, but they were the only people who could judge the relative importance of all demands, and when our importance reached the "top of the house," so our demands began to be satisfied.

The difficulties of keeping the vehicles on the roads were ours, and I can again congratulate all officers and other ranks on the way they worked to overcome their troubles. Critical remarks, therefore, are not to be taken as destructive, but merely to show the difficulties. It is hoped that points brought to light may be of assistance to officers in the future. Remarks which are made intending to point out mistakes are merely a matter of opinion, and I am perfectly convinced in my own mind that excellent reasons can be given as to why a certain number of what would appear to be unpardonable omissions were ever allowed.

One fact, however, must not be forgotten. The chief M.T. vehicle in use for transport purposes in this campaign was the Ford, an American car, as all of my readers are well aware. Thus America had to be depended on for a supply of spares—both vehicles and parts. The difficulty of supply owing to shipping in the first two years of the war was great, and when America herself entered the war, this difficulty must have been multiplied tenfold.

England, for centuries past, has always been in the forefront of the battle, so to speak, whether on land or sea. She has constantly been engaged in small wars—one might almost describe it as constant mimic warfare when compared with the gigantic struggle from which the Empire as a whole has emerged triumphantly.

Mistakes have always been made. England has won her battles through mistakes, but on looking back, can it be said that she has profited much by these same mistakes ?

They are noted, written down, talked about by the professional soldier, seriously discussed at various conferences, and all to what end ?

We had, prior to 1914, a small army of what can only be described as mercenaries, controlled entirely by civilians, who regulated the purse according to circumstances. The purse being a national emergency, every one combined (more or less) to prevent the downfall of the Empire.

Mistakes, therefore, which occurred during a campaign are lost sight of once that campaign is over. There appears to be no reason for rectifying them. We get lulled once more into a sense of false security, and though the soldier tries his best to remedy them, his hands are more or less tied. Rectification generally means expenditure, and this is curtailed because of the above-mentioned fact.

Now to proceed. It has been stated that war in the first place is a matter of transport ; secondly, of supply ; and thirdly, destruction.

The utilisation of mechanical transport in this great war was universal. It had been foreseen for some years past, but not to the extent to which it was eventually employed. As Armageddon spread to other countries, so mechanical transport grew in bulk,

Mesopotamia, from a Mechanical Transport point of view, was entirely an experiment. The campaign was undertaken by India, presumably under orders from the War Office, and once these orders had been given it was left entirely to India to organise and equip the necessary force. When necessary, they could apply to the mother country for help.

It was a big job for India—a country which, since the Mutiny, had only been concerned with frontier fights and small expeditions. Everything India did was on a cheese-paring scale, though doubtless there were very good reasons for it. It would appear that India was looked upon by the home authorities as a country which was quite capable of conducting a strong and possibly long campaign against the Turkish forces in Mesopotamia.

The original force, as we know, was inadequate in every respect, and was apparently not very well equipped.

It was successful in the initial stages, and the one bright spot of the whole war was our success in Mesopotamia ! ! This force advanced almost to Baghdad. Even had it succeeded, Baghdad could never have been held. It retired after the battle of Ctesiphon, where it could not reap the results of a victory, and was locked up in Kut. And everybody knows what happened after that.

The whole expedition, naturally, was not finished, but the first phase of the campaign was over, and any further force sent out was really a new expedition, though a lot of people do not look at it in this light.

The original force which came out had one or two motor cars and half a dozen motor ambulances. For the rest, they depended on the transport as used in India for years past. Practically all the motor vehicles which came out with the original force were lost. It was seen, however, that during certain seasons of the year it was possible to run motors over the whole country. This, though more or less unknown, was similar over all parts. Efforts were then made to get mechanical transport, and this naturally had to be got from England. Beyond motor cars, India had nothing to fall back upon, or, at any rate, nothing useful in any numbers.

I understand that a certain officer, when making out a scheme for the employment of mechanical transport, put down on paper that the services of a good mechanic with the acting rank of staff-sergeant should be obtained. I believe the scheme got no farther than his office, as one or two officers recognised the fact that something larger would have to be attempted. When it was decided to utilise motor transport, some experienced officers should have been sent out to reconnoitre all occupied territory, and to fix on a type of vehicle for future use. This was not done, however, and the campaign went slowly on. A few ambulances were ordered. A company of 30-cwt. lorries was asked for in 1915, and obtained. They were Peerless!

A motor ambulance convoy was requisitioned and arrived, composed of Star ambulances. There was no defined policy behind all this. It was a case of, What shall we ask for next?—or something very similar.

### Base M.T. Depôt

Here again, with regard to this unit, something definite should have been done at the time it was dispatched, in view of the fact that no experienced M.T. officers were available in the country. It was most essential that a unit with main repair shops and stores branch for the whole force should have had provision made for their quick disembarkation and immediate housing. It was the quickness with which it could be got to work that the efficiency of the Mechanical Transport in the country depended.

All the foregoing can be grouped under one heading. The lesson we learn is that it is necessary to adopt some policy before making any decision with regard to the employment of mechanical transport in a country about which very little is known.

### Personnel

We have learned one of the greatest lessons, under this heading, which includes the provision of skilled drivers and tradesmen. It must have been foreseen, by those in the know, that man-power was going to be one of the greatest factors in the war, and that in view of the enormous amount of mechanical transport in use, the provision of drivers and tradesmen would eventually become extremely acute.

The Indians were not altogether unknown. Some had been in France, and though not considered good drivers for the various makes of vehicles that they were put on, they showed promise.

There were numerous taxi drivers and private chauffeurs employed in India. The whole question of training this type of man was left until it was absolutely imperative, owing to there being no British personnel available, to begin training them. This problem might have been tackled earlier.

India as a recruiting-ground offered tremendous possibilities. The employment of mechanical transport had been under discussion for some years past, so the provision of M.T. drivers for an Indian Expeditionary Force ought to have occupied a prominent place in their organisation. It was not until the end of 1917 that any great efforts were made to train the Indian. The process of training was taken up in a rough-and-ready manner, and when the Indians arrived they were untrained.

If definite instructions had been issued, early in 1917, that no more British reinforcements were available, and that India would have to assist, the matter could have been placed on a good footing by the middle of 1917. A steady stream of reinforcements of properly trained, clothed, and equipped Indians would soon have been forthcoming.

### Provision of Spare Parts

When it has been decided to send mechanical transport in any numbers to any campaign, the provision of spare parts should be assured, more especially so when one is dealing with a country in which there are no roads. Allowances, too, should be made for trying climatic conditions.

This force has suffered throughout from a lack of spare parts, the majority of which under ordinary circumstances would have been forthcoming almost simultaneously with the vehicle itself. It is only now, in the beginning of 1919, that spare parts for Ford vehicles indented for in the early part of the previous year are beginning to arrive in any quantities; but knowing the difficulties of the home authorities, it is not surprising.

### Bridges

As soon as it became known that certain types of vehicles were coming out, special bridges should have been made to enable all types of M.T. vehicles to cross either rivers or streams on the line of advance. I mention this especially with regard to the River Hai, over which neither Peerless lorries nor "caterpillars" could proceed. A special barge had to be provided for these vehicles, and later on they were camped at Shumran Bend and took no further part in the advance on Baghdad.

### Roads

I think one of the great lessons learned by everybody, whether with or without a knowledge of mechanical transport, has been the extreme importance and necessity for a thorough provision and upkeep of proper roads. The damage done to mechanical transport vehicles out here has been enormous, because the roads were never properly maintained until 1918.

The difficulties, of course, were numerous, and, as mentioned in a previous chapter, when water is unobtainable the maintenance of roads in Mesopotamia is almost an impossibility. Wells can, however, be dug, and even a large expenditure of money on native labour is more than amply repaid by the efficient working of mechanical transport.

When one is dealing with roads composed of nothing but ground cut off the desert, it is most essential that whenever possible motor roads should be confined to motors alone, and no other type of transport allowed thereon.

### Reinforcements

It is considered that when Mechanical Transport companies are sent out to a country, the necessary number of reinforcements should also be sent in the shape of replacement vehicles.

From the moment an M.T. company takes the field with new vehicles, its workshops begin their proper functions. Because a unit arrives in the country with 130 new vehicles, it is not correct to think that workshops have no work to do until the vehicles show signs of deterioration. Full provision has to be made for its spares and heavy workshop facilities. Casualties must be looked for immediately, and as soon as these occur, the replacement vehicle must be ready in the country.

In addition to the ordinary reinforcements, a percentage over and above those should always be asked for to assist in coping with any small new establishment which may be sanctioned locally, and for which no provision has been made. It might be said that the average time taken to get out vehicles to Mesopotamia after ordering is about nine months, and one can readily appreciate the difficulty of carrying on under such conditions.

The demands from Mesopotamia no doubt at some time upset the authorities at home. But there is one great point about this campaign which cannot occur in any European country. There were no local facilities for repair, and practically no buildings available until Baghdad was reached. No materials suitable for repair to M.T. vehicles were forthcoming in the country, which was a great handicap to the force.

These remarks are embraced here with a view to their

being considered in the event of a further expedition into what might be described as a barren country.

Once Baghdad was reached, material was available, but it was very soon utilised.

## Types of Vehicles

This campaign has shown the necessity for reducing the number of types of M.T. vehicles employed. It would appear essential that any Mechanical Transport Committee which may have the handling of future transport for war should concentrate on producing more or less a standard type of vehicle on the following lines:

1. Three-ton lorry.
2. One-ton lorry (pneumatic tyres).
3. Ten-cwt. lorry (pneumatic tyres).
4. Standard touring car.

Without going into the different types of technical vehicles, such as anti-aircraft lorries, "caterpillars," etc., the above should meet all requirements from a Supply and Transport point of view.

The three-ton lorry is suitable in all countries where there is any attempt at macadamising roads, or even in desert country, such as Mesopotamia, during dry weather.

The original idea for having a 30-cwt. vehicle for the Cavalry, owing to its lightness, might now be washed out.

Three-ton lorries could travel out and feed the Cavalry, and even if there are bridges blown up, it is considered that the time taken to build a temporary bridge capable of taking a three-ton lorry would not be much longer than that to build one to take a 30-cwt. lorry. In any case, there would always be the one-ton pneumatic-tyred lorry to fall back upon. The one-ton lorry fitted with pneumatic tyres could be utilised for all arms, and over any country where Mechanical Transport is able to work. These could also be utilised as workshops for the light van companies, composed of vehicles of their own type.

The van of the 10-cwt. type—by 10-cwt. I mean a useful load—for a journey of 100 miles in a day over average roads is a type of vehicle which could feed many men. They could be utilised for the rapid dispatch of supplies to Cavalry and the rapid transport of troops. They could also be organised as Lewis gun companies, water columns, etc., over practically any type of country.

It is considered that a vehicle such as the Ford redesigned would be most suitable. The redesigning should include the following improvements:

1. Strengthened frame.
2. Differently designed and strengthened springs.
3. Strengthened back axle.
4. Strengthened engine lugs.
5. Stronger rear hubs.

There is no need to go into the facilities and provision of spare parts when dealing with standardised vehicles. It is essential that, when once this standard vehicle is built, a definite period should be laid down for its Army life, and no remodelling introduced for a period of five years, during which time any new improvements which are brought into the Mechanical Transport engineering world can be embodied, discussed, and finally decided upon. At the end of this period, all the vehicles in use should be scrapped. It would be far more economical than trying to keep them on the road.

The above proposition should not affect civilian firms engaged upon the manufacture of mechanical transport vehicles. It should be just as easy for them to make a standard vehicle as to make their own, and civil firms, who would be subsidised, also under the scheme, would have their choice of the three different types as a means of transport in England.

As vehicles were manufactured, so the necessary percentage of spare parts could also be made, whether for civilian firms or the War Department. If necessary, the makers could be subsidised as regards the upkeep of these. This is merely a question of organisation and manufacture.

The same can be said for motor cycles. A standard type should be introduced and adhered to.

The Douglas and Triumph during the campaign have proved their worth, but no doubt there are other makes which would have done equally as well. From an output point of view, smaller firms had to take a back seat, and it was necessary to standardise on two firms which were capable of giving the necessary output. As regards standardising the motor cycle, this is also merely a question of organisation.

### Labour

It is most essential that when a force proceeds to operate in a country such as this a Labour Bureau should at once be established, and all skilled and unskilled men should be registered and classified at the earliest possible moment.

Local conditions always necessitate the provision of more labour than is actually laid down by War Establishments, and it is necessary to have an army of local tradesmen to cope with this. It should not be left to departments to try to recruit tradesmen, and thus vie with each other in a so-called labour market. The question of labour in this campaign was well handled, but was taken up too late; this was no fault of the Director of Labour, but more the fault of a policy that did not foresee the ultimate requirements of this force.

### Salvage

One great lesson which the British nation as a whole has learned is the need for economy. Numerous have been the instructions issued from this Directorate with reference to the conserving of spare parts, all classes of material, and the return of all unserviceable parts. It is most essential that a good organisation should be forthcoming for dealing with those returns.

For some time the Returns Section in this country was part and parcel of the Base M.T. Depôt, which had its Advanced Section at Baghdad. It was found more economical to put this section under the Advanced M.T. Depôt dealing with workshops, and was therefore in a better position to provide the necessary skilled personnel as scrutineers.

A full report has already been rendered with regard to the salvage operations conducted here from a Mechanical Transport point of view, but it might be interesting to relate here the actual value of the spare parts which were reclaimed.

During the year 1917 and the early part of 1918 the value of the parts reclaimed—i.e. spare parts, tyres, etc.—was approximately £9,000. The value between June and September 1918 was also £9,000. Between September and December 31, 1918, it amounted to £17,000, making a grand total up to date of £35,000, reclaimed on what to outside units were unserviceable articles.

This did not by any means represent the actual gain to this force, for the value of spare parts, at a time when there was a great shortage, can hardly be counted in terms of £ s. d. This amount, £35,000, naturally represents the value of the article. This has been taken from catalogues three or four years old, and is not at all the real cash value of the articles in question, so far away from the source of supply.

The Returns Section does not merely comprise the taking in of unserviceable assemblies, sorting them out, and putting the good parts on one side for future use. It should also be capable of handling and dealing with unserviceable parts and putting them into a fit state for repair. Companies in the field are unable to tackle this. It is, therefore, essential that a Returns Section should be part and parcel of some workshop organisation, and not part of the Stores Section.

The above are considered the main lessons which have been learned, and which require attention in future campaigns. There are a number of minor ones, from the A.S.C.

M.T. Company point of view, but it is not intended to go into them.

I think that all officers who have been through this campaign will be thoroughly qualified to undertake a similar campaign should it be necessary.

# M.T. (R.A.S.C.) IN L

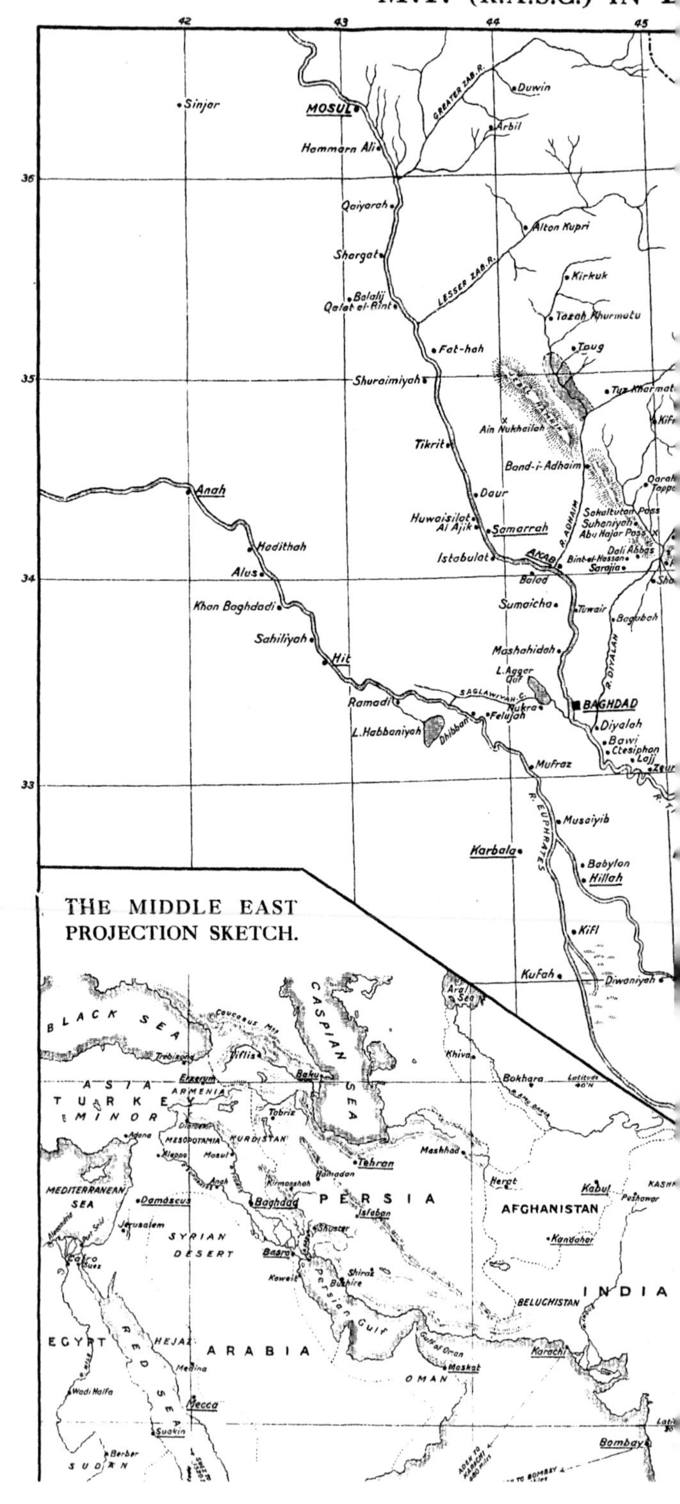

42
43
44
45
36
35
34
33
Sinjar
MOSUL
Hammam Ali
GREATER ZAB R.
Duwin
Arbil
Qaiyarah
Altun Kupri
Shargat
LESSER ZAB R.
Kirkuk
Balalij
Qalat el-Bint
Tazah Khurmutu
Fat-hah
Taug
Shuraimiyah
Tuz Khurmatu
Ain Nukhailah
Tikrit
Band-i-Adhaim
Anah
Daur
Huwaisilat
Al Ajik
Samarrah
R. ADHAIM
Sakaltutan Pass
Suhaniyah
Abu Hajar Pass
Dali Abbas
Hadithah
Istabulat
Akab
Bint-el-Hassan
Sarajia
Alus
Balad
Khan Baghdadi
Sumaicha
Tuwair
Baqubah
Sahiliyah
Mashahidah
R. DIYALAH
Hit
L. Aqqar Quf
SAGLAWIYAH C.
Ramadi
Rukra
BAGHDAD
Dhibban
Felujah
Diyalah
L. Habbaniyah
Bawi
Ctesiphon
Lajj
Mufraz
R. EUPHRATES
Musaiyib
Karbala
Babylon
Hillah
Kifl
Kufah
Diwaniyah
THE MIDDLE EAST
PROJECTION SKETCH.
BLACK SEA
CASPIAN SEA
Caucasus Mts
Aral Sea
Trebizond
Tiflis
Khiva
Erzerum
Baku
Bokhara
Latitude 40°N
ASIA
TURKEY
MINOR
ARMENIA
Tabriz
Adana
MESOPOTAMIA
KURDISTAN
Aleppo
Mosul
Mashhad
Tehran
Hamadan
MEDITERRANEAN SEA
Damascus
Anah
Kirmanshah
Baghdad
PERSIA
Herat
Kabul
Peshawar
Isfahan
AFGHANISTAN
Jerusalem
Port Said
SYRIAN
DESERT
Shuster
Kandahar
Cairo
Suez
Basra
Koweit
Shiraz
Bushire
Persian Gulf
BELUCHISTAN
INDIA
EGYPT
RED SEA
HEJAZ
ARABIA
Gulf of Oman
Karachi
Medina
Maskat
OMAN
Wadi Halfa
Mecca
Suakin
Bombay
Berber
SUDAN

VER MESOPOTAMIA.

# CHAPTER XVI

## Honours and Awards

List of Awards to Officers, N.C.O.s, and Men—Letters of appreciation concerning the good work done on various occasions by the M.T. formations, etc.

Given in this chapter is a list of honours and awards earned by officers and men of the A.S.C. M.T. during the campaign in Mesopotamia.

This list is made up to the middle of 1919. There may be one, or possibly two, further lists published between the time of writing this book and the date of its publication, and it is regretted that it will be impossible under the circumstances to add those names. It is hoped that any officers, N.C.O.s, and men whose names have not been included will accept my apology and regret for their non-inclusion. Occasionally it happens that names have been omitted from *Gazettes*, and the errors rectified later on. Possibly a few names are missing for that reason. The lists have, however, been carefully checked, and it is hoped that all names are correct. Even official lists have numerous errors, such as initials, numbers, etc. Should there be any of these, I trust my readers will pardon me.

| Regt. No. | Rank and Name. | Date of Award. | Order of the Day Number. | Award. |
|---|---|---|---|---|
| | Lt.-Col. Archibald, G. K. | 15.8.17 | — | Mentioned in Dispatches. |
| | ,, Pelly, G. E. | ,, | — | ,, |
| | ,, Gibbons, J. N. | ,, | — | ,, |
| | Major Dickinson, R. P. | ,, | — | ,, |
| | ,, Owen, A. D. | ,, | — | ,, |
| | ,, Reynolds, H. J. B. | ,, | — | ,, |
| | ,, Sykes, R. C. | ,, | — | ,, |

| Regt. No. | Rank and Name. | Date of Award. | Order of the Day Number. | Award. |
|---|---|---|---|---|
| | Capt. Brown, D. A. G. | 15.8.17 | — | Mentioned in Dispatches. |
| | ,, Collings, W. A. | ,, | — | ,, |
| | ,, Vlasto, I. T. | ,, | — | ,, |
| MS/591 | M.S.M. Beckett, A. | ,, | — | ,, |
| M2/048139 | ,, Pellet, T. O. | ,, | — | ,, |
| M/26967 | ,, Stickland, G. J. | ,, | — | ,, |
| M2/021234 | Cpl. Elkin, W. | ,, | — | ,, |
| DM2/131263 | Pte. Mair, M. | ,, | — | ,, |
| | Lt.-Col. Pelly, E. G. | 12.3.18 | — | ,, |
| | Major Sykes, R. C. | ,, | — | ,, |
| | ,, Winlaw, W. W. | ,, | — | ,, |
| | Capt. Aldham, M. S. | ,, | — | ,, |
| | ,, Appleton, A. | ,, | — | ,, |
| | ,, Beard, A. G. W. | ,, | — | ,, |
| | ,, Evans, T. | ,, | — | ,, |
| | ,, Thresh, A. | ,, | — | ,, |
| | Lieut. White, T. L. | ,, | — | ,, |
| M2/020974 | Sergt. Lancaster, R. G. | ,, | — | ,, |
| DM2/180263 | ,, Thomson, C. G. | ,, | — | ,, |
| M2/152572 | ,, Weller, W. | ,, | — | ,, |
| DM2/189500 | Pte. Chellew, J. H. | ,, | — | ,, |
| M2/194918 | ,, Halford, J. | ,, | — | ,, |
| M2/204259 | ,, Harrison, W. | ,, | — | ,, |
| M2/202307 | ,, Hopcroft, F. G. | ,, | — | ,, |
| M2/194535 | ,, Kaye, F. L. | ,, | — | ,, |
| | Lt.-Col. Archibald, G. K. | 27.8.18 | — | ,, |
| | ,, Snepp, E. | ,, | — | ,, |
| | Major Gray, V. S. | ,, | — | ,, |
| | ,, John, N. S. | ,, | — | ,, |
| | ,, Murray, C. de G. | ,, | — | ,, |
| | ,, Parker, E. C. L. | ,, | — | ,, |
| | ,, Reynolds, H. J. B. | ,, | — | ,, |
| | ,, Ray, S. F. | ,, | — | ,, |
| | ,, Rolfe, T. F. W. | ,, | — | ,, |
| | ,, Vallat, F. W. | ,, | — | ,, |
| | ,, Wood, E. B. | ,, | — | ,, |
| | Capt. Broadbent, J. S. | ,, | — | ,, |
| | ,, Brown, D. A. G. | ,, | — | ,, |
| | ,, Ingram, J. S. | ,, | — | ,, |
| | ,, Shurmur, S. E. | ,, | — | ,, |
| | ,, Smith, C. L. R. | ,, | — | ,, |
| | ,, Thresh, A. | ,, | — | ,, |
| | ,, Vlasto, I. T. | ,, | — | ,, |
| | Lieut. Williams, R. H. | ,, | — | ,, |
| | 2nd Lt. Pearson, E. H. G. | ,, | — | ,, |
| | ,, Penman, V. R. | ,, | — | ,, |
| | ,, Hussey, H. N. | ,, | — | ,, |
| | ,, White, J. W. E. | ,, | — | ,, |
| M1/5457 | C.S.M. Atkinson, R. C. | ,, | — | ,, |
| M2/178364 | ,, Blount, A. | ,, | — | ,, |
| M2/201635 | ,, Gordon, J. | ,, | — | ,, |
| M/37387 | ,, Neville, F. | ,, | — | ,, |

| Regt. No. | Rank and Name. | Date of Award. | Order of the Day Number. | Award. |
|---|---|---|---|---|
| M/280878 | M.S.M. Milton, W. J. | 27.8.18 | — | Mentioned in Dispatches. |
| M/22747 | ,, Parsons, G. O. | ,, | — | ,, |
| M2/149171 | ,, Still, F. W. | ,, | — | ,, |
| M2/203394 | C.Q.M.S. Binks, J. | ,, | — | ,, |
| M/25558 | ,, Shields, H. R. | ,, | — | ,, |
| M1/05876 | M.S.S. Foxton, J. J. | ,, | — | ,, |
| M1/5796 | ,, Kilgour, S. | ,, | — | ,, |
| M2/131751 | ,, Lindsey, H. V. | ,, | — | ,, |
| M2/131644 | Sergt. Bulley, J. | ,, | — | ,, |
| M2/148823 | ,, Butt, S. A. | ,, | — | ,, |
| DM2/179120 | ,, Campbell, G. | ,, | — | ,, |
| M2/204251 | ,, Fox, H. | ,, | — | ,, |
| M/316417 | ,, Grenville Morgan, P. G. | ,, | — | ,, |
| M/282704 | ,, Hodgson, M. C. L. | ,, | — | ,, |
| M2/131676 | ,, Kendall, F. G. | ,, | — | ,, |
| M2/131263 | ,, Mair, M. | ,, | — | ,, |
| M2/131602 | ,, Mason, G. L. | ,, | — | ,, |
| M/20536 0 | ,, Shields, E. G. B. | ,, | — | ,, |
| M2/121040 | ,, Smith, W. | ,, | — | ,, |
| M2/131500 | ,, Ward, R. V. | ,, | — | ,, |
| M2/223613 | ,, Wells, W. R. | ,, | — | ,, |
| M2/079503 | ,, Winter, G. V. | ,, | — | ,, |
| M2/131572 | ,, Woods, C. K. | ,, | — | ,, |
| DM2/118180 | Cpl. Broughton, A. | ,, | — | ,, |
| M2/131619 | ,, George, R. W. | ,, | — | ,, |
| M2/204259 | ,, Harrison, W. | ,, | — | ,, |
| M2/156852 | ,, Jobbins, V. S. | ,, | — | ,, |
| M2/131586 | ,, Kebble, A. | ,, | — | ,, |
| M2/167955 | ,, Moulton, W. | ,, | — | ,, |
| M2/150837 | ,, Paterson, J. | ,, | — | ,, |
| M2/152816 | ,, Tite, W. G. | ,, | — | ,, |
| M2/267815 | ,, Williams, A. C. | ,, | — | ,, |
| M2/131808 | L/Cpl. Graham, W. G. R. | ,, | — | ,, |
| M2/131433 | ,, Tomlinson, F. H. | ,, | — | ,, |
| M2/279741 | Pte. Budgen, F. C. | ,, | — | ,, |
| M/131682 | ,, Geddes, T. C. | ,, | — | ,, |
| M/221813 | ,, Jones, A. | ,, | — | ,, |
| M2/131776 | ,, MacPherson, E. | ,, | — | ,, |
| M2/194412 | ,, Phillpotts, J. H. | ,, | — | ,, |
| M2/153231 | ,, Pudney, A. E. | ,, | — | ,, |
| M2/153554 | ,, Shillington, V. G. | ,, | — | ,, |
| M2/194296 | ,, Webb, J. B. | ,, | — | ,, |
| M2/194178 | ,, Greening, C. W. | ,, | — | ,, |
| M2/204295 | ,, Lofthouse, W. | ,, | — | ,, |
| M2/204151 | ,, Mann, A. | ,, | — | ,, |
| M2/203262 | ,, Hudson, G. | ,, | — | ,, |
| M2/176052 | Sergt. Dickensen, S. Y. | ,, | — | ,, |
| | Lt.-Col. Archibald, G. K. | *London Gazette* (page 9650) of 17.9.17 | — | D.S.O. |
| | Major Owen, A. D. | ditto | — | ,, |

| Regt. No. | Rank and Name. | Date of Award. | Order of the Day Number. | Award. |
|---|---|---|---|---|
| | Lt.-Col. Pelly, E. G. | 4th Supplement *London Gazette* 5.2.18 | — | D.S.O. |
| | A/Lt.-Col. Snepp, E. | 5th Supplement *London Gazette* 23.8.18 | — | ,, |
| | T/Major Sellwood, F. G. | ditto | — | Military Cross. |
| | A/Capt. Martin, K. B. | ditto | — | ,, |
| | ,, Appleton, A. J. | ditto | — | ,, |
| | ,, Evans, T. | 4th Supplement *London Gazette* 5.2.18 | — | ,, |
| | ,, Beard, A. G. W. | ditto | — | ,, |
| | Lieut. Linnell, F. S. | 5th Supplement *London Gazette* 23.8.18 | — | ,, |
| | ,, White, T. L. | ditto | — | ,, |
| | ,, Vlasto, I. T. | ditto | — | ,, |
| | T/2nd Lt. Watt, G. | 18.11.18 | 123 | Military Cross. |
| | 2nd Lt. Ravenscroft, L. | 5th Supplement *London Gazette* 23. 8.18 | — | ,, |
| | ,, Lampard, S. M. | ditto | — | ,, |
| | ,, Clatworthy, L. A. | ditto | — | ,, |
| | A/Lt.-Col. Archibald, G. K. | ditto | — | To be Brevet Major, with effect from 3.6.18 |
| | Capt. Pelly, E. G. | 20. 4.17 | 71 | Military Cross. |
| M/205046 | C.S.M. Montgomery, J. | 18.11.18 | 123 | Military Medal. |
| M/340542 | Sergt. Campbell, H. J. | ,, | ,, | ,, |
| M2/222790 | ,, Hill, A. | 2. 6.18 | 110 | ,, |
| M2/034581 | A/Sergt. Ofield, J. | 20. 4.17 | 71 | ,, |
| M2/200886 | ,, Stewart, D. R. | ,, | ,, | ,, |
| M2/131363 | Cpl. Bourke, B. (D.C.M.) | 2. 6.18 | 110 | ,, |
| M2/11576 | Pte. Cunliffe, B. | ,, | ,, | ,, |
| M/317344 | ,, Francis, C. | ,, | ,, | ,, |
| M2/052488 | Driver Stuart, S. H. | 30. 8.18 | 116 | ,, |
| M/336614 | Pte. Graham, C. | 8. 9.18 | 117 | ,, |
| M/334383 | ,, Morris, E. H. | 15.11.18 | 122 | ,, |
| M/336706 | ,, Duckworth, T. | 18.11.18 | 123 | ,, |
| 152909 | ,, Goodman, E. M. | ,, | ,, | ,, |
| M2/203830 | ,, Skilbeck, H. | 1.12.18 | 124 | ,, |
| M2/222216 | ,, Sproule, A. J. | ,, | ,, | ,, |
| M2/136150 | ,, Whybrew, P. C. | ,, | ,, | ,, |
| DM2/180263 | Sergt. Thompson, C. G. | 19.12.17 | 96 | Distinguished Conduct Medal. |

| Regt. No. | Rank and Name. | Date of Award. | Order of the Day Number. | Award. |
|---|---|---|---|---|
| M2/135637 | Cpl. Thorne, R. V. | 2. 6.18 | 110 | Distinguished Conduct Medal |
| DM2/112852 | Pte. Winterbottom, F. | 19.12.17 | 96 | ,, |
| M2/193541 | ,, Sheppard, S. | 2. 6.18 | 110 | ,, |
| M2/119282 | ,, Summers, J. | 19.12.17 | 96 | ,, |
| M2/264498 | Pte. A/M.S.M., now 2nd Lt. Garden, W. G. | 4. 8.18 | 114 | Meritorious Service Medal. |
| M2/14917 | M.S.M. Still, F. W. | ,, | ,, | ,, |
| CMT/2581 | ,, Lawson, H. | ,, | ,, | ,, |
| M/22747 | M.S.S., A/M.S.S.M. Parsons, G. O. | ,, | ,, | ,, |
| M2/131751 | Sergt., A/M.S.M. Lindsey, H. V., Attd. M.G. Corps (Motor) | 24.12.18 | 128 | ,, |
| M1/5457 | C.S.M. Atkinson, R. C. | 4. 8.18 | 114 | ,, |
| M2/101378 | ,, Wagger, W. E. | ,, | ,, | ,, |
| 050221 | ,, Jones, F. J. R. | 24.12.18 | 128 | ,, |
| M4/146433 | Cpl., A/M.S.M. Milton, W. J. | 4. 8.18 | 114 | ,, |
| DM2/164935 | C.Q.M.S., A/C.S.M. Tullie, R. J. | ,, | ,, | ,, |
| M2/131348 | Sergt., A/C.S.M. McKay, R. R. | ,, | ,, | ,, |
| M/21247 | Sergt., A/C.S.M. Protheroe, G. A. J. | 24.12.18 | 128 | ,, |
| M2/203394 | C.Q.M.S. Binks, J. | 4. 8.18 | 114 | ,, |
| M2/070183 | ,, Hoggart, M. | ,, | ,, | ,, |
| MS/3901 | Pte., A/C.S.M. Kirby, F. E. | ,, | ,, | ,, |
| M2/105570 | M.S.S. Perrins, C. J. | ,, | ,, | ,, |
| M1/5017 | ,, Sturrock, J. T. | ,, | ,, | ,, |
| M2/115093 | ,, Bunstead, W. E. | 24.12.18 | 128 | ,, |
| M2/137155 | ,, Bond, T. E. | ,, | ,, | ,, |
| M2/113271 | ,, Harrison, J. | ,, | ,, | ,, |
| M2/192915 | ,, Weir, F. C. | ,, | ,, | ,, |
| M2/131644 | Sergt. Bulley, J. | 4. 8.18 | 114 | ,, |
| M2/131741 | ,, Collings, S. | ,, | ,, | ,, |
| M2/115028 | ,, Cook, F. | ,, | ,, | ,, |
| M2/204132 | ,, Wilkinson, H. O. | ,, | ,, | ,, |
| M2/130904 | ,, Harris, R. W. | 24.12.18 | 128 | ,, |
| M2/152208 | ,, Taylor, W. E. | ,, | ,, | ,, |
| C/2559 | Cpl. Fish, R. | 4. 8.18 | 114 | ,, |
| M2/229792 | ,, Armitage, H. V. | 24.12.18 | 128 | ,, |
| M2/053284 | ,, Hickie, D. | ,, | ,, | ,, |
| MS/1855 | ,, Jacklett, J. W. | ,, | ,, | ,, |
| M2/05277 | ,, Littlejohn, W. F. | ,, | ,, | ,, |
| M2/073835 | ,, Montgomery, A. F. | ,, | ,, | ,, |
| M/26976 | Cpl., A/C.S.M. Stickland, G. J. | 29. 4.17 | 72 | ,, |
| M2/131263 | Pte., A/Cpl. Mair, M. | ,, | ,, | ,, |
| M2/204310 | Pte. Kirkham, J. | 24.12.18 | 128 | ,, |
| S4/085610 | S/Sergt. Perkins, J. F. | ,, | ,, | ,, |
| M/314871 | ,, Walmsley, T. | ,, | ,, | ,, |
| M2/137250 | Sergt. Harvey, D. S. | 10 2.18 | 99 | ,, |

As will be seen, the above mentioned have been awarded the Meritorious Service Medal and appeared in various Orders of the Day. There are other recipients of this award, and though I have no record from Orders of the Day, they have been taken from the *London Gazette* Supplement dated September 22, 1919.

M2/178364 C.S.M. Blount, A.
DM2/151213 ,, Browning, W.F.
MS/768 ,, Clark, R.
DM2/163655 ,, Jervis, C. F.
M2/132497 ,, Milne, J. R.
M/100336 C.Q.M.S., A/Mec. S. Sergt. Hilton, G.
M2/204399 Mec. S. Sergt. Barkley, H. G.
MS/2543 ,, Hotchkiss, T. E.
M2/052739 ,, Jackson, W. C.
M/205121 ,, Malcolm, J. A.
M2/119124 ,, Ryott, L. A.
DM2/189498 Sergt. Bell, J. T.
M2/099594 ,, Davis, A.
M2/098668 ,, Dear, L. A.
M2/120782 Sergt., A/M.S.S. Keeton, W. H.
M2/131676 Sergt. Kendell, F. G.
M2/178931 ,, Koller, C. F., M.M.
DM2/097139 ,, Tongue, R. E.
M2/076637 Cpl. Anderson, F. McK.
M2/168016 Pte., A/Lce. Cpl. Carthew, R.
DM2/228042 Pte. Devoy, J.
M/300469 Pte., A/Lce .Cpl. Evans, T.
M2/203726 Pte. Henwood, C. H.
M/036407 ,, Walter, J.

| Regt. No. | Rank and Name. | Date of Award. | Award. |
|---|---|---|---|
| | A/Capt. Ainsworth, A. A. G. | 21.2.19 | Mention. |
| | T/Capt. Appleton, A. J., M.C. | ,, | ,, |
| | ,, Bean, B. C. | ,, | ,, |
| | ,, Brown, D. A. G. | ,, | ,, |
| | T/Lieut. Conway, J. | ,, | ,, |
| | ,, Chippendall, H. T. | ,, | ,, |
| | T/Major Dickinson, R. P. | ,, | ,, |
| | A/Lt.-Col. Dickinson, H. | ,, | ,, |
| | T/2nd Lt. Daniels, P. E. | ,, | ,, |
| | ,, Dashwood, G. B. | ,, | ,, |
| | T/Capt. Forbes-Leith, W. T. | ,, | ,, |
| | A/Capt. Halford, F. | ,, | ,, |
| | T/2nd Lt. Inglis, W. | ,, | ,, |
| | A/Capt. Martin, K. B., M.C. | ,, | ,, |
| | T/Lieut. Martin, G. C. | ,, | ,, |
| | ,, Masser, H. T. | ,, | ,, |
| | T/Major Parker, E. C. L. | ,, | ,, |
| | T/Lieut. Parker, J. S. | ,, | ,, |
| | A/Lt.-Col. Pelly, E. G., D.S.O., M.C. | ,, | ,, |
| | T/Lieut. Penman, V. R. | ,, | ,, |
| | ,, Petrocochino, A. W. | ,, | ,, |
| | A/Major Player, D. W. | ,, | ,, |
| | T/Major Protheroe, A. H., M.C. | ,, | ,, |
| | T/Capt. Smith, C. L. R. | ,, | ,, |

| Regt. No. | Rank and Name. | Date of Award. | Award. |
|---|---|---|---|
| | T/Lieut. Smith, E. | 21.2.19 | Mention |
| | T/2nd Lt. Scott, C. E. T. | ,, | ,, |
| | A/Major Tobey, G. D. | ,, | ,, |
| | ,, Wright, L. A. W. | ,, | ,, |
| | T/Capt. Ward, R. M. B. | ,, | ,, |
| | T/Lieut. Whatley, L. S. | ,, | ,, |
| | T/2nd Lt. Wisbey, H. | ,, | ,, |
| M/340606 | Pte. Alexander, D. S. | ,, | ,, |
| M2/178364 | C.S.M. Blount, A. | ,, | ,, |
| M2/137455 | M.S.S. Bond, T. | ,, | ,, |
| DM2/179298 | Pte. Bourne, J. S. | ,, | ,, |
| M2/101518 | Sergt. Bord, C. G. (attached M.G. Motors) | ,, | ,, |
| M/303185 | Pte. Boyes, W. C. | ,, | ,, |
| DM2/151213 | C.S.M. Browning, W. | ,, | ,, |
| M2/188328 | L/Cpl. Burton, A. (attached M.G. Motors) | ,, | ,, |
| DM2/195066 | Pte. Chambers, H. E. | ,, | ,, |
| MS/1600 | Sergt. Cockings, P. H. | ,, | ,, |
| M2/204233 | Pte. Cochrane, W. | ,, | ,, |
| M2/073879 | M.S.S. Davey, T. | ,, | ,, |
| MS/1212 | C.S.M. Downs, F. R. | ,, | ,, |
| M/346839 | Sergt. French, C. H. | ,, | ,, |
| MS/1581 | M.S.S. Garrett, W. L. | ,, | ,, |
| M2/316417 | Sergt. Grenville Morgan, R. G. | ,, | ,, |
| CMT/261 | Cpl. Griffin, A. | ,, | ,, |
| M/302020 | ,, Griffiths, T. J. | ,, | ,, |
| M/222451 | Pte. Hall, J. | ,, | ,, |
| M2/113271 | M.S.S. Harrison, J. | ,, | ,, |
| M2/204259 | A/Cpl. Harrison, W. | ,, | ,, |
| M2/203726 | Pte. Henwood, C. H. | ,, | ,, |
| M2/167915 | A/Cpl. Hodges, A. E. | ,, | ,, |
| MS/2543 | M.S.S. Hotchkiss, T. E. | ,, | ,, |
| M2/052739 | ,, Jackson, W. C. (attached M.G. Motors) | ,, | ,, |
| M2/156852 | Cpl. Jobbins, V. | ,, | ,, |
| M2/273129 | Pte., A/C.S.M. Kemp, W. | ,, | ,, |
| M/303089 | Pte. Kirkham, F. | ,, | ,, |
| DM2/151329 | Sergt. MacKenzie, B. | ,, | ,, |
| M2/131602 | ,, Mason, G. L. | ,, | ,, |
| DM2/180515 | L/Cpl. Morgan, W. P. J. | ,, | ,, |
| DM2/195575 | Pte. Postlewhite, J. | ,, | ,, |
| M/21247 | Sergt., A/C.S.M. Protheroe, G. A. J. | ,, | ,, |
| M2/222011 | Cpl. Reynolds, G. A. | ,, | ,, |
| DM2/228348 | Pte. Rippon, J. W. | ,, | ,, |
| M2/133551 | S. Sergt. Rose, E. C. | ,, | ,, |
| M2/018908 | Sergt. Sherrington, W. | ,, | ,, |
| M/25558 | Cpl., A/C.Q.M.S. Shields, H. R. | ,, | ,, |
| M/318706 | L/Cpl. Shroder, F. C. | ,, | ,, |
| M/328005 | Pte. Smith, A. G. | ,, | ,, |
| M2/175081 | Pte., A/Cpl. Smith, G. F. S. | ,, | ,, |

| Regt. No. | Rank and Name. | Date of Award. | Award. |
|---|---|---|---|
| M2/047500 | M.S.S. Smith, W. H. | 21.2.19 | Mention. |
| M/281183 | Pte. Sutherland, J. | ,, | ,, |
| M2/176293 | Sergt., A/M.S.M. Symes, C. W. | ,, | ,, |
| M2/116147 | M.S.S. Taylor, J. C. | ,, | ,, |
| DM2/180263 | C.S.M. Thomson, C. G., D.C.M. | ,, | ,, |
| M/282583 | Pte. Toule, W. H. | ,, | ,, |
| M2/074207 | Sergt. Webber, A. V. | ,, | ,, |
| M/271735 | Pte. Wedderburn, A. | ,, | ,, |
| M2/223613 | Sergt. Wells, W. R. | ,, | ,, |
| M/284284 | Pte. White, T. | ,, | ,, |
| M/318415 | Pte. Yallop, E. E. | ,, | ,, |

*R.A.S.C., Special Reserve*

| — | Rank and Name. | Date of Award. | Award. |
|---|---|---|---|
| | Capt., A/Lt.-Col. Gibbons, J. N. G., M.C. | 21.2.19 | Mention. |

*R.A.S.C. (T.F.)*

| Regt. No. | Rank and Name. | Date of Award. | Award. |
|---|---|---|---|
| | Lt., A/Major Hansen-Hotte, H. | 21.2.19 | Mention. |
| | Lt., T/Major Robinson, H. | ,, | ,, |
| M2/204964 | M.S.M. Price, F. J. | ,, | ,, |

*Dunsterville Mission*

| Regt. No. | Rank and Name. | Date of Award. | Award. |
|---|---|---|---|
| M2/130904 | Sergt. Harris, R. W. | 21.2.19 | Mention. |

| — | Rank and Name. | Date of Award. | Award. |
|---|---|---|---|
| | T/Lt., A/Major Aldham, M. S. | 3.3.19 | O.B.E. |
| | T/Major, A/Lt.-Col. Carty, S. W., M.C. | ,, | ,, |
| | T/Lt., T/Major John, N. S. | ,, | ,, |
| | T/Major Weir, P. | ,, | ,, |
| | T/Lieut. Banks, T. R. | ,, | M.B.E. |
| | T/Lt., A/Capt. Broadbent, J. S. | ,, | ,, |
| | T/Lieut. Davies, S. | ,, | ,, |
| | Lt., A/Capt. Pattinson, E. H. (T.F.) | ,, | ,, |

The above officers also received a "Mention" prior to the grant of the above awards.

## Mentioned in Dispatches

The following names were mentioned in a dispatch from Lieutenant-General W. R. Marshall, K.C.B., K.C.S.I., Commanding-in-Chief Mesopotamian Expeditionary Force, dated February 7, 1919. The list in question actually appeared in conjunction with the King's birthday honours in June 1918.

Capt. and Bt.-Major, A/Lt.-Col. Archibald, G. K., D.S.O.
T/2nd Lt., A/Capt. Banks, T. R.
T/Lt., A/Capt. Beynon, J.
T/2nd Lt. Brennan, J.
T/2nd Lt. Browning, B. D.
T/2nd Lt. Chester Master, A. G.
Capt., A/Major Collings, W. d'A.
T/2nd Lt. Evershed, S. H.
T/Lt., A/Capt. Exton, F. N.
T/Major Gray, V. S.
T/Lt., A/Capt. Hunt, R. C.
T/Lt., A/Capt. Ingram, J. S.
T/Lt., A/Major John, N. S.
T/Lt., A/Capt. Kirwan, T. J.
Major Owen, A. D., D.S.O.
T/Major Parker, E. C. L.
T/Major, A/Lt.-Col. Pelly, D.S.O., M.C.
T/Major Protheroe, A. H., M.C.
T/Capt. Rea, D. B.
T/Major Robertson, C. B.
T/Capt. Ross, A. L.
T/Capt. Sansom, R. N.
T/Major Sellwood, F. G., M.C.
T/Lt., A/Capt. Shurmur, S. E.
T/ 2nd Lt. Smith, E.
T/Capt. Stone, R. B. L.
T/Lt. W. J. L. Stribling.
T/Major Weir, P.
T/2nd Lt. Wilkins, T.
DM2/135568 Pte., A/Cpl. Blake.
M2/178364 C.S.M. Blount, A.
DM2/118180 Cpl. Broughton, A.
M2/192940 Pte., A/M.S.S. Buckingham, A.
M2/044375 Sergt., A/C.S.M. Bull, L. H.
DM2/137982 Sergt. Challand, H.
M2/130879 Sergt. Cleland, H. S.
M2/101394 Pte. Craggs, G. H.
M2/191430 C.Q.M.S. Elson, A.
M2/137260 Sergt. Harvey, D. S.
M2/180902 Pte. Hills, H.
M2/155975 Pte., A/M.S.S. Howman, H. C.
DM2/163655 C.S.M. Jervis, C. F.
M2/205358 Kay, Sergt. D.
M2/200880 Cpl. Kelly, P. G.
M2/138673 Pte. Killin, G. A.
M2/202284 Pte. Laffan, M.
DM2/195148 Cpl. Land, B. J.
M2/202481 Cpl. Mackenzie, A.
S4/157308 Sergt. McHattie, H.
S/19137 S. Sergt., T/S.S.M. Monckton, A.
M2/20284 Cpl. Muirhead, J.
M/37387 C.S.M. Neville, F.
DM2/189296 C.S.M. Parry, A. C.
DM2/138502 Cpl. Reiss, F. A.
M2/222011 Cpl., A/Sergt. Reynolds, G. A.
DM2/206902 Sergt. Roberts, W. H.
M2/119124 M.S.S. Ryatt, L. A.
M/333916 Cpl. Searle, P. A.
DM2/168393 C.Q.M.S. Sugden, P. T.
M/23117 Sergt. Taylor, A. R.
M2/020858 Cpl. C. G. Tipping,
M2/166628 Pte. Tullock, J.
M2/194296 Pte. Webb, J. B.
M/417905 Sergt. White, C. M.
S4/146241 Sergt. Willcocks, J. P.
M/205300 Pte. Wootton, F. L.
M2/166569 Cpl. Worsley, W. G. W.
M2/136692 C.S.M. Wright, W. H.

*Special Reserve, R.A.S.C.*

Lt., A/Major Flack, H. L. (T/Capt. R.A.S.C.).

*R.A.S.C., T.F.*

Capt., A/Major Marshall, T.

*Labour and Porter Corps*

DM2/195173 Pte. Hewitt, F.

*North Persian Force*

T/Lt. Bowen, H. G.
T/Lt., A/Capt. Evans, T., M.C.
T/Major Goodwin, H. G.
T/Capt., A/Major Tobey, G. D.
T/Lt., A/Capt. Wimbleton, E. W.
M/339969 Pte., A/Cpl. Ellis, W. E.
M3/022024 Cpl., A/M.S.S. Hickling, A. J.
M/334980 C.Q.M.S. Jordan, W.
M2/121733 Pte., A/Sergt. Reeves, R.
M/271122 Cpl. Shentall, E.
M2/116147 Mech. S. Sergt. Taylor, C. J.

### King's Birthday Honours

*O.B.E., Military Division*

Capt. A/Major Flack, H. L. (S.R.).
T/Major Parker, E. C. L.
T/Major Protheroe, A. H., M.C.
T/Major Sellwood, F. G., M.C.

*M.B.E., Military Division*

T/2nd Lt. Chester Master, A. G.
T/2nd Lt. Harbottle, D. L.
T/Lt., A/Capt. Kirwan, T.
T/Lt. Martin, G. C.
T/2nd Lt. Pragnell, D. W. A.
T/2nd Lt. Penman, V. R.
T/Capt. Ross, A. L.
T/Lt., A/Capt. Shurmur, S. E.
T/Lt. Stribling, W. J. L.
T/Lt., A/Capt. Wells, R. C. O.

I cannot give the exact date of the following award:

*C.I.E.*

Major R. W. Hildyard-Marris, Burmah M.T. Co. (January 1920).

### *Extract from the Special Order of the Day*

On October 29, at Jift, convoy returning from Shargat had to start again at 12 midnight with water convoy. Lieutenant Pragnall, travelling all night, brought vans to destination in morning.

On November 13, after heavy rain, he successfully took a convoy through to Mosul with rations, the roads being very bad.

M.S.S. Harold Barkley.—Was out on one occasion for three days and three nights in hostile country bringing in and repairing derelict vans.

Sergt. Charles William Avery.—When on duty with a water convoy within range of enemy guns at Fathah, repaired a damaged van under fire and enabled the van to be driven away.

Lieutenant Pragnell was awarded the Military Cross and M.S.S. Harold Barkley and Sergt. Charles William Avery the Distinguished Conduct Medal.

[COPY]

No. A/1972.

HEADQUARTERS, 14TH I. DIVISION,
*January* 11, 1918.

*Memorandum*

I desire to bring to the notice of the Corps Commander the exceptionally good work done by the following M.T. companies, under the command of Lieutenant-Colonel Pelly, M.C., during the recent movements of Matthews Column and the Russians to Pai Tak.

The weather conditions and the roads were very bad. It was the determination and perseverance of all ranks which enabled the column to be fed.

No. 784 M.T. Company
,, 815 ,,
,, 818 ,,
,, 954 ,,

(Signed) W. M. THOMPSON, *Major-General,*
*Commanding* 14*th Indian Division.*

To Headquarters, 3rd Corps.

(11) No. A.M.S. 909/E/767.

HEADQUARTERS, 3RD INDIAN ARMY CORPS,
*January* 12, 1918.

Forwarded.

(Signed) R. G. EGERTON, *Lieutenant-General,*
*Commanding 3rd Indian Army Corps.*

To D.S. and T. at General Headquarters.

*Copy of a telegram from General Hoskins, to O.C.* 789 *M.T. Company, A.S.C., dated March* 15, 1918.

No. B2.

*March* 15, 1918.

Am most grateful for all excellent work you have done.

*From* GENERAL HOSKINS.

[Copy]

No. S/42.

Headquarters Advanced 3rd Corps,
*May* 14, 1918.

*To Director of S. and T., General Headquarters.*

I would like to bring to your notice the excellent work done by No. 3 M.T. Column, under Lieutenant-Colonel Gibbons, during the operations lately carried out by 3rd Corps.

Lieutenant-Colonel Gibbons and his column have worked most arduously, often under very difficult conditions, and the results have been excellent.

I have already written to Lieutenant-Colonel Gibbons and thanked him for his work.

In addition to Lieutenant-Colonel Gibbons's name I should like to bring to your notice the good work done by :

Temporary Captain (acting Major) Player, A.S.C.
,, ,, Robinson, A.S.C.
Lieutenant (acting Captain) D. A. G. Brown, A.S.C.

(Signed) R. G. Egerton,
*Lieutenant-General, Commanding 3rd Corps.*

[Copy]

No. A/1619.

Headquarters, 14th Division,
*December 27th*, 1918.

*Memorandum*

I would like to bring to notice the good work done during the recent operations at Qarah Tappah by No. 971 M.T. Company, under Captain Selwood, and by fifty vans of No. 784 M.T. Company, under Lieutenant Brown.

These two companies encountered considerable road difficulty, and on two occasions were benighted. It was due to their unceasing efforts that the force was able to be supplied.

(Signed) W. M. Thompson, *Brigadier-General,*
*Commanding 14th Indian Division.*

To Headquarters, 3rd Corps.

[COPY]

No. M.S. 926/151.

GENERAL HEADQUARTERS, M.E.F.,
*Dated December* 14, 1917.

*Memorandum*

The General Officer Commanding-in-Chief directs me to request you to convey to the officers and other ranks of the Mechanical Transport convoys comprising representatives from Nos. 729, 730, 784, and 954 Mechanical Transport Companies, Army Service Corps, under command of Lieutenant Prince, A.S.C., and also to Lieutenant Evans, A.S.C., and his water convoy, his high appreciation of the excellent work done by the above-mentioned individuals during the recent operations.

(Signed) L. WILLIAMS, *Lieutenant-Colonel, A.M.S.*

To the D. of S. and T., General Headquarters.

[COPIES]

*Copy of a letter No. Q/*1515/12, *dated October* 15, 1917, *from Deputy Quartermaster-General, M.E.F., to the Director of Supplies and Transport.*

I am directed to convey the Army Commander's appreciation of the expeditious manner in which the reinforcements of springs has been carried out under adverse conditions.

*Copy of a letter No. Q/*1502/5, *dated October* 22, 1917, *from Deputy Quartermaster-General, M.E.F., to the Director of Supplies and Transport, M.E.F.*

I am directed to state that the efficacious and expeditious manner in which the Ford vans have been overhauled reflects great credit on officers and men engaged on this work.

*Copy of a letter No. Q/*1626/8, *dated November* 4, 1917, *from Deputy Quartermaster-General, M.E.F., to the Director of Supplies and Transport, M.E.F.*

The Deputy Quartermaster-General wishes his appreciation of the good work done by the Peerless lorries on the

Nukta-Feluja run, to be conveyed to Lieutenant Williams, A.S.C., and all ranks of No. 596 M.T. Company.

*Copy of a telegram from General Fane, No. Q/6986, dated November 7, 1917, to the Director of Supplies and Transport, M.E.F.*

I should be grateful if you would convey to all Motor Transport employed on water, my thanks and that of all Divisions for all their work and help to us. Am sending this through you as impossible for me to reach them individually.

[Copy]

No. Q/32469/9.

General Headquarters, M.E.F.
*Dated June* 12, 1918.

To D.S. and T.

*Memorandum*

I am directed to forward the attached correspondence regarding the good work performed by 976 M.T. Company, A.S.C., while attached to 13th Division, in order that it may be made known to the Officer Commanding and to the company.

The General Officer Commanding-in-Chief is gratified to hear of the part played by this company, which materially contributed to the occupation of Kirkuk.

(Signed) R. Stuart Wortley,
*Major-General, D.Q.M.G., G.H.Q.*

[Copy]

No. Q/703/910.

Headquarters, 3rd I.A. Corps,
*June* 10/11, 1918.

*To General Headquarters.*

*Copy of a memorandum No. Q/6/139, dated June* 7, 1918, *from* 13*th Division to Headquarters,* 3*rd Corps*

On the departure from my Division of No. 976 Backaxle, I wish to record my appreciation of the particularly good work put in by this unit.

Owing to the great value of the lorries, they have been worked incessantly for long and tiring distances ever since joining my Division, and I have never had a complaint from the officer commanding, and both he and those under his command did all they could in carrying stores to the forward area for the comfort of the Division.

*Memorandum*

Forwarded with the request that this appreciation of their services may be communicated to 976 Backaxle.

(Signed) M. E. WILLOUGHBY,
*Brigadier-General for G.O.C., 3rd I.A. Corps.*

[COPY]

*From the Officer Commanding 33rd Motor Ambulance Convoy, Persian L. of C., to the Assistant Director of Medical Services, Persian L. of C.*

KHANIKIN,
*October* 29, 1918.

SIR,

Before leaving the 33rd Motor Ambulance Convoy to proceed to another formation, I have the honour to place on record my appreciation of the splendid and ready assistance given this unit by the officer commanding the Mechanical Transport formations in Persia and on the Persian L. of C.

I consider that the arrangements of being attached to these formations for technical advice and assistance has been highly successful.

I have the honour to be, Sir,
Your Obedient Servant,
(Signed) W. K. MORRISON,
*Captain, R.A.M.C., Commanding 33rd M.A.C.*

Copy to A.D.T. (M.T.) for favour of his information.

[Copy]

No. Q/E2537/149.

General Headquarters, M.E.F.
*Dated* November 19, 1918.

To D.S. and T.

*Memorandum*

In forwarding to you the attached copy of minute from Commandant Persian L. of C., the General Officer Commanding-in-Chief wishes me to express his satisfaction with the work done by the units mentioned. He entirely agrees with the last sentence of Colonel Moens's minute.

Please convey the above to Colonel Pelly and the units concerned.

(Signed) R. Stuart Wortley,
*Major-General, D.Q.M.G., M.E.F.*

Copy to Colonel Moens, D.S.O.

[Copy]

*Copy of a minute No. A/*1511, *dated November* 8, *from Commandant Persian L. of C. to General Headquarters*

I wish to bring to your notice the good work done by certain M.T. companies between September 13 and the end of September, when there was a question of withdrawing troops from north of Kasvin.

A convoy of twenty-six Peerless lorries of 596 M.T. Company, under the command of Lieutenant Stribling, completed a journey of 354 miles (from Tak-i-Garra to Kasvin) in four days, on two consecutive days spending eighteen and seventeen hours respectively on the road.

Two hundred and four Ford vans of 954, 1054, and 1055 Companies ran 477 miles in six days.

One hundred Ford vans of 1055 M.T. Company, commanded by Lieutenant Kirwin, ran 1,664 miles before returning to their headquarters workshops.

All vans experienced great difficulties on the passes ; in consequence very long hours were worked by all ranks.

That the above long runs were able to be carried out reflects great credit on Colonel Pelly and all the M.T. under his command, and proves the state of efficiency of the M.T. on this line.

[COPY]

*Extract from a report by the General Officer Commanding* 13*th Division to Headquarters* 3*rd Indian Army Corps*

No. Q/15/177.

*Dated May* 28, 1918.

. . . . . . .

5. All Ford vans except those of the 1014 and 1017 Companies are now under orders to leave the Divisional area, and I should like to place on record on their departure my appreciation of the excellent work they have performed.

I would call special attention to their work on the 8th instant, when,although warned that the road was impassable, they pushed forward from Tuz to Taza, spending fourteen hours over the journey.

This excellent performance came at a most opportune time.

[COPY]

A. 87/438.

*The Officer Commanding No.* 1017 *M.T. Company.*

The G.O.C., on the departure of your company from this Division, wishes me to convey to you and all ranks under your command his appreciation of the excellent work performed by all throughout the period the company has been with the Division.

Twice they have rendered the most valuable assistance in maintaining the forces engaged in active operations, the success of which was in a large way due to their unremitting efforts, while throughout the summer over trying roads and recently on long runs in bad weather, the company has cheerfully answered to all calls made upon it.

All whose necessities and comforts have reached them

speedily through your efforts have reason to feel gratitude to you, and in expressing thanks on their behalf, the G.O.C. adds his own with his best wishes for good luck in the future.

(Signed) A. R. GODWIN AUSTIN,
*Major, A.A. and Q.M.G.*

HEADQUARTERS, 13TH DIVISION,
*January* 2, 1919.

[COPY]

GENERAL HEADQUARTERS, M.E.F.,
*Dated January* 11, 1919.

No. Q/2842/1.

*From the Deputy Quartermaster-General, General Headquarters, to the Director of Supplies and Transport*

*Memorandum*

With reference to your No. M.T. 467 of January 8, 1919.

The General Officer Commanding-in-Chief considers that great credit is due to the officers and men of the Advanced Mechanical Transport Depôt for the excellent work done by them during the past year.

They have enabled a considerable quantity of mechanical transport to be kept on the road which would not otherwise have been available, and have thus contributed in no inconsiderable degree to the success and efficiency of the force.

This memorandum should be published in the Depôt Orders.

(Signed) R. STUART WORTLEY,
*Major-General, D.Q.M.G., General Headquarters.*

## CHAPTER XVII

### LIST OF ALL M.T. UNITS, WITH A BRIEF WAR RECORD OF EACH AND OF VARIOUS OFFICERS WHO SERVED WITH EACH FORMATION

THE following chapter contains a complete list of all the Mechanical Transport companies and formations which came out to Mesopotamia between January 1916 and December 1918, or were formed during that period. A short résumé of the operations in which they took part is also given, though it is by no means exhaustive and numerous minor affairs are not mentioned.

It has been difficult to place all the officers correctly with the various units in which they served, and possibly one or two names may be omitted. If so, I trust the omissions will be pardoned. Companies when waiting at the Base prior to dispatch up country often had a rapid change of officer personnel, and it was a difficult matter to keep touch. The changes once a unit got to the front line were many, but for the most part the lists are practically complete. Minor errors as regards ranks, initials, etc., are naturally possible in view of the numerous acting ranks which were given in Mesopotamia.

The names of all M.T. officers who served on the D. of S. and T.'s Directorate or were attached to it, either at Baghdad or Basrah, are given. The names of all inspecting officers of Divisions are also tabulated, though in no special order. At the end of the chapter the situation of all the Mechanical Transport companies in Mesopotamia is shown, with the names of the towns or villages, etc., where each company had its headquarters during January 1919.

Finally, a tabulated statement of personnel and matériel concludes the chapter.

### D. of S. and T.'s Directorate, Baghdad

D.A.D.T.

A/Major N. S. John
*Attached :*
A/Capt. T. R. Banks
Lieut. C. R. A. Hammond
Lieut. G. R. Turner

### Chief Inspectors of Mechanical Transport

Hon. Major E. B. Wood
A/Major C. B. Waterlow
T/Major R. W. Hildyard-Marris
A/Major G. Lynn (I.A.R.O.).

The above officers each held the appointment of Acting Chief Inspectors in the order given.

### D. D. of S. and T., Basrah

D.A.D.T.

T/Major W. W. Winlaw
*Attached :*
Lieut. G. F. Lynn

T/Major A. D. Owen, D.S.O., though graded as a C.I.M.T., was in charge of the Main Stores of the Base Mechanical Transport Depôt, and was employed on that duty for a period of three years.

### Inspecting M.T. Officers Attached to Divisions

Lieutenants Carson, G. C. Martin, C. R. A. Hammond, E. Lee-Wood, R. G. Brydges, P. G. Boyes, C. W. May, A. J. E. McLean, W. H. Churchill, L. O. Daltry, D. N. Payne, H. R. Presland.

## R.A.S.C. M.T. COLUMNS AND COMPANIES IN MESOPOTAMIA

*Chief Transport Officer, Persian L. of C.*

*C.O.*—A/Lieut.-Col. E. G. Pelly, D.S.O., M.C.
*Adjutant.*—A/Capt. A. J. Appleton, M.C.

### No. 1 M.T. Column

Date of formation: November 12, 1917

*C.O's.*—A/Lieut.-Col. E. Snepp, D.S.O.; J. N. G. Gibbons, M.C.
*Adjutants.*—A/Capts. K. B. Martin, M.C., T. Evans, M.C.; 2/Lieut. L. Ravenscroft, M.C.; A/Capt. A. D. C. Halford; 2/Lieut. B. D. Browning.

### No. 2 M.T. Column

Date of formation: November 12, 1917

*C.O's.*—A/Lieut.-Cols. E. G. Pelly, D.S.O., M.C., F. W. Vallatt.
*Adjutants.*—2/Lieuts. A. Whalley, C. Hurry, A. J. W. Wagstaff, A. J. Appleton, M.C.

### No. 3 M.T. Column

Date of formation: November 12, 1917

*C.O's.*—A/Lieut.-Cols. J. N. Gibbons, M.C., E. Snepp, D.S.O.
*Adjutants.*—A/Capt. D. A. G. Brown; 2/Lieut. L. Ravenscroft, M.C.; A/Capt. K. B. Martin, M.C.

### No. 4 M.T. Column

Date of formation: November 12, 1917

*C.O.*—A/Lieut.-Col. H. Dickinson.
*Adjutants.*—A/Capts. M. S. Aldham, A. D. C. Halford.

## No. 5 M.T. Column

Date of formation : March 10, 1918

*O.C.*—Major P. Weir.
*Adjutant*—A/Capt. G. C. Martin.

### Detached Duties

2/Lieut. H. B. Thompson, with Civil Commissioner attached Anglo-Persian Oil Company.
Lieut. H. M. Steavenson, attached A.A.G. 3rd Echelon.

### 596 Company

Company sign : Pioneer. Date of arrival, January 1916

*Officers.*—Capt. Lilley ; A/Majors H. J. B. Reynolds, W. H. A. Turner ; T/Capt. W. W. Winlaw ; Capt. R. M. B. Ward ; Lieuts. H. B. Martindale, W. J. L. Stribling, R. H. Williams ; 2/Lieuts. B. G. Bosher, C. Rickards, W. L. Pratt, J. G. Nicholls ; Capts. W. E. R. Randall, C. Meldrum, J. T. Vlasto, M.C., R. P. Dickinson ; A/Capts. J. A. Earle, Theobald ; Lieuts. Mutch, J. R. Elvin ; 2/Lieuts. R. Stewart, W. S. Reed, R. L. Lawson, Liebert, K. B. Symington, S. H. Bailey, J. G. Aitken, L. P. Wildsmith.

*Attached Officers.*—Lieuts. N. S. John, Campbell-Rogers.

*Operations :*

1916. Fiats : Sannayat, Kut, Shumran, Diyalah.
1917. Adhaim, 2nd Ramadie, Sharban, Qizil Robat, Kifri, Tekrit, Baghdad, Deli Abbas, Jabal Hamrin.
1918. Qasr-i-shirin, Persian L. of C., Mosul.

### 656 Company (23rd M.A.C.)

Company sign : Blue star in white circle on black square.
Date of arrival : May 1916

*Officers.*—Major H. G. Goodwin ; A/Capt. B. C. Bean ; 2/Lieut. J. G. Aitken ; Lieut. M. J. Cahill (attached M.T.) ; 2/Lieuts. L. Hall, T. G. Butt, S. E. Kebbell.

*Operations.*--Base and G.H.Q., Baghdad.

### 729 Company

Company sign : Gollywog. Date of arrival : May 5, 1917

*Officers.*—A/Lieut.-Col. E. Snepp, D.S.O. ; A/Major T. Marshall ; A/Capt. H. S. Jackson ; Lieut. G. E. W. Ward ; 2/Lieuts. W. G. Taylor, T. H. Spink, D. R. Redford ; A/Capts. T. C. Prince, K. B. Martin, M.C., W. Medlycott.

*Operations :*

1917. 1st and 2nd Ramadie, Beled Ruz, Tuwair, Tekrit, Khanakin, Sharban, Qizil Robat, Sakaltutan Pass.

1918. Pai Tak, Kirkuk, Persian L. of C.

### 730 Company

Sign : Harp. Date of arrival : December 31, 1916

*Officers.*—A/Lieut.-Col. S. W. Carty, M.C. ; Major R. C. Sykes ; A/Majors D. L. H. Boycott, W. F. Murdoch ; Lieut. J. G. Howard ; 2/Lieuts. E. F. Knight, W. H. Churchill, C. V. Bowditch, T. M. Burberry ; A/Capt. J. Beynon ; Lieut. Woodward ; 2/Lieuts. F. Ackroyd, W. E. Gibson ; Lieuts. Steavenson, Rhodes.

*Operations :*

1917. 2nd Ramadie, Hit, Beled Ruz, Tuwair, Tekrit Sharban, Qizil Robat, Kifri, Deli Abbas, Jabal Hamrin.

1918. Taki Garri, Resht, Enzali ; Baku, Persian L. of C.

### 773 Company (33rd M.A.C.)

Sign : Tortoise. Date of arrival : October 10, 1916

*Officers.*—Major F. W. Vallat ; Lieut. Nicholls ; T/Capt. F. Forbes-Leith ; Lieuts. R. E. Saunders, S. Davies, B. Reid, H. P. Latham, F. D. Burcher.

*Operations :*

Tigris Front : Cavalry Division, I Corps, III Corps, November 1916 to March 1917.

At Baghdad, March 1917.
III Corps, March to April 1917.
I Corps, May 1917.
At Baghdad, May to June, 1917.
I Corps, July 1917.
III Corps, August 1917 to February 1918.
15th Division, March to April 1918.
III Corps, April to August 1918.
Persian L. of C., September 1918 to date.

783 COMPANY

Sign: Bulldog. Date of arrival: November 16, 1916

*Officers.*—A/Lieut.-Col. J. N. G. Gibbons, M.C.; Majors T. F. W. Rolfe, C. B. Robertson; A/Capt. J. C. Boyce; Lieut. T. L. White, M.C.; 2/Lieuts. J. W. E. White, A. E. Bridger, C. Murray; A/Capts. A. J. Appleton, M.C., M. S. Aldham, W. E. R. Randall; Lieut. T. Kirwan; 2/Lieuts. A. J. V. Graburn, H. H. Munro.

*Operations:*

1916–1917. Sannayat, Kut-el-Amarah, Shumran, Diyalah, Baghdad, Mushaidie, Istabulat, Samarah, Baqubah, Mendali, The Hai, 1st and 2nd Ramadie, Khanakin, Beled Ruz, Tuwair, Sharban, Qizil Robat, Kifri, Tekrit, Jabal Hamrin.

1918. Qasr-i-Shirin, Sharban, Qizil Robat, Pai Tak, Kifri, Kirkuk, Persian L. of C.

784 COMPANY

Sign: Squirrel and nut. Date of arrival: November 6, 1916

*Officers.*—A/Lieut.-Col. E. G. Pelly, D.S.O., M.C.; Major V. S. Gray; A/Capt. A. C. W. Beard; 2/Lieuts. V. W. Dean, G. C. Martin, T. H. Stanley, J. A. Grant; A/Capts. T. Evans, M.C., D. A. G. Brown; 2/Lieut. E. H. G. Pearson, Pawson, Dalrymple; Lieut. Carson.

*Operations :*

1916–1917. Sannayat, Kut-el-Amarah, Shumran, Diyalah, Baghdad, Mushaidie, Istabulat, Samarah, Baqubah, Mendali, Khanakin, Beled Ruz, Adhaim, The Hai, 2nd Ramadie, Hit, Tuwair, Tekrit, Kirkuk, Sharban, Qizil Robat, Kifri, Jabal Hamrin.

1918. Sharban, Qizil Robat, Pai Tak, Persian L. of C.

### 788 Company

Sign : Rabbit. Date of arrival : February 1917

*Officers.*—A/Capts. S. S. Porritt, C. C. Holland; 2/Lieuts. R. E. Pither, E. W. T. Hichens, H. B. Waddington, F. D. Crump.

*Operations :*

1917. Sannayat, Kut-el-Amarah, Shumran, Tekrit, The Hai.

1918. Pai Tak, Persian L. of C., Tekrit.

### 789 Company

Sign : Black cat. Date of arrival : February 1917

*Officers.*—T/Major T. F. W. Rolfe ; Capt. V. B. L. Helme ; Lieut. Eldridge ; 2/Lieuts. E. H. Sharp, D. I. Laurie, L. W. J. Warren.

*Operations :*

1917. Sannayat, Kut-el-Amarah, The Hai, Tekrit, Shumran.

1918. Pai Tak, Persian L. of C., Euphrates Front.

### 815 Company

Sign : Figure eight with line down middle. Date of arrival: August 15, 1917

*Officers.*—Major E. C. L. Parker ; Capt. G. E. Worthington ; A/Capt. J. S. Broadbent ; Lieut. M. J. Cahill ; 2/Lieuts. S. M. Lampard, M.C., J. D. Slinger, A. T.

Boundford, L. O. Daltry, D. N. Payne; Capt. V. B. L. Helme, G. S. Briggs; 2/Lieuts. H. B. Rogers, J. N. Gilles, N. J. Walton, Hogarth.

*Operations :*

1917. Beled Ruz, Tuwair, Khanakin, Tekrit.

1918. Kirkuk, Taki Garri, Resht, Enzali, Pai Tak, Persian L. of C.

818 Company

Sign: Black cat. Date of arrival: August 15, 1917

*Officers.*—A/Lieut.-Col. Dickinson, H.; Major H. G. Goodwin; Capt. B. D. Grant; Lieut. C. H. Burrell; 2/Lieuts. H. G. Bower, E. J. Pocock, C. E. T. Scott; A/Capt. E. C. Robson; 2/Lieuts. L. Ravenscroft, A. G. Smith, E. Winn, J. Singleton; Lieut. H. P. Stidolph.

*Operations :*

1917. Beled Ruz, Tuwair, Tekrit.

1918. Kirkuk, Pai Tak, Persian Patrol Work, Persian L. of C.

901 Company

Sign: Triangle with circle in centre. Date of arrival: May 1917

*Officers.*—T/Major S. S. Marshall; A/Capt. W. Medlycott; 2/Lieuts. A. N. Campbell, W. G. Jacoby, G. W. Jeffrey, T. Evans, M.C., H. W. Teeton, D. S. Moore.

*Operations :*

1917. Tekrit, Tigris Front, Mosul, Persian L. of C.

902 Company

Sign: Black butterfly. Date of arrival: May 1917

*Officers.*—Capt. T. Capel; A/Capt. D. A. G. Brown; 2/Lieuts. R. Gibson, A. H. Ratcliff, B. D. Browning, A. Stanbury, S. C. Bagg.

*Operations :*

1918. Mosul, Euphrates Front, Persian L. of C.

### 903 Company

Sign: Black shield, forked lightning. Date of arrival: May 1917

*Officers.*—T/Major V. S. Gray; A/Capt. F. M. Dimond; T/Capt. T. C. Prince; 2/Lieut. G. F. Carrington, C. G. Hill, J. H. Buckley; Lieut. F. A. Curtis; 2/Lieut. J. A. Grant.

*Operations:*

1917. Sharban, Qizil Robat, Deli Abbas, Jabal Hamrin.

1918. Kirkuk, Kifri, Chaman-Kupri, Tuz, etc., Mosul, Persian L. of C.

### 911 Company (39th M.A.C.)

Sign: Five legs in a circle. Date of arrival: August 17, 1917

*Officers.*—Major C. B. Robertson; A/Capt. J. A. Earle; 2/Lieuts. A. Ross, H. P. Latham, H. B. Ward; A/Capt. R. C. Hunt; A/Major E. H. Pattinson; 2/Lieuts. H. P. Stidolph, L. W. W. Davis, H. B. Thompson.

*Operations:*

1917. III Corps, October 1917 to November 1918.

1918. Kirkuk.

### 953 Company

Sign: Four D's. Date of arrival: August 16, 1917

*Officers.*—Major C. de G. Murray; Major E. C. L. Parker; Capt. C. L. R. Smith; A/Capt. T. Kirwan; 2/Lieuts. V. R. Penman, J. Brennan, J. F. Nicholson, E. H. Reynolds.

*Operations:*

1917–18. L. of C. Company, stationed Baghdad.

### 954 Company

Sign: Rising sun. Date of arrival: August 17, 1917

*Officers.*—Major R. H. C. Plews; Capt. W. Mark; A/Capt. J. R. B. Handyside; 2/Lieuts. G. B. Dashwood,

J. A. Forbes, F. Rylands, V. L. B. Sergent, H. N. Hussey, E. P. Innocent, C. E. T. Scott, E. G. Evans.

*Operations :*

1917. Beled Ruz, Tuwair, Sakaltutan Pass, Sharban, Qizil Robat, Kifri, Kirkuk, Persian L. of C.

### 968 Company

Sign: Red and white. Date of arrival: October 1917

*Officers.*—Major P. Weir; Capt. R. G. Swanson; Lieut. H. G. Warlow; 2/Lieut. E. Francis; A/Capt. E. L. Boultbee.

*Operations :*

1917. Jabal Hamrin.
1918. Kirkuk, Persian L. of C.

### 969 Company

Sign: Red and white. Date of arrival: September 8, 1917

*Officers.*—Capt. G. E. Worthington; A/Capt. F. M. Dimond; Lieut. F. B. Hallowes; 2/Lieuts. S. Kendall, H. P. Peyton.

*Operations :*

1917. Jabal Hamrin, Kifri, Diyalah.
1918. Kirkuk, Mosul, Persian L. of C.

### 970 Company (40th M.A.C.)

Sign: Domino—the four-blank. Date of arrival: September 18, 1917

*Officers.*—A/Major A. J. Petrocochino; A/Capts. C. N. Draper, A. J. Smith; 2/Lieuts. F. C. R. Douton, R. H. Henderson, H. B. Ward.

*Operations :*

1917. 2nd Ramadie.
1918. Khan Baghdadi, Anah, Mosul.

### 971 Company

Sign: Dog. Date of arrival: September 5, 1917

*Officers.*—Major F. C. Selwood, M.C.; A/Capt. J. S. Ingram; 2/Lieuts. J. Spencer, D. W. A. Pragnall, L. S. Whatley; Capt. F. M. Dimond; 2/Lieuts. R. E. Pither, F. G. Connor, L. A. Clatworthy, M.C.

*Operations:*

1917. 2nd Ramadie, Beled Ruz, Tuwair, Tekrit; Sharban, Qizil Robat, Sakaltutan Pass.
1918. Khan Baghdadi, Anah, Mosul.

### 976 Company

Sign: Red triangle with white circle. Date of arrival: Packards, September 16, 1917

*Officers.*—Capt. C. I. Clark; A/Major R. P. Dickinson; 2/Lieuts. E. H. G. Pearson, J. R. Elvin, L. F. Wildsmith, A. M. Gibson, R. C. Baskett; Capt. R. Rippon; 2/Lieut. A. H. Bull, W. March, J. E. H. Kirkwood.

*Operations:*

1917. Nil.
1918. Taki Garri; Resht, Enzali; Pai Tak, Persian L. of C.

### 1013 Company

Sign: Ace of spades. Date of arrival: January 17, 1918

*Officers.*—A/Major F. G. McKim; A/Major G. D. Tobey; A/Capt. E. W. Wimbleton; 2/Lieuts. D. H. Hedges, C. S. Southey, D. W. Cameron, H. Wisbey, A. Ogilvy; A/Capt. J. S. Ingram; 2/Lieut. J. G. Nicholls.

*Operations:*

1918. Khan Baghdadi, Anah, Taki Garri, Resht, Enzali, Persian L. of C.

### 1014 Company

Sign: Dragon. Date of arrival: January 24, 1918

*Officers.*—A/Major L. A. N. Wright; A/Capt. A. C. Humphrey; 2/Lieuts. W. H. Wilcocks, M. H. G. Munro,

A. J. E. McClean; A/Capt. D. H. Christmas; 2/Lieuts. J. N. Gillies, J. G. Nicholls, W. G. Jacoby.

*Operations :*

1918. Khan Baghdadi, Anah, Kirkuk, Mosul.

### 1015 Company

Sign : Squirrel. Date of arrival : January 24, 1918

*Officers.*—A/Major D. W. Player ; A/Capt. F. D. R. Wylie ; 2/Lieuts. S. A. Beckham, W. Spires, H. T. Chippendall ; Lieut. R. M. B. Ward ; 2/Lieut. A. H. Ratcliff.

*Operations :*

1918. Taki Garri, Kifri, Resht, Enzali, Kirkuk, Persian L. of C.

### 1016 Company

Sign : 14 lb. weight. Date of arrival : January 6, 1918

*Officers.*—Capt. R. C. Stone ; A/Major A. J. Petrocochino ; Capt. C. N. Draper ; A/Capt. W. G. de Courcy ; 2/Lieut. S. J. O. Panchaud, P. Westacott, C. H. Crews, D. N. Campbell.

*Operations :*

1918. Khan Baghdadi, Anah, Kirkuk, Persian L. of C.

### 1017 Company

Sign : Ace of hearts. Date of arrival : January 24, 1918

*Officers.*—A/Major H. Robinson ; A/Capt. R. C. Hunt ; 2/Lieuts. W. A. Empey, P. E. Daniels, G. S. Shaw, A. W. Petrocochino.

*Operations :*

1918. Kirkuk, Kifri, etc.

### 1018 Company

Sign : Butterfly. Date of arrival : January 24, 1918

*Officers.*—A/Major Hansen-Hotte ; A/Capt. G. Graham ; 2/Lieuts. G. Watt, H. J. Newbury, D. C. Eastwood, I. W. Sandell, J. P. Thorne.

*Operations :*

1918. Kifri, Taki Garri, Resht, Enzali, Pai Tak, Kirkuk, Persian L. of C.

### 1019 Company

Sign : Lion rampant. Date of arrival : February 23, 1918

*Officers.*—A/Major A. E. Scoby; A/Capt. P. S. Harrison; 2/Lieuts. A. G. Chester-Master, W. H. Richards, S. H. Evershed, P. J. C. Bovill, W. S. Percival, H. L. L. Brown.

*Operations :*

1918. Mosul, Persian L. of C.

### 1020 Company

Sign : Ring broken in three places. Date of arrival : February 23, 1918

*Officers.*—Capt. R. G. Swanson; Major T. F. W. Rolfe; Lieut. F. L. Eldridge; 2/Lieuts. C. H. Boissier, C. J. W. Daniell, A. J. V. Graburn, N. M. Pullen; Capt. D. L. H. Boycott; A/Capt. W. Evans; 2/Lieuts. E. Francis, E. T. Butteriss, J. G. Nicholls, D. N. Payne, H. Smith, H. T. Chippendale, W. H. Richards, J. O. Crombie, T. M. Burberry.

*Operations :*

1918. Persia.

### 1023 Company (Burmah)

Sign : Skull and cross-bones. Date of arrival : January 21, 1918

*Officers.*—Major R. W. Hildyard-Marris; Capt. G. Lynn; 2/Lieuts. G. R. Cockman, E. Bruce, E. G. Fleming, E. L. Bayley, H. L. L'O. Brown, C. V. Bowditch, E. R. Allen, C. H. Stork.

*Operations :*

1918. Khan Baghdadi, Hillah, Persia, Mosul.

### 1024 Company (Burmah)

Sign : Peacock. Date of arrival : July 1, 1918

*Officers.*—Major G. E. Cunningham ; Capt. Webster ; A/Major E. G. Fleming ; 2/Lieuts. C. F. Pyett, A. J. Bennison, J. P. O'Shea, D. J. Ross, Capts. C. N. Draper, E. W. T. Hichens ; 2/Lieuts. H. L. Rose, E. H. Sharp, A. J. F. Wagstaff, H. W. Teeton, E. L. Bayley ; A/Capt. G. R. Cockman.

*Operations :*

1918. Persia.

### 1028 Company

Sign : Two spanners crossed. Date of arrival : January 6, 1918

*Officers.*—A/Capt. G. D. Tobey ; Capt. D. L. H. Boycott ; A/Capt. T. Evans, M.C. ; 2/Lieuts. C. R. Thompson, D. L. Harbottle ; A/Capt. E. W. Wimbleton ; 2/Lieuts. R. E. Pither, L. O. Daltry, G. R. Turner.

*Operations :*

1918. Khan Baghdadi, Persian L. of C., Mosul.

### 1054 Company

Sign : Ace of diamonds. Date of arrival : June 7, 1918

*Officers.*—A/Major C. L. B. Francis ; A/Capt. E. L. Boultbee ; Lieut. N. L. Huggins ; 2/Lieuts. C. M. Bowser, E. H. Wilson, G. E. Field, P. L. Griffiths, R. D. Chapman, L. W. J. Warren, C. G. Cowlishaw, C. H. Stanley.

*Operations :*

1918. Persia.

### 1055 Company

Sign : Snake. Date of arrival : June 7, 1918

*Officers.*—T/Major P. Weir ; A/Major G. L. R. Smith ; Capt. E. M. G. E. de Wilton ; A/Capt. T. Kirwan ;

Lieut. R. Maiden; 2/Lieuts. F. S. Rainbow, F. S. Adcock, H. C. Mitchell, C. H. Gibbs, J. N. Gillies, H. B. Rogers, L. O. Daltry, A. T. Boundford.

*Operations :*

1918. Hillah and Persian L. of C.

### 1056 Company

Sign: Question mark. Date of arrival: June 7, 1918

*Officers.*—Major H. L. Flack; A/Capt. F. N. Exton; Lieut. H. S. Pick; 2/Lieuts. R. Stewart, A. E. Vequeray, W. S. Percival, A. D. Atkins, T. Owen.

*Operations :*

1918. L. of C. Company, Headquarters at Basrah.

### 1071 Company

Sign: None (left country on formation). Date of formation: March 28, 1918

*Officer.*—O.C. T/Capt. S. S. Porritt.

### 1072 Company

Sign: None (left country on formation). Date of formation: March 23, 1918

*Officer.*—O.C. A/Capt. F. R. Buckley.

### 1073 Company

Sign: None (left country on formation). Date of formation: March 28, 1918

*Officer.*—O.C. A/Capt. C. Meldrum.

### 1091 Company (45 M.A.C.)

Sign: Switch key. Date of arrival: September 6, 1918

*Officers.*—Capt. J. J. C. Allen; A/Capt. H. L. Huggins; 2/Lieut. H. C. Gambell, H. Ardern, R. B. Vick.

*Operations :*

1918. Mosul, October to November, 1918.

### 1093 Company

Sign : Four black-and-white check squares

*Officers.*—A/Capt. C. Fergusson ; Lieut. B. B. Alder ; 2/Lieut. C. S. Fisher.

### 1094 Company

Sign

| | | X |
|---|---|---|
| | O | |
| X | | |

*Officers.*—Capt. C. H. Russell ; Lieuts. H. J. Betts, H. E. Pidduck.

### 1095 Company

Sign : Red lion couchant

*Officers.*—Major K. E. Hartridge ; Lieuts. B. F. Petre, J. B. Ledgard.

### 1096 Company

Sign : Six Diamonds

*Officers.*—A/Major J. G. Kay ; A/Capt. C. W. Hacking ; Lieut. H. E. Collier.

### 1097 Company

Sign : Touchwood charm

*Officers.*—O.C. Capt. W. H. A. Turner ; Lieut. J. C. L. Henneguy, J. Hamer.

### 1098 Company

Sign : Green on white square 

*Officers.*—Capt. J. B. Henderson-Roe ; Lieut. H. H. Pine ; 2/Lieut. F. R. Harman.

### 1099 Company

Sign: Yellow on black 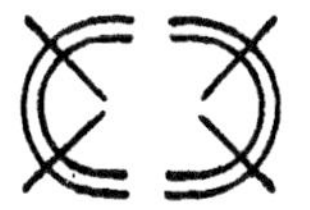

*Officers.*—Major J. H. Blundell; Lieut. H. W. Langtry, J. F. Cargin.

### 1100 Company

Sign: Bird in blue in yellow circle in red circle on yellow square

*Officers.*—Major C. E. Fidgeon; Capt. A. G. Woodhams; 2/Lieut. W. Eggert, A. T. James.

### 1110 Company

Sign: Black and white 

*Officers.*—Major P. C. Franklin; Capt. E. W. Terry; 2/Lieut. W. Melloy.

### 1111 Company

Sign: Acorn in black circle with white outer ring

*Officers.*—Major G. M. Oakes.

### 1114 Company

Sign: White cock on black ground. Date of arrival: Autumn 1918

*Officers.*—A/Major C. H. Reynolds; A/Capt. O. B. Cox; Lieut. S. H. Bailey; 2/Lieuts. G. L. Dupré, C. F. Bennett, R. G. Wyer, W. Davies.

*Operations:*

1918. Persia, Mosul.

### 1115 Company

Sign: Yellow man-faced dog on drum. Date of arrival: Autumn 1918

*Officers.*—Capt. G. T. Miller; A/Capt. F. L. Cater; 2/Lieuts. C. H. Fison, J. Bower, R. E. S. Feilden, C. G. Cowlishaw, R. J. Ilsley, J. W. Hart.

*Operations:*

1918. Mosul.

### No. 1. Floating Workshops

Sign: Lifebuoy, plug, and anchor

*Officers.*—Major R. C. Sykes; Capt. H. C. Gould; A/Capt. A. A. G. Ainsworth; 2/Lieuts. W. Steriker, S. W. C. Gibson, E. P. Innocent, A. Baxter, R. C. Brydges; A/Capts. J. A. Earle, F. R. Buckley; 2/Lieut. H. P. Peyton.

### Advanced M.T. Depôt

Sign: Shield

*Officers.*—Capt. Sutcliffe; Major R. C. Sykes; A/Lieut.-Col. S. W. Carty, M.C.; A/Major E. H. Pattinson; A/Capts. R. C. O. Wells, E. C. Robson, P. G. Boyes, I. W. Sandell, W. Evans, S. F. Rich, F. A. B. Farquharson, T. R. Banks (attached D. of S. and T.); 2/Lieuts. N. J. Walton, E. D. Waller, A. Whalley, H. Smith, G. W. Sadler, H. P. Peyton; Lieuts. G. W. Grabham, F. Ackroyd; 2/Lieut. F. D. Crump, J. L. Bell, C. A. A. Gubbins, V. H. Marlow, L. V. Colato, W. G. Garden, W. J. Coker, W. I. Thomas, J. A. Seager, D. H. Rignall, A. W. M. Robertson, A. L. Dunstan, E. T. Coates, J. Coulthard, A. B. Smyth, C. H. R. Laming, L. A. Smith, R. H. Lee, E. Clifford, C. J. M. Gwatkin, E. T. Butteriss, J. E. Groom, C. R. A. Hammond (attached A.D.T., M.T.); Capts. S. S. Porritt, C. Meldrum; 2/Lieuts, W. S. Percival, C. E. A. Grimshaw; Lieut. Campbell Rogers; 2/Lieuts. B. G. Bosher, A. J. F. Wagstaff, H. L. I. Rose, J. O. Crombie; W. G. Jacoby, R. E. Saunders, B. M. Wilmott, H. B. Waddington, J. W. E. White, R. G. Brydges, S. W. C. Gibson, J. H. Buckley, C. H. Stork, H. J. Brocklebank.

BASE M.T. DEPÔT, NO. 695 COMPANY

Sign: Magneto

*Officers.*—A/Lieut.-Col. G. K. Archibald, D.S.O.; A/Major W. d'A. Collings; Capt. D. B. Rea; A/Capts. S. E. Shurmur, R. N. Sansom, J. Beynon; 2/Lieuts. A. C. de Fraine, J. S. Parker, S. V. Stanley, T. Wilkins, J. J. Stubbing, S. G. Morris, O. L. Denny, A. E. Jones, E. H. Reynolds, H. G. Danks, W. A. Crinks, G. F. Lynn, E. Anger, R. A. Donkin, L. Funston, J. A. Manes, J. F. Beaver, C. R. Nightingale, J. H. Pountney, J. R. B. Handyside, P. L. Griffiths, C. R. Howard, E. R. Allen, C. H. Stork; Major F. W. Vallat; A/Capts. B. D. Grant, T. Capel, C. Meldrum, R. C. O. Wells, E. C. Robson, H. C. Gould, J. A. Earle, T. R. Banks; Lieuts. H. B. Martindale, R. Savage; 2/Lieuts. Backhouse, C. H. Burrell, E. J. Pocock, F. D. Burcher, L. Hall, E. H. Wilson, H. W. Teeton, Harrild, G. L. Potter, F. D. Crump, T. Owen, Hyland, W. Taylor, E. Winn, C. R. Murray, G. E. Field, E. L. Bayley, Mallinson, H. Bennett, E. P. Innocent, H. H. Keal, W. G. Taylor, Pendleton, C. E. A. Grimshaw, J. E. Groom, Pezare, G. J. Welch, Rhodes, Purdue, G. Hakewill, H. M. Enderby, A. E. Jones, Curtis, Tozer, Hogarth, Pethwick, B. Reid, D. E. Johnstone, Braithwaite, A. G. Steavenson.

Officers of this unit who were in charge of the Ahwaz detachment of Mechanical Transport: Lieut. I. Campbell-Rogers, 1916–17; Lieut. F. Liebert, 1917–18; Lieut. W. Melloy, 1918.

695 Company (*continued*), Base M.T. Stores

Sign: Magneto

*Officers.*—Hon. A/Major A. D. Owen, D.S.O.; A/Capt. R. Lloyd; 2/Lieuts. J. Conway, A. Munro, H. W. Pike, H. W. Birdsall, A. V. Lloyd, E. W. Willett; Hon. Major E. B. Wood; Capt. A. Thresh; A/Capt. R. B. Stone; 2/Lieuts. E. H. Reynolds, C. W. Stidolph, J. D. Slinger, V. B. L. Sergent, L. L. Cruttenden, L. H. Crispe, W. B. Smith, R. H. Coggan, H. T. Masser.

695 Company (*continued*), Advanced M.T. Stores Section

Sign: Magneto. Date of arrival at Baghdad, June 1917

*Officers.*—Capt. A. Thresh; A/Capt. R. B. Stone; 2/Lieuts. H. T. Masser, W. B. Smith, W. S. Reed, T. Singleton, J. O. Crombie, L. H. Crispe, C. W. Stidolph, R. H. Coggan, G. R. Turner, S. Rothwell.

The officers of the Stores Section were part of the establishment of the Base M.T. Depôt, and are merely shown separately on account of the sections being detached from their "parent unit."

962 Company (Base M.T. Workshop)

Sign: Micrometer screw gauge

*Officers.*—T/Major S. F. Ray; T/Major F. W. Vallat; A/Capts. M. S. Aldham, E. Smith, R. B. Pardon, A. Macdonald; 2/Lieuts. L. W. J. Warren, H. M. Enderby.

Light Armoured Motor Batteries [1]

Sign: White lamb on blue background

14th: Lieut. F. S. Linnell, M.C.; 2/Lieut. B. M. Wilmot, W. J. Coker.

6th: 2/Lieut. H. Lambert, J. E. H. Kirkwood, A. J. F. Wagstaff.

7th: 2/Lieut. H. L. Rose.

[1] These Light Armoured Motor Batteries are shown because, though not R.A.S.C. units, they were dependent upon the R.A.S.C. for men, vehicles, spare parts, and repairs.

8th : 2/Lieut. W. Inglis.
13th : 2/Lieut. W. Statham ; Lieut. A. A. G. Ainsworth.
15th : Major A. H. Protheroe, M.C. (Technical Adviser to L.A.M.B.) ; 2/Lieut. F. S. Rainbow.
*Operations.*—1917-18 continuous.

### Anti-Aircraft Section

92nd, 93rd, 80th, 118th, 59th, Pom-Pom Anti-Aircraft Section and Railway Armoured Motor Battery. None of these units had R.A.S.C. officers.

## SITUATION OF M.T. UNITS ON JANUARY 16, 1919

### Ford Van Companies

| | | | | | |
|---|---|---|---|---|---|
| 729 | Co., | hdqrs. | Baghdad, | detachments | Tekrit, Qizil Robat. |
| 783 | ,, | ,, | Baghdad, | ,, | Tekrit, Qizil Robat. |
| 730 | ,, | ,, | Kermanshah | | |
| 784 | ,, | ,, | Baqubah, | ,, | Tekrit, Khanikin. |
| 815 | ,, | ,, | Karind | | |
| 818 | ,, | ,, | Kasvin | | |
| 953 | ,, | ,, | Baghdad | | |
| 954 | ,, | ,, | Baqubah, | ,, | Khanikin. |
| 971 | ,, | ,, | Ramadi, | ,, | Tekrit. |
| 1013 | ,, | ,, | Kasvin. | | |
| 1014 | ,, | ,, | Shargat | | |
| 1015 | ,, | ,, | Khanikin | | |
| 1016 | ,, | ,, | Qasr-i-Shirin | | |
| 1017 | ,, | ,, | Shargat | | |
| 1018 | ,, | ,, | Khanikin | | |
| 1019 | ,, | ,, | Baghdad | | |
| 1020 | ,, | ,, | Qasr-i-Shirin | | |
| 1023 | ,, | ,, | Hillah | | |
| 1024 | ,, | ,, | Karind | | |
| 1054 | ,, | ,, | Sahneh | | |
| 1055 | ,, | ,, | Kermanshah | | |

## Heavy Lorry Companies

| | | | | |
|---|---|---|---|---|
| 596 Co. | (Peerless), | hdqrs. | Khanikin, | det. Baghdad. |
| 976 ,, | (Packhards & Fiats) | ,, | Khanikin | |
| 1114 ,, | (Peerless) | ,, | Khanikin, | ,, Tekrit. |
| 1115 ,, | (Peerless) | ,, | Baji | |

## Motor Ambulance Convoys

| | | | | | |
|---|---|---|---|---|---|
| Det. | 23rd | M.A.C. | Baghdad | (656 Co. R.A.S.C. att.), | Stars. |
| ,, | 33rd | ,, | Kasvin | (773 ,, ,, ,, ), | Fords. |
| ,, | 39th | ,, | Khanikin | (911 ,, ,, ,, ), | ,, |
| ,, | 40th | ,, | Baji | (970 ,, ,, ,, ), | ,, |
| ,, | 45th | ,, | Baghdad | (1091 ,, ,, ,, ), | ,, |

## Caterpillar Companies

| | | |
|---|---|---|
| 788 Co., | Tekrit | (attached 159th Siege Battery). |
| 789 ,, | Samarah | ( ,, 157th Heavy ,, ) |
| 901 ,, | Jift | ( ,, 246th Siege ,, ) |
| 902 ,, | Baghdad | ( ,, 257th ,, ,, ) |
| 903 ,, | Qizil Robat | ( ,, 269th ,, ,, ) |
| 968 ,, | Khanikin | ( ,, 384th ,, ,, ) |
| 969 ,, | Baghdad | ( ,, 177th ,, ,, ) |
| 1028 ,, | Baghdad | ( ,, 395th ,, ,, ) |

## Light Armoured Motor Batteries

| | | |
|---|---|---|
| 6th | L.A.M.B., | Ramadie, No. 322 Co. R.A.S.C. Workshop unit attached. |
| 7th | ,, | Baghdad. |
| 8th | ,, | Baghdad. |
| 13th | ,, | Baghdad. |
| 14th | ,, | Mosul. |
| 15th | ,, | Kasvin. |

### M.T. Companies at the Base

695 Company, Base M.T. Depôt.
962 Company, L. of C. Heavy Repair Workshop.
1056 Company, L. of C. Ford Van Company.
23rd M.A.C. Star Ambulances (No. 656 Company R.A.S.C. attached).

### New Units at the Base: partly arrived and in process of being demobilised

| | | | | | |
|---|---|---|---|---|---|
| 1093 | Company | (Ford Vans) | 1098 | Company | (Ford Vans) |
| 1094 | ,, | ,, | 1099 | ,, | ,, |
| 1095 | ,, | ,, | 1100 | ,, | ,, |
| 1096 | ,, | ,, | 1110 | ,, | ,, |
| 1097 | ,, | ,, | 1111 | ,, | ,, |

Finally, it will be of interest to record here the total number of vehicles and men comprising the Mechanical Transport Section of the Mesopotamian Expeditionary Force on January 1, 1919. These numbers can be compared with those given in Chapter V as being in the country at the end of 1916.

### Personnel

| R.A.S.C. | British Officers. | British other Ranks. | Indian other Ranks. | Other Nationalities, approximately. | Total. |
|---|---|---|---|---|---|
| Mechanical Transport | 368 | 8,457 | 2,909 | 1,000 | 12,734 |

### Vehicles

| | | | |
|---|---|---|---|
| Lorries, 3 ton | 560[1] | Other motor cars | 121 |
| ,, 30 cwt. | 685[1] | Armoured cars | 97 |
| Ford vans | 3,279 | Motor cycles | 1336 |
| ,, cars | 396 | Tractors | 40 |
| ,, ambulances | 405 | Fowler trucks | 22 |
| Other ambulances | 72 | Fire engines | 7 |
| Total | 7,020 | | |

[1] These figures include all workshops and technical vehicles.

*Printed for*
Forster Groom & Co., Ltd.,
*by*
*Hazell, Watson & Viney, Ld., London and Aylesbury.*

Printed in the United Kingdom
by Lightning Source UK Ltd.
113567UKS00002B/70-72

9 781845 741341